Southeast
to
PANAMA

Susan:

Thank you always for being such a good friend.

Love,

Bob Devine

ROBERT C. DEVINE

For Patricia

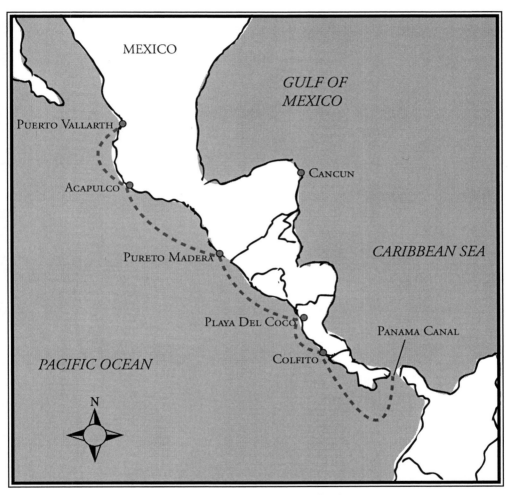

Dotted line designates route of delivery

CHAPTER ONE

The telephone call

I hear the telephone in the house from the back yard. After several rings my wife answers. From my distance I know the caller is somebody she recognizes, her distant muffled voice is filled with pleasure and delight. "Robert," she ultimately calls through the screen door, "its Allen Daniels from Mexico. He has a question for you."

"Ok, I'll be right there." The wheels turn inside my head as I make my way up onto the large deck on the back of our house and into the kitchen where I am handed the telephone together with a raised eyebrow by my wife Pat.

"Hola, Allen. How are you?"

"Quite well. Everything and everyone here is good. Pat tells me that you guys are OK."

"Pretty much so. The weather is still cool and rainy, but hopefully summer is not too far away. The weather in Puerto Vallarta must be good?"

"Starting to get hot and humid, but not bad yet. Listen, the reason for the call is to ask if you are interested in helping me transport Athena from here to Ft Lauderdale, Florida."

"Wow, what are the particulars? When do you plan to depart and what is the anticipated delivery time?"

"I am thinking that we are ten days away from departure. I would like you here two or three days beforehand. I estimate a four-week delivery. I will pay for your round trip airline ticket, fifty cents a mile and meals,"

"I'll need to talk with Pat. Can I e-mail you with my decision?"

"Sure. I know this is on very short notice. Paco and I would really like to have you join us."

1

"Thanks. It will be like old times, huh?"

"Right. Take care and let me know."

The line goes dead before I can say goodbye.

Pat stands across the kitchen with the knowing look of disruption written across her face.

"How much did Allen tell you?" I ask.

"Not much, but I could tell by your end of the conversation that it is a boat delivery."

"You're right of course." I watch her face for signs of approval or rejection.

"When and where?" she asks.

"Leave Puerto Vallarta in ten days for a four week delivery to Florida. The boat is Athena."

"No wonder Allen wants you to go as well as you know the boat."

"I'm sure that is part of it. Paco is going as first mate. It will be somewhat of a reunion."

"And you get to fulfill your dream of going through the Panama Canal," she says with a half knowing smile.

"As a matter of fact, yes," I reply. *And cross the dreaded Tehuantepec*, I say to myself.

"Well you better get busy with whatever you need to do. It is something you have always wanted to do, so get going."

I cross the kitchen to give her a hug and kiss.

With that, I know I need to find air tickets ASAP. I need to get sufficiently committed so that when the realization hits my wife of how long I will be gone, it will be more difficult for her to have a change of mind.

I climb the thirteen stairs to our bedroom loft to where my computer is located. Within minutes I am confirmed through Newark and Houston to Puerto Vallarta. I e-mail Allen providing him with the specifics of my arrival date and time as well as the ticket price.

"I'm all set," I inform Pat returning to the downstairs.

"Well, you need to get things done around here before you leave so I don't have to do them," she says with some slight sarcasm in her voice.

"I'll get as much done as possible," I respond trying to keep the conversation positive.

"You know how much needs to be done in the spring around here."

"Yes I do," seems like the best answer. I knew her enthusiasm for the trip would wear thin quickly.

I decide to make a checklist of mutually approved tasks. The next week will be busy and interesting.

✍

Incredibly the time has passed with lightning speed. Now comfortably seated in 2A on Continental Express to Newark, I feel comfortable in that I have tended to all of the agreed upon items, plus a few extras. I reflect on the very early rising this morning, the hour plus drive to the Portland Jetport and my goodbye hugs and kisses. Pat seemed upbeat in spite of the prospect of my long absence.

The sky to the east is cloudless allowing bright sunshine to enter the cabin. *A good omen for a safe trip*, I think as the steward serves fresh hot coffee.

Relaxed, my mind turns to what lies ahead. Certainly this will be the most extensive and probably the most challenging of all the times I've helped Allen move boats. As a certified 100-ton United States Coast Guard Captain, a marine surveyor and published author, he is considered one of the best yacht transporters in the world. He and I together with Paco, a Mexican National, have made a good team over a number of years. We think alike and watch out for each other, important factors when on the open seas. I'm prepared for a voyage of high adventure, good fellowship and new sights to see.

The approach into Newark Airport takes us to the west of New York City now profiled against the sun and clear morning air. The twin towers of the World Trade Center together with the Empire State Building and the Chrysler Building dominate lower Manhattan. On final approach I catch a glimpse of the Statue of Liberty majestically standing guard over New York Harbor. Minutes later we are parked on the tarmac.

Thirty minutes later I am welcomed aboard Flight #602 to Houston. "Your seat assignment is 11 F," says the pleasant gate agent.

"Thank you," I respond upon receiving my ticket stub. I make my way down the loading ramp before stepping into the cabin to find my seat. I have little time to settle in before the main cabin door closes and we push off the gate.

"Our flight time is three hours and forty minutes," is about all I hear from the overhead speaker. The rest of the message I tune out having heard it often enough over the years. With the empty seat between us, my fellow passenger and I spread out.

Taxi, take off and climb out to our cruising altitude is routine followed by a light breakfast. After which I read (I have brought several books along), make numerous notes to my travel ledger (my bible for recalling names, places and happenings) and sleep (the early morning rise and frantic pace getting to the jetport combine for a needed nap).

The three hours pass quickly. Our descent, landing and taxi into Bush Intercontinental Airport go smoothly. Our arrival is on time, a few minutes before eleven AM. I deplane at terminal C knowing my departure is from international terminal D.

"Hello, how are you," I ask son number two, Thomas, from a pay phone.

"Good, we are all well. We wish you were staying rather than passing through."

"I know. My planning was not the best when I put this together. Anyway, I want to let you know that mother was fine this morning. I know she is going to be lonesome during my absence."

"We'll call and check up on her."

"I appreciate that. Say hello to Maria and the kids. I need to go."

"OK, take care and have a good trip."

The aircraft is a Boeing 737 already parked and waiting at the gate. I find a seat in the lounge where I can watch passengers arrive and check in. I try to imagine what may be the purpose for my fellow travelers in taking this flight. Many I guess are honeymooning, others celebrating an anniversary and a few like me are on business.

"Continental flight number 1325 is ready for boarding to Puerto Vallarta. Please have your boarding pass out for processing," informs the gate agent.

I gather up my briefcase and camera bag to queue up.

"Welcome aboard, Mr. Devine. Glad to have you with us today," offers the agent.

My seat assignment in mid cabin is on the isle beside a middle-aged woman travelling with a pre-teen child. We exchange hellos as I strap-in.

Push back, taxi out and take off are smooth and effortless. We climb to altitude before the seat belt sign goes out during which I read.

"My name is Sarah, what's yours?" asks the young lady from her window seat.

"Sarah, it is none of your business. Leave the gentleman alone," exclaims the older woman.

"I don't mind," I respond. "My name is Bob."

"I apologize for my granddaughter's poor behavior. I'm Helen, please forgive us."

"Not at all. Nice to know you Helen and Sarah."

"Why are you going to Puerto Vallarta?" asks Sarah despite Helen's stern look.

"I am to help a good friend deliver a sailboat to Florida."

"Cool, can I come along?"

"Nonsense," responds Helen. "You know better."

"Sliced turkey or ham/cheese?" asks our flight attendant.

Helen and I choose turkey, Sarah asks for ham. We eat in relative silence, each of us enjoying our sandwiches and soft drinks.

"Have you done this sort of thing before?" asks Helen now finished.

"Yes, this will be my fifth delivery and by far the longest. Prior trips have been from Puerto Vallarta up the coast to San Diego taking from ten to twelve days. We expect to take four weeks for this."

"Don't you get seasick?" asks Sarah.

"No. Fortunately I have always been good on the water. No stomach or head problems if I watch what I eat and drink."

"What does your wife think about you being away for so long?" asks Helen.

I chuckle as I wonder just how to answer. "Actually she has been a good scout. She knows how much I love the water and has tolerated my absence."

"Where do you live?" asks Sarah.

"Mid-coast Maine. A rather small town called Townsend."

Over Helen's face comes a mask of disbelief. "I am originally from Townsend." Without blinking, she adds, "My maiden name was Pinkham."

"I know the name," I respond. It is one of four or five families that are very prominent in the area and can trace their roots back for generations.

"Oh, Grandmother," I hear from the window seat, "Bob doesn't care about you being a Pinkham."

"Of course, I'm sorry."

"No apology necessary. I understand the significance of the name. Do you ever visit the area?" I ask.

"Occasionally, mostly for family reunions. Admittedly I have not spent any real time since I graduated from high school and went off to Smith."

Now it is my turn to do a double take. This is a special lady. Smith College is and has been a tough school to get into academically and is very expensive. I am willing to bet that she is one of a handful of local students ever to get into Smith.

"I had a girlfriend at Mount Holyoke College while stationed at Westover Field. She and I would go up to Smith for dances and other social events."

"Did you marry her?" asks Sarah.

"That is none of your business young lady," evokes Helen.

"No, Sarah, I didn't. We were from two very different worlds. We dated for just a short period of time before we went our separate ways."

"How sad," says Sarah.

"Not at all." I respond. "I eventually went on to take up residency in Southern California where I met my wife. We celebrated our thirty-seventh anniversary this past February. I believe things worked out just fine."

"I'm sure it did," comments Helen.

The flight remains smooth with clear visibility. Below us is the sprawling city of Monterrey, Mexico with its associated smoky blue haze.

Helen I calculate must be my age, in her mid-sixties. She is well dressed, but not overly so, her hair and makeup make her an attractive woman. Wishing to keep the conversation going, I ask how long she plans to be in Puerto Vallarta.

"Not long, perhaps two weeks. I need to return home to my business."

"Grandmother has her own business," inserts Sarah.

"I represent two dozen clients who have me buy and sell items for them over the Internet."

"Interesting," I say.

"It keeps me busy and active in the business world."

"Grandmother and grandfather once owned a computer company."

"Are you and your husband still involved?" I ask.

"Grandfather died two years ago," explains Sarah.

"I am very sorry."

"It is OK," says Helen looking away. She recovers quickly to say, "I miss him but have learned that the best therapy is to keep busy."

Feeling awkward at the sobering turn in the conversation, I turn to my open book.

"Please don't think you have offended me," says Helen.

"Grandmother gets weepy every so often."

I now sense a strong bond between these two. Despite their age differences and the usual grandmother authority figure, they act more like sisters.

I feel the pilot reduce power to begin our decent. The flight attendants scurry about the cabin passing out Mexican immigration papers and collecting the last of the service items.

"Where will you be staying," asks Helen.

"On board the boat. It is fully air conditioned, has a full galley and generally has lots of food and drink."

"You sound like you know the boat."

"I do. My wife and I stayed on board her for two months while our sailboat was under repair"

"Here is my son's telephone number. Please give us a call before you leave so that we may have dinner. I would like you to meet him and my daughter-in-law."

"Thank you. I will call."

I set about the task of completing my immigration forms. They are much easier to complete than in past years, however there is still the tricky part where a signature is required on the back of the form that is easily over looked. I check that my passport is in order and file both items away for customs clearance.

We are in fast decent as the ground rushes up to meet us before the tires scuff the runway and we come to a chattering stop before turning left off the runway and onto the taxiway.

"I always hold my breath on landing," says Helen.

"It can be a little wild here at times," I say, "especially in the late afternoon when the sea breeze can cause disturbed air."

"I'm just glad we are here," chimes in Sarah.

As the engines shut down a mob of ground personnel converge upon us, including a ramp used for deplaning. The forward cabin door eventually opens to the heat and humidity of the day. I am struck by the intense brightness of the afternoon sun as I make my way down the steps and across the tarmac to the customs entrance where inside, it is cool and comfortable. The queues to the custom agents are eight to ten deep, the penalty for sitting aft in the cabin. Helen and Sarah are just ahead of me.

The passenger mood reflects the anticipated fun and relaxation of visiting this holiday/vacation destination. Custom officials, I sense, try not to spoil the feeling as they process us through with little delay.

After a cursory look at my passport, the agent stamps it together with my visa form allowing me to remain in the country for sixty days. It seems very mechanical; however I know they are trained to detect folks trying to enter the country illegally.

I gather my paperwork, camera bag and briefcase to proceed to baggage claim and the more interrogating part of the immigration process. My duffel bag comes bumping towards me looking none the worse for the trip. I give a sigh of relief knowing that too often bags having to make two connections can be lost for days.

'Now the fun part,' I think. With all my articles in hand, I walk to the baggage inspection area where baggage is inspected on a random "luck of the draw" basis. You are required to push a button on a pole that in turn illuminates either a red or green light, much like a traffic signal. A red light signifies that your baggage will be searched; a green light allows you to pass without inspection.

"Senor, please press the button," instructs the woman attendant. She is dressed in a smart business suit with an identification tag clipped to her left lapel. She stands next to the pole holding a clipboard. 'Polite but firm' I think as I approach the round black button about waist high. Instantly upon pushing the button, the green light illuminates.

"You may pass. Thank you and enjoy your visit," she offers.

"Thank you," I respond, thankful for my good luck.

In exiting I look for either Allen or Kate.

Now beyond the noise and confusion of welcoming voices, I set down my gear in the center of the cavernous main building where I can see and be seen. I catch out of the corner of an eye Helen and Sarah leaving escorted by what I guess are several family members.

CHAPTER TWO

Welcome to Mexico

C̲arlos Mendoza is not pleased.

Once again he is faced with a difficult decision. Either conform to the cartel's orders or face certain hardships. He holds a gaily-wrapped package with a pink bow that was delivered minutes ago. The contents are not for him to see. He walks to a window and looks out on the busy street below. Frustrated he asks *How many more times will they dictate so much?*

After ten minutes I come to the conclusion that I am rideless. The terminal building has emptied, leaving me standing conspicuously alone. Knowing both Allen and Kate, I figure they got busy and forgot.

It is not that I cannot find my own way to the marina, I say to myself as I head for the taxi stand exit. The sliding doors open to the blast furnace of heat and humidity from outside. *To think that just a few hours ago I was in sixty degree weather and now this.* I feel a little foolish dressed in jeans and sweatshirts while around me are folks in shorts and tank tops.

"Where do you go?" asks the attendant from inside her air-conditioned booth. It is necessary to first come here to purchase your taxi fare.

"Marina Vallarta," I reply.

"One hundred pesos, por favor."

"It is too much," I find myself saying. "It is less than three miles."

"This is the price," she answers in an indifferent voice.

I can feel myself starting to sweat even though I have been outside for less than five minutes. I recall on a prior trip I decided to take the shuttle bus that took forever, as well as leaving me with a considerable walking distance to my destination. The other option is to walk. I pay the one hundred pesos, receive a receipt and walk towards the line of taxis.

"Buenos tardes," offers the first driver in line.

"Good afternoon," I respond placing my duffel bag in the open trunk. I slide into the passenger seat handing the driver my paid receipt. The vehicle is a recent model Volkswagen. He starts the engine, which brings cool air from the air-conditioner. He must not have been sitting long as the interior temperature is not at the sweltering point.

"Where you go, Senor?"

"Marina Vallarta, close to the yacht club. I will show you as we get close."

Traffic is heavy with construction on the roadway departing the airport adding to the congestion. We stay on the less traveled frontage road before making a right turn at a shopping plaza that takes us to the marina. We wind around a golf course with its many beautiful homes, pass several high rise condos and hotels that stretch along Banderas Bay before reaching the cobblestone drive leading to the yacht club.

"Turn left at the next opening," I instruct the driver.

He nods in recognition.

We make the left turn but can travel only a short distance as vehicles are parked on both sides of the narrow street. Stopped, I find it is a tight squeeze to open my door wide enough to get out; however, I do manage to gather my belongings from inside together with my duffel bag from the trunk. I tip him and walk the twenty or thirty steps to where I turn left and proceed to Kate's canvas shop. It is considerably cooler here because her shop is set in under a wide overhang that protects it from the sun and rain. From the walkway, across a grassy area of thirty feet, are the waters of the marina shimmering in the late afternoon sun.

Reaching the shop, both doors are closed and there are no lights on inside. I have a slight panic attach thinking she may be gone. A push on the right hand doors reveals that it is unlocked. I step inside to the delight of cool air. No one is visible.

"Is anyone here?" I call out.

"Yes there is," is the voice of Kate from behind the partitions used to create an office enclosure.

I set down my bags as she comes from her office.

She is best described as being tiny. Several inches under five feet, she weighs perhaps ninety pounds and wears a size four. But she is a tough businesswoman and not to be under estimated because of her size. She has built a solid business serving the boating community for their canvas needs.

"Hola," we say together with big hugs.

"You are looking good," she says.

"Thank you and so do you," I reply.

We exchange family information.

"Allen should be along soon," she says. "He and Paco have been spending full time on Athena. There was much to be done."

"Are they still thinking in terms of leaving in two days?"

"I believe so. I haven't heard anything different. I know he is looking forward to having you here."

She slips into her office to answer the telephone.

I look around the familiar surroundings of her shop. Although it has been two years, it could be yesterday that I was last here. Bolts of new cloth, thread, aluminum tubing is stored on one side of the forty by forty-foot space. A cruiser's lending library consisting of mostly paperbacks line the front wall. A four-foot wide worktable with sewing machines that run the entire length of the opposite wall. Various pieces of canvas, patterns and hand tools are scattered about, attesting to work in progress. To the rear in one corner is her office together with a bathroom. In the other corner is a small kitchen primarily used to make coffee. Another workbench fills the center back wall with numerous hand tools and bins for spare parts.

"Your mural still draws attention," she says returning.

"Does it now?" I say shifting my attention to the wall behind the sewing machine tables. The mural is a painting of the marina measuring roughly twenty-four by twelve feet. Its focal point is the signature lighthouse that stands watch over the marina together with the surrounding condos, restaurants, boat slips and watercraft. I painted it from a photograph I took by enlarging it, (the photo) gridding and transferring it by corresponding blocks to the wall. It was a fun project requiring about a month to complete.

"Allen wants us to meet him at the boat. We'll get you settled in and then go to dinner."

"Sounds good to me," I respond.

Gathering my gear once again, I wait outside in the warm, moist evening air as Kate locks up for the night. There is a light breeze off the marina, giving some relief to the sticky temperature. We walk out to her parked van on the street that I had entered earlier.

"I still have old reliable," she says.

Old reliable is a Chevrolet van, vintage 1980, now with well in excess of two hundred thousand miles. The interior has been stripped out leaving only the two front seats. She has lined the entire inside with rug material to help sound proof and lend a little class. Tonight the van is relatively empty, only a few items belonging to Allen.

I throw the duffel bag in behind the passenger seat together with the camera bag and briefcase. Kate has the engine running as I settle in and click into my seatbelt.

"She sounds good," I say.

"I keep my fingers crossed each time I turn the key."

She backs out of the narrow street onto the main road. The van chatters along the cobblestone street that runs around the perimeter of the marina having to slow periodically to traverse the many speed bumps. The Mexican policeman, as the speed bumps are commonly referred to, are very effective in keeping speed to 25 or 30 mph.

There remains a deep purple glow from the last vestures of sunlight in the western sky. It is that magical time between day and night when the world seems to relax and reflect on the day's activities. My watch shows it is a few minutes after six thirty PM.

Arriving at our destination, Kate navigates the van into a parking space, shuts off the engine and slides out her door to the ground. I follow her towards pier G where at the rod iron-gate she punches in the security code. She pushes it open allowing us to proceed down the ramp onto the floating dock. All shapes and sizes of boats line the dock. Many are in transit while others have not moved in months. We reach Athena, berthed at the far end of the dock where Kate rings the doorbell located next to the boarding ladder to alert Allen of our arrival. She nimbly climbs the three stairs to the deck, turning to reach for my camera bag and briefcase. I muscle the duffel bag under the lower lifeline onto the deck before scrambling aboard.

"Welcome aboard," booms Allen's voice from inside. "Glad to have you here."

"Good to be here," I manage to say before being smothered and beaten on the back by one of Allen's famous bear hugs.

"Stow your gear and let's go eat," he says. "You can decide later where you want to sleep. Roger is in the forward port cabin; otherwise the place is yours with the exception of my captain's quarters."

I wrestle the duffel bag through the cockpit and down the companionway to the main salon. A quick look around tells me that physically, very little has changed in my absence. It remains spacious and elegant with bright colors, rich woods and deep carpeting.

I carry my gear into the aft starboard cabin, dropping everything on one of the two single bunks. I step into the head to splash water on my face, quickly change into a pair of shorts, a lightweight shirt and thongs. I now feel and look a little less like a tourist.

I find Allen and Kate waiting in the cockpit. "You look hungry. Let's go," he says.

We walk to the head of the dock to the promenade, more often referred to as the malecon, where we turn left and proceed a short distance to one of several open-air restaurants that line the walkway.

"Food from Chile sound ok?" asks Allen.

Kate and I nod approval.

As is the custom of most restaurants here there is a display, under cover, of the entrees offered this evening. Tonight, several cuts of prime beef are featured together with chicken and chops. These together with the aroma of meat cooking on the open grill, makes me realize just how hungry I am.

From behind a lectern positioned at the entrance steps the maître de.

"Welcome Allen, Kate and guest. May I offer you a table?" he asks.

"Yes," replies Allen. "Franklin, meet a good friend, Bob."

"It is a pleasure, Senor."

"Thank you," I respond.

Franklin seats us to the rear and away from the other patrons. We order drinks and choose from the menu.

"This is a nice looking restaurant," I comment. I count thirty tables, all with white tablecloths, folded napkins and lighted candles. The interior is done in simple bamboo with white canvas panels lacing in-between. Ceiling fans and hanging plants complete the décor. The kitchen and preparation areas are to the rear, visible but not obtrusive. The steaks, chops and chicken are cooked outside the kitchen on an open grill that is fired by hard wood, clearly visible to the patrons.

"Franklin is one of my customers," says Kate.

"I thought that may be the case by the canvas work above."

Our waiter delivers drinks.

"Salud," we say to one another as we raise and touch glasses.

My cold Pacifico beer tastes good. It goes down smoothly and quickly.

"Did you have a good trip down?" asks Allen.

"Yes, everything went according to plan. I met a most fascinating couple on the leg coming into here. They are a grandmother and granddaughter who live in Texas but have a home here as well. Interestingly, the grandmother was born and raised through high school in Maine. She is from an old and well known family."

"What is her name? Perhaps we know them," asks Kate.

"I failed to get their last name. I do have a local telephone number that I have been invited to call for dinner arrangements before we leave.

Which begs the question, when are we leaving?"

"I'm holding off on the final decision until tomorrow. We have multiple concerns with regards to the port engine that Paco has been unable to fix. Greg has agreed to look at it in the morning."

"And who is Roger?" I ask.

"He is a young man who we have known for about three months. He is the nephew of one of our good friends. He has been working for Kate and based on this work experience, I hired him to help us. For his age, he exhibits a good deal of boating knowledge and skill."

Our dinners arrive which we consume with gusto. We decline any desert or coffee.

"What are the plans for tomorrow?" I ask.

"We have a 08:00 hour meeting on board. The four of us can review what needs to be completed. I have saved the provisioning, safety and inventory for you as in the past."

"Ok. Thanks for dinner."

"Don't get use to eating like this too often; it is more expensive than our budget allows," grins Allen, paying the bill.

"I understand."

"Thank you and come again," says Franklin as we leave.

"I'm going to walk the malecon for a while before turning in," I announce.

"See you in the morning."

"Goodnight Bob, see you sometime tomorrow," says Kate. She and Allen, hand in hand, head back to the parked van as I head off in the opposite direction.

CHAPTER THREE

The scheme

Mendoza walks across his office to a painting on the far wall. Lifting it off its hook, he reveals a wall safe. Spinning the dial with familiarity, he opens the door and places the package inside. Closing the door he spins it locked and replaces the painting checking that it is hung correctly. Satisfied that everything is in order, he flicks off the lights while closing and locking the handsome mahogany door.

As is his custom, he walks to and from his apartment, a modest distance of ten blocks that he feels helps keep him in shape. A bachelor, he has little reason to hurry. Walking also helps him to think.

Born of a Mexican father and an American mother, he has his father's good looks and his mother's intelligence. In his early years he lived in Texas with his mother after his parents' divorce. Upon high school graduation he returned to Puerto Vallarta in order to help run the family import/export business that passed to him upon the unfortunate early death of his father. Now at age forty he finds himself modestly financially and socially successful by dealing in a variety of questionable occupations under the umbrella of the import/export business. Considered by many as unsavory, he is recognized by others as an individual that can handle most kinds of difficult situations. His suspected association with the cartel is an example of his underworld connections.

He stops and enters a small bar. The country western music stirs memories of his days in Texas. Focusing, he sees the familiar sights of the bar interior where a young lady stands behind the bar.

"Come in, Mr. Mendoza," she says with the wave of a hand. "Your booth tonight, sir?"

"Yes, please"

"Right this way," she says coming from behind the bar. "What can I get you? The usual?" she asks after he settles into the tiny booth.

"Please."

"Be right back."

It is not much of an establishment he thinks looking around. The main attraction is a jukebox together with a small dance floor. Ten booths set along the back wall together with a like number of tables with chairs scattered around fill the remaining space. *However, it makes money and that's what counts.'*

"Here we are," says the barmaid returning. "Can I get you anything else?"

"I'm looking for the boys."

"Haven't seen them tonight. Shall I call?"

"Yes."

"Be right back."

Carlos takes a swallow of the cold beer. He stretches his long limbs out while trying to relax and plan his strategy. He knows he is hungry but that will have to wait. His stomach welcomes the nourishment of the beer.

"They can be here within thirty minutes," says the returning barmaid.

"Thanks," he says waving her away.

Despite the early evening hour, the malecon is crowded with throngs of walkers. Although the temperature remains in the eighties and the relative humidity about the same, there is a cooling effect from the waters of the marina. Carriages with babies, toddlers and youngsters with their family members gaily parade along the broad pedestrian walkway. Couples, hand in hand, young and old, vacationers and locals all enjoy the procession. The restaurants, bars and boutiques are filled with shoppers, browsers, eaters, drinkers and the curious. There seems no shortage of people here this evening.

My walk takes me to the far end of the marina, close to Kate's shop and the closed yacht club. The building, badly damaged in an earthquake last year, is showing signs of nonuse and neglect. It seems a shame that what was once so active a place now is empty and dark.

I peek through the padlocked rod iron gate into the interior. The empty and discolored kidney shaped swimming pool lies straight ahead, while to the right is the graceful mahogany bar, the scene of many race stories. A circular staircase located beyond the end of the bar accessed the harbor master office, located above on the second floor. I recall the story told that he was in his office at the time of the tremor, nearly finding himself on the ground floor through a gaping hole.

Feeling tired from the long day's activities; I start back towards the boat. The malecon remains active as it is early by Latin American time. The evening meal is most often not eaten before now, nine o'clock. The restaurants and bars are getting busy.

Thank goodness the security gate is open because I'm not sure I would remember the combination. It may have changed in my two-year absence. I make a mental note to ask Allen.

The dock is empty although I hear a distant television playing from one of the boats. Burgee's and boat flags flap in the evening breeze, disturbing the quiet of the night under a canopy of stars.

Reaching Athena, I climb aboard and proceed to the cockpit door where I find it unlocked. Stepping inside I am welcomed by the refreshing feel of air-conditioned air. I hear the TV playing from the main saloon. Roger must be aboard.

At the companionway I descend below where I am able to see someone sitting on the floor, his back against the couch in the forward lounge. He quickly gets to his feet and comes forward to greet me. "Hello, I'm Roger. Are you Bob?"

"Yes. I'm sorry if I alarmed you."

"No problem. I was too involved in this film."

"I'm glad to meet you," I say shaking hands. He has a firm grip. He is well over six feet, weighing two hundred twenty pounds on a muscular frame. I estimate he is in his mid-twenties. Clean-shaven with a fresh military style haircut, he is casually dressed in blue jeans, T-shirt and is barefoot.

"Do you have any gear I can help you stow?" he asks.

"No, thanks. When I was aboard earlier I put my things below in the aft starboard cabin."

He returns to his seat, such as it is. "I'm afraid there is very little to eat or drink," he says.

"I'm fine. I had a big dinner not long ago."

"You must be tired. Did you come from Maine today?"

"Yes. I left Portland this morning with stops in Newark and Houston. Actually, it has not been a hard day when I consider I sat in a seat most of the time."

"Still you must be weary."

"I am and without appearing rude, I am going to excuse myself for bed."

"I understand."

"I understand we have an 08:00 meeting," I say making my way toward my cabin.

"Yes. Allen will be here before then, probably by 06:30."

"Then for sure I need some shut eye. I'll see you in the morning."

Below I find sheets, blankets and a pillowcase to make up the bunk. I do a haphazard job of getting them on, but really don't care. I wash up, brush my teeth and slip into my hastily made sack. Snapping off the reading light the cabin plunges into semi-darkness. I lie awake listening to the waves lap against the boat's side. I realize that I have failed to call my wife. It is much too late to call now. I fall asleep feeling a little guilty. I hope she will understand.

"Hello Mr. Mendoza," the one young man says as spokesman for the three.

"Have a seat, fellows. Order what you want."

The barmaid turns away without needing to be told.

Each of the men is in their late twenties, sport military haircuts and are solidly built. They could be poster boys for an exercise equipment company.

"Thanks for coming on short notice," starts Carlos after drinks are delivered.

"Let me be brief and to the point."

They are familiar with meetings of this nature, as he has employed them on many occasions. They have been paid handsomely for their services and have learned not to ask questions or get greedy.

"My sources tell me that your new friend Roger is leaving within the next few days on a private boat?"

"Yes," answers the spokesman.

"How well do you know him?"

"As well as we know each other, I would say," answers one of the others. They all nod in agreement. "In his few months here he has never given us reason to doubt his integrity or honesty."

"I need you to convince him to take a package to Panama, quietly."

"We don't see that as a problem," says the spokesman after surveying the faces of his accomplices.

"My offer of payment is five hundred dollars to him. One half now, the other half upon delivery. You will each receive two hundred dollars with the same payment schedule. I'll give full details upon his acceptance."

"We'll set it up immediately. I'll contact you tomorrow evening," says the spokesman.

"Very well. Good night," announces Mendoza as he rises to leave.

CHAPTER FOUR

Preparations

The boat is quiet at a little after seven AM, yet I suspect my other ship-mates are already on board. I shower, shave and dress leisurely in shorts, tie-shirt and boat shoes before entering the main cabin. The sun streams in through the overhead hatches further brightening the rich colors of the sofas, chairs and carpeting. I pause in the spaciousness and comfort of the area where memories of the two months my wife and I lived aboard are all about. It seems like only yesterday rather than two years ago.

Facing forward and elevated by twelve inches above the main cabin sole is the lounge with its overstuffed, deep plush full-length sofa stretch-ing the width of the cabin. Large oversized throw pillows are evenly dis-tributed across the back. A huge mahogany coffee table occupies the cen-ter with numerous magazines and books spread about. Windows behind the sofa allow full view of the deck forward, now covered with drawn curtains. The space is ideal for the three to four couples (The number for which the boat is designed to carry) for socializing and/or to watch the giant television located in one corner.

Crossing the width of the cabin to the galley, I find fresh hot coffee.

The galley is separated from the main cabin by a bar, ideal in serv-ing guests a buffet meal. The shelves created under the bar contain space for a large assortment of dry goods, including cereals, cake mixes, flour, spaghetti, etc., etc. The space above holds a complete setting for twelve of English bone china tableware. A six-burner combination gas and electric cook top range sits to the right and perpendicular to the counter, a large convection oven beneath. A microwave rests above. Along the outside bulkhead, parallel to the counter, is a two-compartment stainless steel sink with disposal. Above the splash rail are windows providing a look

19

at the outside world, today allowing this morning's bright sun to enter. Underneath are several shelves for the many pots and pans needed to prepare the assortment of meals served onboard. Finally a large capacity stainless steel floor to ceiling refrigerator/freezer completes the galley. Beside it is a nice size work counter where the coffee maker and toaster are kept.

From the cockpit area, I hear the distance voices of Allen and Paco. Topping off my coffee I start towards the steps leading out of the cabin. I run my left hand along the top surface of the handsome mahogany formal dining table as I start aft. It is situated to the left of center of the main cabin allowing ample space to pass between it and the galley.

I pause once again to admire the built-in china cabinet containing a splendid collection of Waterford crystal. I open the solid double doors where the sunlight reflects off the glassware, radiating warmth throughout the room. Carefully closing the doors I carry on towards the voices above.

Allen, Paco and Roger are seated at the large oak table that forms part of the cockpit on the starboard side. Here is where my wife and I would usually have meals, play cards, write cards and letters and generally hangout. The table sits eight comfortably, four facing forward, four aft on comfortable full-length colorful cushions.

"Good morning all," I say approaching the table.

"Buenos días, Roberto," says Paco as he advances to give me a bear hug.

"Did you rest well?" asks Allen.

"Much better than I had expected," I respond.

Roger expresses his good morning as I slide in beside him.

"If we are ready, let's get started," says Allen. "It is my hope that we can be underway in two days. Bob, is that enough time for your inventory and provisioning?"

"I believe so," I respond. "I feel I know the boat well enough to be able to identify and record all safety items today and provision tomorrow."

"Paco, how about you?"

"As you know I am waiting for Greg to look at the port engine. I have been unable to find exactly an oil leak and as you know and I am worried about low compression on two cylinders. He told me he would be here today, early. Otherwise, everything else is OK."

"You need to call him and make certain he remembers. You know how forgetful he can be."

"OK. I'll call him on the VHF as soon as we are done."

"I'd suggest you go up to his shop."

Paco nods in understanding.

"Roger, how goes things with you?"

"Good. I plan to work on the ground tackle today including an oil change of the windless. I'll do standing and running rigging afterwards."

"OK. Then we'll work towards being ready in two days' time. Keep me updated with any problems and we'll meet again in the morning."

Roger and Paco depart immediately.

"Bob, it is good to have you here. Thanks for coming," says Allen.

"I'm pleased to be here and am looking forward to the trip."

"We truly need to be out of here in two days. The bank is giving me a bad time about money. It seems that suddenly, after all this time; they have decided that they want the boat in Fort Lauderdale, yesterday." The bank to which Allen refers is the lien-holder of the boat.

"Based on what I just heard, we should be ready to go."

"I hope so. My big concern is the health of the two engines. They have high hours and have not been well maintained. The oil leak is, I feel, a blow-by caused by worn rings which are part of the low compression problem. It is why we have asked Greg's evaluation."

"Well, if anyone can find a solution it will be Greg. He did a great job for us on Eastwind."

"The problem is getting him and keeping him here long enough to diagnose and give a recommendation. It is not like I am asking him to do it for free."

With that, he slides out and goes below to his cabin located immediately aft of the cockpit to answer his cell phone.

I go below to my cabin where from my briefcase I extract a legal sized yellow ruled writing tablet and number two pencils. On the tablet I draw a rough flat sketch of the boat looking from above. I designate bulkheads and cabin spaces as points of reference, labeling larger spaces. The bow is to the top with the stern to the bottom of the sketch. My purpose is to be able to identify quickly any trouble spots.

Without delay, I begin forward and work my way mid-ship and then aft, recording the various intake and exhaust through holes on the sketch. I test the working condition of their related gang valves for ease of operation. I secure a wooden plug to each for emergency use. In addition I record on the sketch the location of emergency fire extinguishers, checking their content and date last serviced. It is not particularly difficult work; however it does require persistence and a degree of perseverance to locate each of the roughly fifty through holes that are scattered throughout the boat. Any of them if damaged or fail from fatigue can allow gallons of seawater to enter the boat creating a potentially dangerous situation.

By noon I have completed that portion of the survey. I have found two fire extinguishers out of date, requiring service. Paco agrees to drop them off at a local shop for servicing on his way home.

Athena is equipped with a halogen fire system providing protection to the two engine compartments. The fire retardant containers register in the fully charged range, which is about all I am able to check out. Flare guns and flares are found in date and in good shape. Sufficient life jackets with lights and whistles are found and recorded as being located in an aft locker on the aft deck. Two ten-foot boat hooks are stored port and starboard attached to the outside of the cockpit. An eight-man life raft rests in its cradle lashed to the fore deck, properly showing a recent passing inspection tag. Two EPIRB's (Emergency Position Indicating Radio Beacon) are located and noted as in date. One is in the cockpit mounted on a bulkhead to the left of the ship's wheel, the other is mounted on a stantion outside adjacent to the controls for raising and lowering Athena's tender.

The tender is a 22-foot inflatable Zodiac, powered by a 200 horsepower Suzuki outboard. It is suspended at the transom by an electric powered hydraulic boom. My inspection reveals that the Zodiac has a fire extinguisher, flare gun and flares, life jackets, medical kit, VHF radio, bottled water and flotation cushions.

Allen finds me sitting at the cockpit table. It is 3:00 PM.

"How is it going?" he asks.

"I believe I'm about done. Do you have time to look over my findings?"

"Sure. I need a break."

He slides onto the bench across from me while taking the several pages of inventory and my sketch. His ruddy good looks are the epitome of a sea faring captain. His mustache, eyebrows and full head of hair are bleached white from hours in the sun. Clean-shaven, his face, neck, arms and hands are brown as a berry. Barrel chested, his two hundred plus pounds are evenly distributed over a six foot three inch frame. He peers through a pair of weather beaten eyeglasses that remain tethered to him by a cord around his neck.

"Good job," he says after several minutes. "I'll have these laminated and placed in the emergency manual."

"How are things going in the engine room?"

"I am not sure. Greg has been on and off the boat since just after our meeting. No news is good news, I hope."

"Do you have a provisioning list?' I ask.

"Sure do. I'll go get it. In fact let's spend a few minutes reviewing it for adjustments."

Looking forward I can see Roger standing waist deep inside the chain locker working on the electric windless. Rows of anchor chain, stretched fore and aft, are laid out drying on the deck after having been washed, measured and painted according to length. He is dressed in a swimsuit; his sun-tanned body sleek with sweat. No question that he is in good physical condition.

Allen returns from below, sliding in beside me. I am familiar with the list having used it on previous occasions. We adjust items up and down, adding some, deleting others. When completed there are two hundred items covering frozen foods, fresh vegetables, canned goods, dry goods, diary and meat/poultry/fish. This we calculate should be sufficient to feed the four of us for ten days to two weeks. Next provisioning should not be needed until Panama, if then.

"Unless there is something else, I'm going up to make a couple of phone calls," I say.

"No nothing more go ahead."

On the Malecon I find a pay phone where I dial my wife, hoping I'll find her home. She answers on the third ring with a cheerful hello. I learn she has been busy and that overall she is doing well without me. I promise I'll call again before leaving before saying I love her and hanging up.

Next I place a call to Helen. The telephone rings several times before the familiar voice of Sarah answers.

"Hello Sarah, this is Bob from the airplane yesterday. Do you remember?"

"Yes, I do. How are you?"

"Fine, thank you. May I speak with your grandmother?"

"Are you coming to see us?"

"Well I thought I would see what your schedules look like. It looks like we will be leaving day after tomorrow."

"Hold on, I'll go get her."

The telephone goes clunk as Sarah apparently drops it. I can hear her call to her grandmother. Several minutes go by in silence.

"Hello Bob. How are you?" is the voice of Helen.

"Very well and how are you?"

"I am feeling good, a little tired from the trip down, but overall fine. Sarah tells me you may be leaving soon?'

"Yes. If all goes well, we could be on our way day after tomorrow. So I thought if I was to meet the rest of your family I should call today."

"I'm glad you have. I told my son about you and the fact that you live in Maine. He is anxious to meet you. Are you free this evening?"

"Yes, that would be fine."

"Good. He wants to know more about the sailboat trip as well. Do you mind?"

"No, not at all."

"Let me give you directions as to where we can meet. Do you have a pencil and paper?"

I write them down, set a time of six thirty to meet and thank her.

Arriving back on board I find Allen, Paco and Greg huddled in the cockpit.

"Bob, good to see you," says Greg standing to offer his hand.

"Good to see you. You're looking well."

"Thanks and so do you."

The two years since I last saw him have been good to him. He has put on several pounds around the middle, but not excessively so. An American in his forties, he is married to a Mexican lady, has learned the lingo and enjoys life in Mexico. Trained as a diesel mechanic he has had no problem finding work in and around the marina.

"Come join us," says Allen. "We are about to make a decision."

I slide in beside Greg.

"According to Greg, he feels that the oil leak is unfixable," starts Allan.

"Actually, it is not so much an oil leak," injects Greg, "as it is a blow-by condition caused by worn pistons and rings. Both engines are twenty years old, have been worked hard and not been well cared for. They need a complete overhaul, which is probably not cost effective. The port engine more than the starboard is showing her age and is the reason we see so much oil residue. It is my opinion that if operated at reduced power with frequent oil and filter changes, say at every one hundred operating hours, you have a good chance of them making the trip."

"We have checked compression in all cylinders and found them all are below specified levels," adds Paco.

Roger joins us from below, freshly showered and nicely dressed.

"The turbochargers operate normally, engine oil pressures are normal and steady, no signs of excess vibration and both engines sound good," continues Greg.

"We have replaced all fuel injectors," reminds Paco.

After a few moments of silence Allen speaks. "OK. It sounds to me that you two feel we a good chance of making it. Am I right?"

"Yes," answers Paco. "I think if we red line at 2750 rpms with one hundred hour oil and filter changes, we can make Florida."

"Then it is a go. How much more do you have left Paco?"

"Service the two generators and a few other minor items."

"And you, Roger?"

"Ground tackle is complete. All that is left I can have completed by noon tomorrow."

"Bob, you can provision in the morning."

With that, Allen thanks Greg and asks for his bill.

Departure is set for Friday morning.

CHAPTER FIVE

The pitch

I *consider myself a lucky individual* thinks Roger Andrews as he walks along the street leading to his favorite bar. He feels particularly good about himself this evening. Smartly dressed in a colorful open neck sport shirt, neatly pressed trousers and a pair of sandals he strides along with the confidence of a man enjoying life. At age twenty-six years, in excellent health, single and with a new job, he feels as if he has the world by its tail.

Reaching the bar, he steps inside to the welcome relief of air-conditioning.

Removing his sunglasses it takes him a minute for his eyes to adjust to the darkness.

"Hi Roger," calls a familiar female voice. He knows it source as coming from behind the bar located to the right of the room.

"Hello, Diane," he responds moving into the room now that his sight is improving. "How are ya?"

"Good. Hey you look great. Got a hot date?"

"Nope, just felt like cleaning up for a change."

"The usual?" she asks.

"Please."

He moves to the back of the smallish-sized beer hall where there are booths lining the back wall. The place is virtually empty he observes slipping into the far right booth.

"Here you are my friend, a nice cold Pacifico," says Diane.

"Thanks, I'll run a tab."

She turns to return to the bar. He watches her leave admiring her blue jean clad firm fanny sashay away from him. He smiles knowing that it would not take much encouragement from him to land her in bed.

Realization quickly sets in as he reminds himself that she would come with lots of baggage. Two small children, a jealous ex-husband, no money and lord knows what else.

No not Diane, I have better sense than that. Besides my parents would disown me. *I wonder how they are*, he asks himself. *It has been a year since I last saw them and months since we talked.*

The beer has a mellowing effect. Now relaxed from a full day of work in the sun he calls for another.

Some folks would call him a drifter; he considers himself more of an adventurer, having followed his instincts in a quest to see the world. Since his separation from the US Navy he has wandered, zig zagging the globe over the past two years. His love of boats, the water and his navy seal training has provided him with an ability to earn an income, although modest. Now, within the next few hours, he will be departing on a sixty-five foot catamaran bound for Florida via the Panama Canal. This, he reflects, is symbolic of his continued good luck in his exploration of new places to visit.

The bar is getting busy, as he looks at his watch. Nearly nineteen hundred hours. Funny he muses; *I guess I'll always think in terms of the twenty-four hour clock. My friends should be here soon* looking towards the only door. *I wonder what it is that is so urgent that they need to see me tonight.*

Puerto Vallarta, he reflects, has been more or less his home base for the past ten months. Arriving from Mazatlan to visit an uncle and aunt who have retired here, it was through them that he met the Daniels'. His work for Kate for several months building a reputation for hard work and dependability led to the present job offer.

The door opens as three young men roll in. They like Roger are well known to Diane who directs them towards where he is seated. They shake hands before seating themselves.

"Beers all around?" asks Diane.

"Yes, mamm," come a collective answer.

"None for me," adds Roger. "Two is enough for me on an empty stomach."

"What's up with you guys?" asks Roger after Diane leaves. "Why the big hurry to get together?"

Collectively there is a look of indecision before one of them speaks. "We have a favor to ask," he begins. "We have a package that we would ask you to deliver to Panama."

"Actually we are not asking for ourselves, but for a friend," chimes in one of the others. "A business friend."

"Here we are, guys," says Diane placing a galvanized bucket of six iced beers in the table center. "I'll be back to check on you."

There is a silence around the table as each takes a long pull from their individual bottles. Roger unsure what to say remains quiet trying to sort out why these three before him with such a weird request.

"What does the package contain?" he finally finds words to ask.

"We don't know for sure."

"Who is the business friend?"

"We are not at liberty to say."

"You must think I'm nuts to agree to taking a package with unknown contents from a secret source out of one country and into another. The answer is no."

"There is a lot of money involved if you will agree."

"I cannot believe this is happening. How can you possibly think money would change my mind?"

"Look, we know this has the ring of something illegal and corrupt. However, we feel we know the business individual well enough that he would not ask us to do anything against the law."

"He is a well-known citizen who would have no reason to place us or him in harm's way," offers one of the others.

"He is offering to pay for services rendered, nothing more," says another.

"The risk is minimal to you. No one would have reason to give second thought to suspecting anything illegal being carried by a private boat," offers a third, now gathering addition confidence.

"But you cannot even tell me what it is I would be carrying."

"We would if we knew."

"Don't you think it is unusual, even strange, that the contents are unknown?"

"Only if you did not know the man making the request."

"I don't know," says Roger, his mind in turmoil. Why are these guys trying to complicate my life? "How much is he willing to pay?" he blurts out, sorry afterwards for letting a break in his defense armor show through.

"Five hundred dollars."

Roger nearly chokes. He suddenly finds it difficult to speak.

"Half now, the balance upon delivery in Panama."

"The final details will be delivered to you with the package upon your departure."

"Is there a departure date and time?"

"Yes," says Roger somewhat recovered. "Friday morning at 10:00 hours."

"Good, we can meet here tomorrow night."

"Not so fast. I haven't agreed to anything."

"Would you say that you are at least interested?"

"Perhaps. But, I need time to think it over. I'm not prepared to give an answer right now."

"Can we meet tomorrow evening for your decision?"

"OK, but don't count on my saying yes," says Roger as he scoots out of the booth and heads for the door.

"We'll pay the bill," shouts one of the men as Roger hurries outdoors into the evening twilight. Instinctively he decides to walk to better be able to think.

The old section of the city is still quiet, it being too early by Mexican standards to eat dinner. Familiar with this area he takes the less traveled

streets and sidewalks where he tries to bring to reality the pros and cons of the proposal. Finally he arrives at an outdoor sidewalk café where he finds an empty table and seats himself. Although hungry he picks at his meal. Emotionally disturbed and confused he is unable to eat. He makes his decision. *No. It is far too risky.*

CHAPTER SIX

Puerto Vallarta at night

Public transportation by bus in most of Mexico, certainly so in Puerto Vallarta, is often an adventure. The vast majority of buses are old and not well maintained. Most have no air conditioning; therefore cooling comes from open windows from which comes the dust and smells of the roadway.

Seats have little padding and are often too thin to provide any cushioning.I question as to whether the buses have springs or shocks as every bump in the road seems transmitted directly to the frame. Imagine if you will the vibrations caused by the many cobblestone streets of Vallarta on your back and bottom. The single largest advantage to riding them is that they are cheap. Tonight to ride from the marina to the old section of the city, a distance of ten miles, costs two pesos, or about twenty cents. Upon boarding I am surprised to see several empty seats. Normally at this hour, it is standing room only. I sit beside an older woman, who I guess is a maid on her way home.

We rumble along stopping to take on and let off passengers. It takes us ten minutes to get to Paseo Diaz Ordaz, a one way street that features a wide pedestrian walk to our right and the waters of Banderas Bay beyond. To our left is a narrow sidewalk fronting the multitude of shops, boutiques and restaurants comprising the newer downtown commercial section. Many of these places of business are just now reopening after the afternoon siesta and in most cases will remain open until the early morning.

The bus rattles along the five or so blocks on Diaz Ordaz to make an S turn following the curve of the Bay and passing the Cabrillo de Mar or Seahorse statue to our right. My memory recalls that the statue was recovered from the ocean floor after many years as part of a sunken Spanish galleon. After restoration it was placed here depicting the cities trademark of hospitality and love of the sea.

Continuing, we pass the city's municipal building to our left and the tree shaded Plaza de Armas to the right, followed by three blocks of shops lining both sides of the narrow street. Now another S curve before crossing up and over the Rio Cuale River. The river geographically divides the new from the old parts of the city. An island, created in its middle, is host to scores of more shops and boutiques, affectionately referred to as 'gringo gulch.'

It is here that the film director John Huston brought Richard Burton and Elizabeth Taylor in 1965 to make the movie Night of the Iguana. Burton and Taylor's romance blossomed on the banks of the Cuale creating an international scandal that put Vallarta on the world map. Their individual houses with the connecting pink arched bridge still remains today as a popular tourists attraction. Taylor's house, Casa Kimberley, is now a bed and breakfast as well as a museum of sorts, as it contains everything she left when she sold the house in the 1980's.

A handsome statue of Huston sitting in his director's chair can be found nearby in a lovely courtyard, not far from one of his favorite restaurants. In spite of commercialism of the area, it is a pleasant place to come for a few hours of browsing, sightseeing and excellent food.

Now the street name changes to Ignacio Vallarta, the cities namesake, paved in cobblestones. We rumble along for six blocks before turning left onto Basillo Badillo where we come to a jolting stop at the bus terminal. By now there is only a hand full of passengers remaining.

Disembarking, it is a few steps to my connecting bus where Mismiloya is hand written in white shoe polish across the windshield. Fortunately it is about to depart as my time to meet Helen draws near. I pay the necessary two pesos and take a second row seat.

The bus is nearly empty as we start out. Within a block, the bus turns right onto Mexico 200 where we climb the moderate grade that takes us south following the seacoast. The two-lane road turns and twists as we rise above sea level. The sun, about to set, is a blaze of color to our right. To the left is visible the many homes and condos that are literally wedged into the rocky cliffs we are skirting. Our progress is slow as we make numerous stops to take on and let off passengers.

After what seem like an eternity, we arrive at the hotel where I am to meet Helen. I enter the hotel grounds and proceed toward the spacious open lobby. I've admired this property each time I've driven by, but never had the occasion to visit.

Set back from the road, it is guarded by high hedges, lush lawns and colorful flowerbeds. Bougainvillea, still in color despite the lateness of the season, is plentiful throughout the gardens.

Steps from the circular covered drive take me to the spacious and nicely appointed lobby where I find Helen and Sarah waiting in high back wicker chairs. They stand as I approach them. Helen speaks as we shake hands, "Bob, it is so good to see you."

We exchange pleasantries as if we were old friends rather than newly acquainted.

"The hotel can take us to my son's home. Please wait," asks Helen, departing for the front desk.

"So, what is new in your life since we saw each other?" I ask Sarah.

"Not much. I have been busy with a few of my friends going to the beach and learning to sail."

"Like in sailboat sailing?"

"Ya. I mean yes. Dad and Mom enrolled me in a sailing school. We sail mostly Hobe cats."

"That's great. I learned to sail when I was about your age. That was before fiberglass boats so my experiences were in wooden prams and a variety of homemade boats that my father built."

"I'm just a beginner, but I really like it."

Helen returns saying that the hotel's shuttle will pick us up momentarily. We start towards the steps and driveway.

"Grandmother, Bob is a sail boater."

"Is that so?"

"And his father built wooden boats."

"Well, you certainly know a lot in such a short period of time."

"It's fine Helen. I enjoy our conversations."

The shuttle pulls up and stops so we may get aboard. It is an electric cart capable of carrying six adults and their luggage. It is covered by a canvas white top and a jaunty yellow fringe, beige leather seats equipped with seat belts. Helen rides up front while Sarah and I take the middle seat. The driver suggests we strap in for the ride. He is a Mexican, tall and slender, I would guess in his late twenties. His dark complexion is in sharp contrast to the starched white hotel uniform he wears. It is obvious that he knows my two companions, as there is an easy banter between them as we start off.

"I'm sorry Bob for not introducing you before. Please meet Juan Carlos, our driver," says Helen.

"Bueno Juan Carlos. I am pleased to meet you," I respond from my back seat.

"Senor, it is my pleasure as well."

"We have known Juan Carlos for a long time," says Sarah from beside me. "He is a good friend."

He takes us around to the back of the hotel, before turning left or north following a brick pathway paralleling a stretch of white sandy beach and now up a grade to an elevation of fifty feet for a lovely view of the sweeping coast line of Banderas Bay. Juan Carlos stops the cart so we may enjoy the view.

"Bob, below is a most wonderful beach for swimming and sun bathing. Sarah and I come here often for both."

"Very pretty," I reply, attempting to fix a mental picture of the grandeur.

We now turn inward away from the water and climb another fifty to sixty feet. We pass through a thick grove of palm trees, their leaves swaying gently in the evening breeze, before coming to a rod iron gate as part of a well-built six foot high stone wall that runs off in both directions. We pass through the open gate onto the grounds of what appears to be a private home. Juan Carlos maneuvers the cart, remaining on the cart path through the well-kept lawns to the paver brick circular drive. He takes us the remaining distance before setting the brake and assisting Helen while Sarah and I unstrap and climb out.

A quick look reveals an attractive single story ranch house built of native stone and tile set among well-manicured gardens. A winding walkway takes us to a handsome set of mahogany doors.

"Hello gang. You are right on time. Bob, I'm Meredith, Helen's daughter-in-law and Sarah's mother. Welcome to Casa Vista."

"It is a pleasure. Thank you for inviting me."

"Come in. Please feel at home."

From the entranceway the house opens into a spacious living room featuring two oversized sofas and several easy chairs center on a large mahogany coffee table. A brightly colored throw rug accents the tile floor under the furniture. The room is high vaulted built from native hardwoods lacquered to a high shine accentuated by brass ceiling fans and fixtures. The inside walls carry the theme of native stone, dispersed with sliding glass doors that provide access to a covered patio and a kidney shaped swimming pool. Wall coverings include several oil paintings and tapestries, all in a Mexican theme that I recognize from Oaxaca.

"Make yourself comfortable," says Meredith. "Helen and Sarah have gone to freshen up and Matt, my husband, will be right along."

Alone for a moment, I stand by a door that offers a view of the patio and pool and where I can see the reflected lights of Puerto Vallarta on the waters of Banderas Bay in the distance.

I know why this is called Casa Vista, I say to myself.

"Hi Bob, I'm Matt. I'm Helen's son. Good to meet you," he says offering his right hand as I turn to meet him.

"Nice to meet you and thank you for the invitation," I say as we shake hands.

"It is our pleasure. Please come have a seat," moving towards the sofas and chairs. "What can I get you to drink?"

"A beer would be fine," I respond.

"I'll get it," says Meredith. "What do you want Matt?"

"Beer will be fine."

I sit in one of the chairs. The open doors allow a delightful breeze to enter.

Both he and Meredith, I would estimate, are in their late forties or very early fifties. They both are trim, tanned and seemingly fit from what I guess are from outdoor activities Matt is clean-shaven with closely trimmed thinning brown hair. He wears a logo golf shirt, neatly pressed khaki trousers and brown open toe sandals. Meredith has her auburn hair trimmed neatly to an easy care style, very little makeup and beautiful smooth skin. A red dress, sandals and white cotton short sleeve sweater complete her attire.

"You have a beautiful home," I say once seated.

"Thanks you," says Matt. "We are close enough to the city for shopping and entertainment, but far enough away that we don't get the noise and confusion."

"I can see the lights of Vallarta. The view must be special during daylight hours."

"It is. We are out on a peninsula that affords us an unrestricted view of the bay. The house was designed and built by my parents."

"I understand from Helen that you have a home in Texas?"

"True. We are fortunate that my business permits me to have the better of two worlds."

Meredith arrives with two cold bottles of Pacifico with frosted mugs together with her glass of white wine and an assortment of crackers and cheeses. She sets everything on the coffee table.

"Help yourselves. Helen will be along in a minute and I believe Sarah is on the computer."

"Thank you," I say pouring my beer.

"Helen indicates that you are about to depart on a voyage through the Panama Canal on a sailboat," says Meredith joining us on the end of one of the sofas.

"Yes. We are scheduled to be underway this Friday morning," I say while helping myself to crackers and cheese.

"And you are delivering it for a client for pay?"

"That is also correct," I respond with a smile. "I get paid for something I love to do."

"Is the client accompanying you?" continues Meredith.

"No. A bank in England owns the boat."

Helen joins us. She has changed into a smart looking skirt and blouse. Her silver hair is pulled back into a bun with a large stickpin running through it. Light makeup and perfectly even white teeth highlight an unblemished complexion.

I start to rise from my chair.

"Please stay seated Bob. There is no need to get up for me. Can I get anything for anyone?"

"We all indicate no. She excuses herself to the kitchen.

"Mother still enjoys getting dressed up to go out," says Matt.

"My mother was the same," I relate. "She was always the best dressed in the group. I don't believe she ever owned a pair of blue jeans."

"Neither does Helen," chuckles Meredith.

"I know the boat," says Matt returning to the previous topic.

"Athena," I respond.

"Yes. She has been extensively written about in the local papers and several boating magazines. She is considered somewhat of a hard luck boat, surrounded by mystery and unexplained occurrences."

"I didn't know that," says Meredith.

"One article I recall described how shaken the captain was that brought her into Puerto Vallarta. He refused to take it further because of her erratic behavior."

Helen returns from the kitchen with her white wine. She joins Meredith on the sofa. "I've heard part of the conversation," she says. "What is this mystery all about?"

"Well, there is no question that she has a design defect in high seas," I say. "She is set so low in the water that waves become trapped underneath her superstructure causing an upward hydraulic effect that stalls forward progress."

"Admittedly, I know very little beyond what I have read." says Matt. "Other stories tell of mysterious unexplained occurrences such as equipment malfunctions and strange illnesses to crew and passengers."

"I've not heard or experienced any of this in my time onboard," I remark.

"How did she get here?" asks Meredith.

"The story goes that she had been in La Paz, Baja Mexico previously. It was there that the bank repossessed her and hired the captain mentioned earlier, who assured them he could deliver her to Florida for resale. For reasons unknown to me, he got her as far as here where he dumped her off, never to be seen again. After the bank got news of the defection, they contacted my friend Captain Allen Daniels to finish the trip who declined because she was in such bad condition. Refusing to believe his appraisal of her condition, the bank allowed her to remain virtually unattended for months, although they did pay slip fees and gave Captain Daniels a small stipend for minor repairs and cleaning."

"What a shame," says Helen.

"The bank listed her with several yacht brokerages in Mexico and California, but to no avail. I think a big reason she didn't sell was the asking price. The bank never believed that she had depreciated as much and refused to lower the price. Finally, someone woke up to the realization that their only hope to recover any of their investment was to spend the necessary funds to get her seaworthy and to pay Daniels to get her to Florida where the resale boat market is strongest." I pause for another cracker and cheese before continuing. "It has taken three months to get her ready. Daniels found it necessary to take her to Mazatlan to have the bottoms cleaned and painted in a boatyard that could accommodate her 25 foot width."

"I'm guessing that because an English bank holds the mortgage that she is of English origins?" asks Matt.

"Yes. Constructed, I believe, in Southampton, England in 1978. The only one built, she was designed exclusively for charter work to carry three or four couples in complete comfort. Each couple has their own air conditioned stateroom with full bath, a stereo radio/tape system and lots of privacy if desired. Common areas consist of a dining room, full galley or kitchen, a lounge for social activities and a full array of water sports."

"Sounds wonderful," says Meredith.

"She did very well in her first ten years of service in the British Virgin Islands where she was kept busy and made money. After that and again for reasons that I am not certain, she passed through a series of owners until she was brought to La Paz."

"You say she is a catamaran?" asks Matt.

"Yes," I answer in between a swallow of beer. "Sixty-five feet in length, twenty-five feet in width and draws six feet of water. She is a cutter-rigged sloop with two Volvo Penta diesel engines. She is capable of six to seven knots of speed in smooth water."

I look up as Sarah appears from the bedroom end of the house. She also has changed into a skirt and blouse, her short blond hair neatly parted in the middle and held back under a barrette. Like her mother and grandmother she has clear smooth skin although bronzed by the sun. Her smile reveals a small retainer.

"I'm ready whenever you guys are," she says headed for the kitchen.

"Another beer, Bob?" asks Matt.

"No thanks, I am fine."

"We thought we would eat out tonight," says Meredith. "I hope you do not mind."

"We'd like to take you to one of our favorite places," says Helen.

"It's called Archie's Wok," calls Sarah from the kitchen.

"I know the place," I respond. "We have gone there often over the years."

"Then perhaps we should be on our way," indicates Meredith. "It can be busy even at this time of the year."

"Would you care to see more of the house?" asks Helen.

"Yes, if you wouldn't mind."

Helen takes me on a brief tour of the inside, pointing out special features as we go. "Charles and I built this as a retreat," she offers as we step out on the patio. "He loved it here especially for the view," she continues as we circle the pool area. The tour ends in the kitchen where the family has assembled for departure.

"Out this way," indicates Matt leading us out to the garage.

I have a moment in which to reflect. It is indeed a beautiful home and a gorgeous setting.

CHAPTER SEVEN

Dinner with friends

"**W**hat is his answer?" asks Mendoza.

"He wants to think it over," answers the spokesman.

"Why? Haven't I offered enough money?"

"Perhaps, but I think he is afraid of being caught."

"Everyone has a price. Double the offer. When do you see him again?"

"Not until tomorrow evening."

"That is too late. You must see him before. Go tomorrow morning to convince him."

The spokesman leaves the way he came in, through a back door. He is careful not to be seen as he stays in the shadows of the back street.

With Matt driving the family Suburban, the trip down to old Vallarta takes only a few minutes. Luckily he finds a parking space on the one way dead end street just steps from the restaurants entrance. The street, only one block long, terminates at the bay at Playa de los Muertos, the beach of the dead, which city officials have long tried to rename Playa del Sol.

"One of the benefits of Vallarta in the summer is that you can find on occasion a place to park," says Matt as we all leave the car to walk up the inclined street.

Archie's, tucked away here is nearly obscured by glitzy silver/gold stores, souvenir shops and the more typical outside patio style restaurants. Its exterior is very modest with the use of white stucco, rod iron bars covering

four exterior windows and a dimly lit sign featuring a Chinese wok

38

suspended over the three steps leading inside.

A young lady, who I suspect may be one of Archie's daughters, greets us as we enter. We follow her through the first seating area to an elevated section directly above where we are seated at a round table with Helen seated to my right. A third section of the restaurant is terraced above us, creating three distinct dining rooms. The lower or ground floor through which we entered, provides space for the kitchen, a small liquor bar, seating for twenty-five to thirty and at the very far opposite corner from the bar and kitchen are two tiny restrooms.

The cuisine is Oriental, featuring many Thai dishes. Archie, a native of the Philippines was employed by John Huston as his personal cook, traveling the world with Huston, meeting and marrying his wife Cindy, before coming to film Night of the Iguana. They decided to settle here and open this restaurant about 1980. Unfortunately he has since passed away; however, his wife and three children continue to carry on with the tradition of great food.

Our waitress introduces herself, explained the evening's specials, pours water, spreads napkins on each of our laps and takes our drink orders.

"How do you know Archie's?" asks Helen.

I explain my wife's and my long association with the area in having kept a sailboat here for many years both before and after retiring. "The Daniels' were the first to introduce us and we would come often when in town."

Our drinks arrive together with menus by our cheerful waitress. "I'll be back for your dinner orders," she says.

"Salud," offers Matt raising his glass in the traditional toast of good health and friendship.

"How come you don't sound like a Mainer?" asks Matt. "Most of mother's families have a very distinctive accent."

Helen frowns in the direction of her son.

"We have only lived in Maine for a few years since retirement in 1994."

"Why Maine, of all places?"

"No single reason," I answer. "Certainly the quality of life is a factor as is the natural beauty of the state. Other contributing factors are the people and their values."

"Unfortunately Mathew has had very little exposure to where I was born and raised," injects Helen. "Except for a few family reunions, he and for that matter even I have not spent any long periods of time in Maine in years."

"You mentioned earlier Matt, that you are an attorney by training, but do not practice law. May I ask what you do?" I ask hoping I have not overstepped my bounds.

"I am the CEO of our family's charitable foundations."

"Oh," is about all I can say. My mind whirls attempting to understand.

Matt grins as he recognizes my dilemma, but defers to Helen for any explanation.

"Tell the story, grandmother," says Sarah, now fully involved in the conversation.

"I remember you saying on the airplane that you dated a young lady who was attending Mount Holyoke. What year was that?" asks Helen.

"1952," I answer wondering what this has to do with Matthew's answer.

"I was in my sophomore year at Smith then," she reflects. "I graduated in 1955. It took me a little longer than others to get my degree. In 1954, the year I was to graduate, I met Charles my future husband. My education suddenly seemed unimportant. We were married in the chapel at Smith in 1955 after which we set up housekeeping in Boston where Charles finished at MIT the following year."

Our salads arrive.

"Bob are you a New Englander?" asks Meredith as a way to keep the conversation going, but allowing Helen to eat her salad.

"Yes, born in Massachusetts. I left after high school and like you folks have not returned except for family affairs."

"I thought I heard a broad A once or twice," she says with a smile.

"I thought I had lost that long ago."

"After graduation, Mother and Dad settled in San Jose, California. Dad was born there, so it seemed the best place to put down roots," offers Matt.

"Charles was a constant tinkerer. After a day's work he would spend hours in our garage. His passion was electronics," inserts Helen.

"The short story version is that he developed one of the first circuit boards for use in computers and other electronic devices," says Matt.

"Our company exists today, although we are no long involved in its management. The wealth created by becoming a public company, allows us through our foundations to help others," says Helen with a sparkle in her eye.

"And that is where I come in," says Matt. "With mother and the board of directors, I oversee the day to day running of the various trusts, investments, charitable requests and distribution of funds."

It makes sense now.

Dinner is served. Our efficient waitress serves us and leaves with the promise she will check back shortly.

Over dinner the conversation is light and breezy with topics including Sarah and her sailing, Matt leaving on a business trip, Meredith's boutique and Helen's E-shopping business. There is good exchange between them with periods of friendly family fun poked at one another.

I finish what has been an excellent meal to sit back and relax as the table is cleared. I order coffee but no dessert.

"Might I ask Matt, if the new gymnasium back home was made possible by the foundation?"

"Yes, dedicated by Dad and Mom in 1990."

"That was a wonderful day," says Helen as tears well in her eyes.

Over coffee we discuss the schedule of ports of call for the transit. I try to the best of my ability to give a time line when we expect to be at the Canal and on to Florida. "There are so many variables," I say, "that it is difficult to say for sure when we will reach Ft Lauderdale."

"I may be down to the boat tomorrow morning," says Matt. "I'd like to see her and to meet Daniels."

"I'll let him know. About what time should I say?"

"Eight AM."

"We should be on our way," says Helen. "Can we give you a lift back to the marina?"

"It is not necessary," I respond. "The bus runs until midnight and the terminal is just up the street."

"As you wish," she says rising from her chair to descend the steps to the main room. Matt pays the bill while the four of us proceed outside into the warm night air.

"Bob, I am so glad we had this opportunity to be together," says Helen.

"Thank you for allowing me to meet your family," I say with a kiss on the check and a hug.

"Sarah, be careful when sailing. Perhaps when you come to Maine you will look me up."

"I would like that," she says as we shake hands.

I say goodbye to Meredith with a hug.

"I'll see you in the morning," says Matt offering a firm handshake.

The walk to the bus terminal takes me past several shops, restaurants and bars. The narrow sidewalk bustles with activity as I weave in and out avoiding the multitudes.

Reaching the terminal I find the marina bus. I step aboard, pay my two pesos and settle into a vacant seat. Several others come aboard before the driver backs us away from the loading area. At the traffic light he turns left onto Ave. Constitution, the one way street leading out of the old section. This street is no less bumpy than its counterpart. Soon we cross the Rio Cuale and on towards the marina.

The ride of thirty minutes affords me the opportunity to reflect on the evening events. I could not have imagined that I would be given a firsthand account of how one of America's most respected companies got its start as well as being narrated by one of the founding members. I also feel fortunate in that I was taken in and made to feel so comfortable as part of the family. It shall be an evening to remember.

Departing the bus, the walk to the marina and on to Athena's berth takes just a few minutes. Although it is midnight, the malecon remains active, as are the restaurants with late evening diners. I am again fortunate to find the entry gate unlocked. There is no activity on the dock, only the evening breeze causing a halyard somewhere above to slap against its metal mast as well as the gentle flapping of flags and burgees. I unwittingly disturb a sleeping heron perched on a bowsprit, scaring him as much as myself. Squawking his displeasure, he soars aloft into the star filled night.

Heart pounding, I reach the boat and quickly scramble on board. I refasten the lifeline before entering the cockpit where only a small lamp illuminates the cabin indicating that Roger has turned in for the evening. Quietly crossing the main cabin and descending below, I enter my cabin. It is as I had left it; no maid service today I chuckle.

With little fanfare I prepare for bed. Another busy day lies ahead I remind myself as I switch off the reading light. I need to be up early enough to let Allen know we may have company at eight.

Sleep comes fast.

CHAPTER EIGHT

Preparations for departure

"**S**o, you got an earful about Athena's dark background," says Allen. "Who again is this chap from whom you got all this information?"

We are seated at the cockpit table. It is 06:45.

"He is the son of the woman I met on the plane," I explain. "His name is Mathew."

"I have heard many of the same stories and rumors but have found nothing to substantiate them."

"I guess I'm only mildly curious," I say. "During all the time I have spent on board, I've not seen anything unusual or abnormal."

"So there you go. I'll see you at the eight o'clock meeting."

The spokesman nervously sips his coffee while playing with his watch. It is nearly 07:00, the usual time that Roger finishes his morning run. If he sticks to his normal routine he should be passing the small café at any moment. The spokesman has rehearsed his speech several times. He hopes that the extra money offered will help convince Roger that he would be foolish to decline. He plans to emphasize the minimal risk factor and the favor he would be doing for his buddies. He admits however, that he doesn't know Roger all that well and therefore isn't certain how greedy he may be. Also, he inwardly wishes he knew more about the contents of the package.

As anticipated, Roger comes into view running along the nearly disserted malecon. The spokesman stands and steps out onto the sidewalk in order to be seen. "What brings you here?" asks Roger still running in place. I am hoping I could have a few words with you." "If it is about the package, my answer is still no."

"Can we sit and talk for a minute, please?"

Reluctantly and against his better judgment, Roger takes a seat opposite the spokesman.

"Can I get you anything to drink or eat?"

"A bottle of water would be fine."

The spokesman signals the waiter and orders as Roger towels down from the morning workout.

Sensing a need for quiet, the spokesman allows time for the water to be delivered and for Roger to take several swallows. He knows that what happens in the next few minutes will determine his ability to gain Rogers cooperation. He rehearses his presentation once again.

"Hola, Paco," I say upon finding him stacking boxes and cartons on the aft deck. Although only 07:30, it is quite warm and humid.

"Hola, Roberto. How are you?"

"I am fine. Can I help you?"

"Yes. Hand these items to me in the engine rooms."

There are two piles, each containing engine filters, belts and oil. He goes below where he opens the starboard engine access hatch. I hand down the items designated starting with the engine oil. We then move to the port engine's access hatch where the same procedure occurs.

"Good morning, Bob," says Roger as he comes aboard from his morning run. "Meeting at eight?" he asks.

"I believe so," I answer.

"See you then," he says headed for his cabin.

Paco sticks his head out saying, "Thanks for your help."

"You're welcome. Meeting at eight o'clock," I remind him.

Returning to my cabin I cool off with a wet towel. Even at this early hour the outside air is enough to cause a healthy sweat. I sit on my bunk to further relax, cool off and ponder the day's activities.

Headed for the meeting, I stop at the galley for coffee before entering the cockpit and sliding into the forward bench. Paco sits beside me followed shortly by Roger to sit across from us. It is 08:00 sharp.

Allen comes from his cabin below carrying several pieces of paper. He slides in beside Roger on the aft settee before spreading the multiple page weather faxes.

"As you will see," he starts, "the weather up and down the Mexican coast is good. We are under a stationary high-pressure system that will assure us of good weather for the next three or four days." He turns the papers so that we may individually look. "Looking out five to six hundred miles shows no disturbances, "he continues while displaying a second page. "Wind direction and speeds are favorable from the west with sea swells at two to three feet. High tide tomorrow is at 15:00 hours. By leaving at 12:00 hours we can expect a good push out of Banderas Bay from the outgoing tide as we round Cabo Corrientes at 18:00 hours. Any questions so far?"

We each shake our heads, no. Typically, Allen is very thorough.

Folding the weather faxes, he turns to two other papers. "I have a draft authorization from the bank for sufficient money to see us to the canal. At Balboa I will receive a second draft for the balance of the trip. I need to go to Banamex today to access the funds. Additionally, I have the bank's authorization to physically move the boat from here to Florida.

Lastly, I have been in contact with our agent in Panama, who is now aware of our transit and will prepare the necessary paperwork. Can I answer any questions?"

I ask if he plans to file a float plan.

"No. Unlike in the states, there is not a government agency that keeps track of civilian boat movement. However, Kate has our intended ports of call and estimated times of arrival. I generally keep in contact on a regular basis via single sideband.

If there is nothing else for me, let's go around the table for updates from you."

Paco starts. "I need to service the two generators and the Yamaha outboard. I have everything on board to last the entire trip based on one hundred-hour oil and filter change. I have a few other items, such as inspect and clean the air conditioners. I could use a helping hand with cleaning evaporators and condensers."

"I'll help," offers Roger.

"Then I should have no problem being ready by morning."

"Roger, how about you?"

I have only to finish making the lightning arresting devise. I have all the materials I need and can help Paco whenever he wishes."

"Good. Bob, you can go ahead with provisioning. We can ride together. I'll do my banking while you shop. Departure will be at 10:00 hours. I'll arrange for port clearance to Acapulco. Let's go to work. Bob, I'll be with you in a couple minutes."

I pour myself the last of the coffee and find two pieces of old bread for toast. While waiting for Allen, I go aft into the port side pontoon where

I recall a small sleeping area with a double sized bunk. The space shares a head with a shower; toilet and hand sink with a similar space forward that I figure Paco will use. There are storage drawers for clothing and other personal effects, together with a small hanging closet. A porthole lets in good daylight while a reading light over the bunk looks ideal for nighttime reading. This is ideal for me.

"Allen, unless you have an objection, I am going to move aft into the small cabin in the port pontoon," I say in passing his cabin.

"None at all. You'll probably get a better ride back there."

"Thanks. It won't take me long to move my gear. Call me when you are ready."

I gather together the few items which I have used placing them into the duffel bag. Striping the bed, I take the sheets and pillowcase to the laundry room to be washed later. Within minutes I am satisfied that I am leaving the cabin as well as I had found it.

The new cabin, although smaller, proves to be more than adequate for my needs. I make up the bed, find clean towels, store my gear and test the night light.

Realizing the time, I head for the cockpit where I find Allen talking with Matt outside on the fantail. Matt must have come aboard without my hearing him. I hesitate disturbing them because their body language suggests a deep conversation.

After several minutes, they shake hands and Matt departs. I'm tempted to say hello, but decide against it, remaining inside until Allen joins me.

"Did you see your friend's son? Allen asks.

"Yes, just briefly before he left."

"Nice fellow, we had a good visit. All set below?" he asks.

"I believe I am going to be very comfortable."

"Good. Let's go," he says opening the sliding cockpit door and stepping out into the mid mornings heat and humidity.

"I trust you have good news," exclaims Carlos Mendoza.

"I do," says the spokesman. "He has agreed to carry the goods for the new amount offered. He will meet us tonight to finalize the arrangement."

"Very well, I'll have everything ready when you come back."

"Won't you be joining us?"

"No, no. There is no need for me to attend. I have complete confidence in your ability to handle matters." With the wave of a hand, he dismisses the young man.

"I have made arrangements with Kate to borrow her van," says Allen as we make our way to the ramp leading up to the malecon. "I'll drop you off at the market while I go to the bank."

The van, parked in the shade, is reasonably cool when we climb inside. Backing out of the one way street, he carefully maneuvers the aged beast over the cobblestones with tender loving care. Our destination is reached in very little time where I am dropped off at Commercial Mexicana, the large supermarket that anchors the mall. I proceed to the office of Roberto Perez, the store manager. He is a good friend who has helped us before and speaks excellent English.

"Hola, Roberto," he says shaking my hand. "It is good to see you again my friend."

"Thank you Robert. It is good to see you as well."

"Captain Allen said you would be in this morning. I have two of my best people to help you with your shopping. Come with me and I will introduce them to you."

He takes me to the employee lounge located to the rear of the market. It is crowded with numerous off duty cashiers, baggers, stockers and general staff. He leads me to a table where several young people are seated, introducing me to Jose and Maria Osuna, who I learn are second cousins.

"I will leave you in their capable hands," announces Roberto before leaving.

"Let me begin by thanking you for helping me," I say placing the three page list on the table.

"We'll try our best," answers Jose in perfect English.

Both are I estimate to be in their late teens, well groomed with clean white starched uniforms and nicely polished black shoes.

"Are you in school?" I ask Maria.

"Yes, presently I am in my final year of what is the equivalent in the United States of high school."

"And you Jose?"

"I am also in my final year."

"Excellent," I say. "Good luck to you both."

Now seated with each on a side, I spread the lists out for them to review.

"Each item is written first in English, then Spanish followed by quantities. As you locate an item, check it off on the list. If unable to find an item, leave it the space blank."

"I would ask that Jose be responsible for frozen, Maria for dry while I work on fruit and vegetables. Use your best judgment in substituting brands that you cannot find as mentioned before. Can I answer any questions?"

"Where should we meet when we have completed the list?" asks Jose.

"Good question. I'll ask Roberto to have a checkout line designated for our exclusive use. Either he or I will let you know which line number it will be. Anything else?"

"If we have problems, can we find you?" asks Jose.

"I should be around the fruits and vegetables. Captain Allen will probably float between us. Do you know what I mean by float?"

"He will move around helping as needed," answers Jose.

"Right you are. OK, let's get started."

Entering the large confines of the market, we select our shopping carts and proceed to our areas of assignment. This is certainly the easiest way to accomplish the provisioning task. I can recall the first time that I attempted to do this entirely by myself it literally took forever.

I am delighted when the produce manager comes forward to introduce himself.

Shaking hands, I thank him and show him my list. Without hesitation he takes it and whirls into action using hand signals and Spanish towards two stockers who have suddenly appeared. Quickly I realize that this is an added effort by Roberto to make this a painless experience. I am impressed. The carts fill quickly. I feel guilty that I am not taking a more active part; however, there is very little I can do other than stand and watch.

I find Roberto by his office together with Allen. I ask if a separate checkout line can be created, to which Roberto agrees.

Allen excuses us as we walk back towards the produce section.

"The bank was very slow," he indicates. "They had to double check on the authenticity of the transfer like I haven't been doing this for over a year. And of course I had to produce two pieces of identification, even though the branch manager knows me by sight. I guess it was the large dollar amount of this one that had them nervous."

Jose and Maria greet us with a big smile. They indicate that everything listed was found and that the carts are ready to be taken to the checkout area.

Roberto waves us to line number ten where soon there is a beehive of human activity at the station including a very capable female checker, two or three baggers together with Jose, Maria and Roberto. Once the dry goods are assembled, I have two baggers take them to the waiting van parked just outside in the shade under the large overhang.

We stack to the front just behind the two passenger seats where I figure first in is last out, best for non-perishables.

Finishing, we return for the next load. We get further assistance from two additional baggers who load both frozen and dairy. Lastly is produce. The loading is done smoothly in less than five minutes. Time now is precious, as we need to quickly get back to the boat, off load and get the perishables into refrigeration.

Closing the back of the van, I hurry inside to say thank you and goodbye to Roberto and his helpful staff. Afterward, Allen and I waste little time getting back outside, into the van and underway. I estimate it is close to ninety degrees inside. It is just past twelve noon. We rumble over the cobblestones ever mindful of the five dozen eggs that are stored somewhere behind us.

Looking over to Allen, I ask, "When are we going to learn to do this in the relative coolness of the night?"

"Good question," he answers with a grin. "We have done it enough times now that you would think we should have learned something."

He takes the van to the end of the dead end street leading into the marina where we park in a loading zone.

Immediately I climb out, open the rear doors and gather as many bags of produce that I can carry. Allen likewise, we head for the boat. Again fortunately the security gate is open so we are able to proceed without delay.

Reaching the boat we find Roger on the fore deck. He comes aft and assists with our bundles to the galley.

"Can you find Paco to help us?" asks Allen of Roger. "The two of you bring the two wheel dolly. We are parked next to Greg's shop."

Returning to the van, I gather the remaining small bags of produce and the beginning of frozen goods. We decide that Allen will remain at the van to wait for Paco and Roger while I remain on board to begin putting items away.

"Ok," I respond as I start off. Reaching the security gate I pass the boys with the two-wheel cart.

"Allen is waiting," I indicate.

Reaching the connecting ramp leading down to the floating dock, I realize that the incline is very modest due to the near full tide. 'This is the tide that will help carry us out of the bay tomorrow afternoon,' I say to myself.

I find it necessary to maneuver around several projects occurring on the boat dock. One couple has decided to empty the contents and clean their dock locker with the contents now scattered about. Jim, from Jedi is scrubbing the bottom of his dinghy that fills half of the dock. He looks up and asks; "Need any help?" as I pass.

"I could in getting through the life line and onto the aft deck," I answer.

Dropping his scrub brush, he hurries ahead of me to climb onboard. Now he reaches down to take several bags placing them in the shade of the awning. It is a big help for which I am grateful. Once everything is aboard, he carries many items into the boat and to the galley.

"Thank you very much," I say once all is below.

"Oh, you're welcome. I'm just piddling around, trying to get ready to go north."

"Where to?"

"San Carlos. I store the boat there every year. I am late this year because I have been in the States up to a week ago."

"Well, I appreciate the help. Thanks once again." I sense he would like to stay and visit, but I need to get these many things put away. Thankfully he doesn't offer to stay and help. He is known on the dock as an overly friendly type that doesn't know when to go home. He is single, probably never been married and not the most hygienic. Some individuals who have been on board his boat say that it is in need of fumigation. Apparently he is a pack rat who never throws anything away.

I load the frozen goods into freezer units, recording their location in a spiral logbook. Vegetables are placed in the one side of the two-compartment sink where I run tepid water while adding three to four drops of microdyn. Here they remain for twenty minutes to kill any bacteria. I have most of the perishables unbagged and in various stages of disinfection before the dry and paper goods arrive.

"Any place special you would like these to go?" asks Paco of the three bags he brings down.

"No, anyplace will do," I answer without paying particular attention.

"And these?" asks Roger.

"What do you have?" I ask.

Mostly frozen with some fresh meats mixed in."

"If you can separate the two, the frozen can go below. The other can be put in the refrigerator unit up here."

Roger takes little time to complete the sorting and placement of the items he brought down before returning above for additional items. I look through the bags brought down by Paco to find that all items are nonperishable, so can be dealt with later.

The process continues until all fruits and vegetables are sanitized and put away. Several more loads of nonperishables arrive, to the extent that the main cabin sole is covered. Roger helps to separate items. We work well together in deciding what quantities of pork chops, steaks, sausage, and bacon are enough for one meal for the four of us. All are carefully marked and put away for ease of finding when needed.

Cooking on board in the past has been more the responsibility of Allen than anyone else. He has tended to be the one who makes up the evening meal menu and generally cooks whatever he has decided upon. Most often his meals are surprisingly tasty and filling, although on one occasion he got heavy

handed with the red wine he was using in a sauce and I thought I would

never get over the heartburn. I drank gallons of water for two days to put the fire out.

Paco cooks on occasion, especially if he catches fresh fish, which he marinates then bakes. The results are outstanding.

My role has been in keeping the galley clean. The big challenge is the cleanup after either of them. On many occasions I have wished the roles could be reversed.

The last of the items are now onboard. Roger and I sort out the last of the refrigerated goods, mark and put them away. Next the dry goods are separated and they also are stored away according to their use and need.

Of the twelve large loaves of bread, ten go into a freezer. Two of the three five pound tins of coffee are put into the freezer.

The process continues until all items are put away where they can be found when needed. The master list of where any item may be located is placed between the sugar and flour canisters. Hopefully this will serve as a guide to whoever is preparing the meal as to where to look for whatever they need without having to ask Roger or myself. This is wishful thinking as I have learned from prior trips.

Finally done, we each make ourselves a good size ham and cheese sandwich, open a bag of potato chips, a jar of dill pickles and a soft drink. Retiring to the lounge, we sit on the cabin floor before turning on the television. The clock above the set indicates it is 1500 hours.

Relaxed we watch an old cowboy movie playing on HBO. I doze off for a ten-minute power nap, waking to hear Allen rustling about in the galley. He joins us with his sandwich by sitting on one of the sofas that form the semi-circle to the lounge.

"What's happening?" he asks.

"Roger was good enough to help me," I answer. "I believe I am ready except for a little clean up."

"I am expecting Thad (electrician & radio man) from Mine Too to come over and give our electronics a final check," says Allen. "Paco tells me that he is completed with his items, again thanks to Roger."

"No problem," says Roger.

"And your status, otherwise?" he asks Roger.

"All set. I need to put a few tools away and secure the forward chain locker. Otherwise I am done."

"I have obtained our departure clearance from the Port Captain to Acapulco," Allen summarizes. "Once we have fuel, we can go."

"Are we eating onboard tonight?" I ask.

"No I think not. I expect Paco will want to be with his family. Kate and I probably need to spend time together as well. So you two are on your own. Bring me the receipts and I'll reimburse."

"If you don't mind Bob, I plan to have dinner with a buddy tonight. I hate to leave you alone."

"No problem," I answer. "I'll go up to Porto Bello and renew old acquaintances."

The doorbell rings.

"Probably Thad," says Allen as he gets up from the sofa and moves towards the cockpit stairs.

Roger clicks off the now forgotten TV movie. "I'll see you later," he says as he ducks down the companionway to his cabin.

Cleanup in the galley takes only a few minutes. I make a pot of coffee. It seems that there is always a pot brewing. I fill two mugs to take them to the cockpit where I can hear Thad doing a series of radio checks. Allen is nearby, monitoring results on a meter. Putting down the mugs where they both acknowledge their thanks, I head for my cabin.

The late afternoon sun reflecting off the shimmering water streams in through the porthole creating a dance of light and shadow on the bulkhead. It produces a warm and inviting feeling to this small but adequate space I shall call home for the next few weeks. I stretch out on the bed just as a test. It will be fine I predict. I put away the last of my items, wash up and return to the cockpit.

"Hello, Robert," calls out Thad, looking up briefly from his work.

"Hi, Thad."

"You are looking well," he continues. "How is Pat?"

"She is well. Loves Maine and keeps busy with her ceramics."

"Give her my best when you speak to her next."

"I shall. In fact I need to call her this evening."

Not having anything specific to attend to, I slide into the forward settee to observe and relax. Allen and Thad keep a lighthearted banter going between them while performing the various tests.

Allen and Kate have known Thad and his wife Eileen for many more years than Pat and I have. They (the Daniels) introduced us to them at one of the many parties we attended upon our arrival.

This is Thad and Eileen's second marriage. They enjoy each other in a relaxed, vagabond life living aboard a forty-foot sailboat.

I recall with pleasure the time we cruised together from Mazatlan to Ixtapa, each in our own boat. We made many stops en route, anchoring in remote bays and inlets where we fished, swam, sun bathed, drank beer and looked out for each other. In Zihuatanejo, we join up with a dozen additional cruisers to spend several weeks riding the hook (anchor) inside that towns beautiful bay. It seems there was a party every evening in a different restaurant or on some ones boat, where Thad usually held center stage. However, when they are "under way", they are serious boaters. Both are members of the Coast Guard Auxiliary and have thousands of miles under their keels. By training he is an electronics repairman, at one time owning his own company, she I believe is a former nurse.

"Allen, I believe I am done here. All components check out good. You guys are good to go."

"Then it's cerveza time," announces Allen turning to open the refrigerator located under the hand sink.

"They may not be cold," I say.

"OK, then let's go up to the bar next to Kate's shop. I bet their beer is cold."

Thad gathers together his tools and test equipment. "I'll meet you there," he says departing through the sliding door to his waiting dinghy.

I quickly go below for my hat, sunglasses and money. Returning to the cockpit, Allen is telling Paco our plans. Paco indicates that he is ready to leave for home.

We take the dinghy despite the short walk around the marina. The sun, now low in the western sky, casts long shadows from the three and four story condos ringing the basin across the open water. It remains hot and humid even in the shade.

We approach "A" dock where scores of tenders are tied off in a helter-skelter manner requiring that we push and shove them aside in order to get close enough to off load. Once the dingy is secured, we hike up the inclined ramp to the malecon and head for the bar. It is not difficult to find because it is the only place with activity. Many of the other tiendas (restaurant/bars) remain closed for siesta. We settle in on two stools at the bar to wait for Thad.

This bar has been popular with the gringo cruising community for as many years as I have been coming here. The owner provides good service, cold beer and a small selection of sandwiches. His prices are reasonable and the place is clean. He has not tried to make the bar something it is not.

"Hi Allen," greets the bartender. "What can I get for you and your friend?"

"Rum and coke for me. What about you, Bob?"

"A beer, please. A Pacifico."

"Right away, Senors."

He leaves to fill our orders.

"I'm going over to the shop for minute," informs Allen sliding off his stool. "I should be right back."

Left alone, I gaze out over the marina. Everything is in shadows except for the upper half of the signature lighthouse and the very top of a few condos.

Fleecy cumulus clouds are piled one upon another above the distant Sierra Madre Mountains, a pillar of snowy white upon which the infinite colors of sunset play. Activity on the water consists of a sailboat with mainsail up, gliding down the channel. The late afternoon breeze moves her along on a nice broad reach.

"Here you are," announces the bartender disrupting my solace.

"Thanks. I expect Allen will return shortly together with one other."

"Fine, let me know when I can help."

After squeezing the lime into my beer, I take several swallows, savoring the refreshing taste. There is nothing better than a cold beer on a hot day. This one is no exception.

A couple arrives taking stools across the U shape bar. They, like so many others are boaters, retired or on a sabbatical of some sort. They are tanned from exposure to the sun, wear loose fitting comfortable wash and wear clothing and appear to be enjoying life.

Further activity on the water catches my attention. Coming to the dinghy dock is both Thad and Eileen. What a pleasant surprise to see her. They like us earlier, fight their way through the maze of dinghies before being able to tie off.

"It looks like there will be four of us," I inform the bartender.

"No, I believe it will be five," he says motioning behind me as Allen and Kate approach.

I slide off my stool to greet Kate. She has apparently closed shop early in order to relax and spend time with Allen before departure.

We exchange hellos as Thad and Eileen arrive.

"Bob, it's good to see you," says Eileen as we give hugs and kisses.

"Same here. I didn't think I'd have a chance to see you."

"It worked out well," she says.

At the bartender's suggestion, we sit at a table rather than remain at the bar. Once seated and drinks ordered, the conversation centers on catching up with each of our lives since last we saw one another. There are many questions regarding Pat and our lives in Maine. There is much to talk about. We reminisce about sailing trips, who is still cruising and those who have given it up.

The time passes far too quickly before we need to say goodbye. Thad and Eileen return to their boat by dinghy while Allen and Kate depart to the van to drive home. The twilight of the evening now casts a purple vale over the marina. There is still a breeze causing small ripples on the water's surface, otherwise the only disturbance to the tranquil scene is the trailing wake from Thad and Eileen's distant dinghy.

CHAPTER NINE

Chance meeting

Finding a pay telephone, I place a call to Pat. She picks up on the third ring with a cheerful, "Hello."

"Hi there, how are you?" I respond.

"I'm good. Are you ready to go?"

"Yes, tomorrow at noon on the outgoing tide. We are provisioned and except for fuel, all is in readiness."

She fills me in on a couple household items and the weather, while I tell her

about having seen Thad and Eileen, Jim from Jedi and a little about last evening with Helen and her family.

"I'll call from Acapulco."

"Ok. I'll look forward to hearing from you."

"I love you."

"And I love you."

"Bye."

"Be careful."

"I will," I say hanging up.

Relieved with the positive news, I decide it is time to eat. It is several minutes past seven PM and about my dinner time. My restaurant of choice is Porto Bello, Italian, located in the marina on the malecon. Despite being under dressed, I decide to go none the less.

There seems less of a spring in Rogers's step this evening as he makes his way along the streets of the old section of town. His mind is in turmoil as he tries to focus on the impending meeting. He never considered himself greedy; however, the lure of being paid one thousand dollars has had an over powering effect. The question, is the risk worth the reward? He wished he knew.

Reaching the bar, he hesitates before entering knowing that this is his last opportunity to walk away, to not take the risk, to continue with his uncomplicated life. But, he also knows that he is expected inside and he must admit that inwardly, he feels that he can pull this off.

Inside he is met with the familiar sounds and smells of the aged bar. It takes several seconds for his eyes to adjust to the dim light of the smoke filled room. Diane offers her usual cheerful greeting before nodding her knowing head towards the back.

He finds the three in their usual booth. Sliding in beside the spokesman, Roger asks where is the mysterious businessman, expecting him to be present.

"He decided it best not to attend," answers the spokesman. "Besides we can conduct our business without him."

"I really don't like this," says Roger.

"Relax. There is little to worry about," says another of the three.

"Easy for you to say. You're not the one taking the risk."

"Come on fellows," says the spokesman. "Let's not get cold feet now."

From beside him the spokesman produces two items. One is a parcel, measuring six inches by four and two inches deep, neatly wrapped in colorful yellow paper with a white ribbon and bow. The other is an envelope, also yellow with the appearance of being a greeting card to compliment the package.

"Happy birthday," says the spokesman with a wink. "You will have to wait until you get to Panama to open your card."

Roger, taken aback, stares at the two seemingly harmless items on the table.

"This is it?" he asks.

"This is it," answers the spokesman.

"This is what some businessman wants taken to Panama and is willing to pay one thousand dollars for its delivery?" ask Roger in disbelief. "What possibly can be of such value in this small package?"

"We don't know and don't care," answers another of the three.

"We have learned from prior experiences with our businessman not to ask questions," comments the spokesman.

Recovering somewhat, Rogers mind starts to work. 'Certainly,' he concludes, 'these will be easy to conceal on board. If asked, he will answer truthfully that he is taking a gift for a friend from a friend. The one thousand dollar payment may be a problem to explain, however."

"What about the money. When and where do I receive it?" he asks realizing that the question seals his fate. He is now fully committed.

As before, another envelope appears from the spokesman. "Here is half of the amount; the remainder will be given to you by the pickup person upon delivery of the package. Final instruction as to where to deliver the package is contained in the card envelope, not to be opened until after the canal transit."

Silence falls over the table as the bulky envelope changes hands. Roger, tempted to look inside, decides to simply place it in a pocket. Suddenly he feels uncomfortable with a strong urge to leave. He gathers together the package and card before sliding out of the booth.

"Good luck and thanks," says the spokesman.

Roger walks to the door, never looking back.

Activity on the malecon is light even though most shops, boutiques and restaurants are now open. Still it is much too early for the throngs of people that can be expected later this evening. I reach Porto Belo quickly to find that I can be seated inside immediately at the station of one of our favorite waiters, Miguel who greets me with a huge smile and firm handshake.

"Hola senor, it is good to see you."

"Hello Miguel, I'm pleased to be here."

We exchange small talk before I order a glass of wine. He excuses himself and heads for the bar.

Spreading my nicely starched napkin on my lap, I relax as a bus boy pours ice water while another brings a basket of warm bread with butter.

I am seated inside, in the air-conditioned section where it is delightfully comfortable. Outside seating, under a large awning, relies on cooling from the evening breeze and overhead fans. Equally as many seats are inside as out; however, the inside in our opinion has more charm and comfort. Mahogany wood paneling accentuated with mirrors over fine wallpaper, bronze scone light fixtures and ceiling fans together with artwork creates a delightful room of color and elegance.

Miguel delivers my wine.

"Are you ready to order," he asks.

"Yes. The spaghetti with meat balls in marinara sauce."

"Bueno and your salad dressing?"

"Italian, please."

"I'll be just a few minutes with your salad," he says.

"Are either of the owners in tonight?" I ask.

"Yes. Mario."

"Ask him to come by for a minute, please."

Si, Senor."

The wine and buttered bread provides a warm feeling of well being. I need to not fill up and not be able to eat my dinner.

From my table I am able to watch activities both inside and out. Despite the early hour, they are about one third occupied. Based on the number of wait staff, there is little question that they are expecting a good size crowd. Except for the lovely lady who seated me, the rest of the staff is male. Each is dressed in starched white shirts with black bow ties, black trousers and vests. All are conversant in English and Spanish. A few are fluent in French and Portuguese.

Miguel brings my salad. "Mario will be over soon," he says.

Mario and his partner are Brazilian. They met while in college and formed an alliance to someday go into the restaurant business. After several years of going their separate ways, they reunited to establish Porto Bello about ten years ago and have thrived. In the six or seven years that we have been coming here we have always given them high marks. It is pricey, but we never minded for the quality of the food and service has been worth every penny.

My salad finished, I order a second glass of wine.

Now totally relaxed, I try to focus on the next several days and the trip ahead. I'm pleased that we are leaving so soon. My calculations say that it should take us two and one half days to reach Acapulco. If we are able to average seven to eight knots of speed, we should enter Acapulco Bay in the early morning of our third day.

Miguel startles me from my trance. "Here is your dinner, Senor," he says placing a large bowl of steaming spaghetti before me.

"Thank you, Miguel."

"Is there anything else I may bring?"

"No, this is quite sufficient, thank you."

With a slight bow he turns away to attend to his other patrons.

Tucking the napkin under my chin, for I am notorious about getting sauce on myself, I proceed to indulge in one of my favorite dishes. I savor every bite knowing what lies ahead in the way of rolling seas and suspect meals. Finished, I place my knife and fork in the empty bowl and return my napkin to my lap. Reflecting, I wonder where I have managed to put it all.

"Coffee and desert, Senor?" asks the ever attentive Miguel.

"Just decaffeinated coffee, please."

"As you wish," answers Miguel clearing the table.

There have been numerous parties seated during my meal. A party of ten has taken a table near me where there is a birthday party celebration in progress with great fanfare. Seated at the table head, the birthday gal is enjoying the attention her husband at the other end and her guests are showering upon her. It must be a significant age she has achieved.

My coffee is served together with a brandy, compliments of the house.

"Mario apologizes," informs Miguel. "He will be along shortly."

I pour the brandy into the coffee to give it a rich, robust taste warming body and soul.

I spot Mario coming my way. He looks just as I remember. Tall and trim at two hundred pounds, he is clean-shaven and nicely tanned. In his early forties, he is dressed in a white, loose fitting white shirt open at the neck and sleeves rolled up. He moves gracefully among the many patrons who call his name and seeks his attention. Reaching me he extends his hand in a firm handshake before seating himself across from me.

"Robert. It is good to see you. How long are you here for and where is your lovely wife?"

I fill him in on the purpose for my visit and give him an update on Pat.

"Are you still single?" I ask.

"Yes, no one yet. I am too busy to get married," he answers with a smile.

I ask about his partner who I learn is visiting with his wife in the United States. Our conversation lasts for ten minutes before he excuses himself to leave. "Thank you for coming," he says.

I ask for the check in preparation of leaving. The inside seating area is full, so I know Miguel will appreciate my table for customers waiting outside.

I finish my coffee to the realization of how tired I am. I pay the bill providing Miguel with a nice size tip and my warm regards.

The heat and humidity of the night hits like a stone wall as I exit. I observe the outside seating area as full as I start for the exit when I hear my name called from somewhere within the multitude of diners. It is a male voice, someone I think I recognize, but I'm not sure.

"Bob, over here. In the corner."

Suddenly I feel that all eyes are upon me as I search for the source.

"Over there," points a waiter.

I weave in and out of the close set tables while attempting to avoid waiters, bus boys and patrons until I identify my caller as Matt. He is standing as I approach the table while three other men remain seated.

"I thought that was you. I hope I haven't embarrassed you," he says as we shake hands.

"No, but I did wonder who would know me."

"Can you join us?"

"Yes, of course."

A bus boy brings a chair.

"Bob, let me introduce my companions. Jorge Posada, Miguel Valentino and Carlos Mendoza." Each rises to shake my hand. "Would you like coffee or an after dinner drink?" Matt asks.

I decline and thank him.

Matt explains to them how we know one another and a brief overview of the delivery of Athena to Florida.

"I want to apologize Bob, for this morning. I had hoped to get to the boat by eight o'clock; however, I got a late start."

"I did see you for a fleeting minute, just as you were leaving."

"I met Allen. He explained that you and he were leaving for provisions. He invited me to return later, which I was unable to do."

"We leave at ten tomorrow."

"I know, but you guys are going to be too busy to have me hanging around."

"What is your time line to reach the canal?" asks Mendoza.

"Two weeks if we are able to maintain a good speed," I answer.

We spend a few minutes in idle conversation before I excuse myself to return to the boat. I say goodnight to the three men before Matt walks with me to the exit for a final handshake and goodbye.

Thankfully it is a short distance to the boat ramp where once again the security gate is open. The dock is quiet except for the flutter of flags and burgees in the evening breeze. I am watchful for the bird, but he is somewhere else tonight.

Aboard, I slide open the unlocked cockpit door and enter the coolness of the interior. I doubt that Roger is onboard. It is too early for him to be in bed; otherwise he would be watching TV. I leave the door unlocked, proceeding down to my aft cabin.

I prepare for bed finding that my little space is more than adequate. The compartment is very comfortably cool from an air supply source I find I can adjust. There are two reading lights at the head of the bed providing ample light for reading. Not tonight however, as I am unable to focus on the printed page. I snap off the reading lights. The cabin falls into semi-darkness. Sleep comes quickly.

CHAPTER TEN

Underway

Day 1. Tuesday.

Sliding feet first off of the bunk, (it is enclosed on three sides) I find much to my surprise it is six thirty. I shower, shave and dress in shorts and a tee shirt in anticipation of a day spent mostly in the out of doors. A pair of canvas deck shoes and a ball cap round out my attire. I slather on a generous amount of sunscreen on exposed arms, legs, face and ears as past experiences have taught me how tough the sun can be on my skin.

Allen I find is in his cabin on his computer. He looks up upon hearing me enter. "Buenos días, Roberto."

"Buenos días, Allen," I respond.

"How did the night go?" he asks, leaning back in his chair to stretch his large frame. "Did you sleep well in your new quarters?"

I answer in the affirmative as well as give him a brief rundown of dinner and the telephone call to Pat.

"Kate and I stayed home where we had a quiet dinner, watched a little TV and went to bed early."

He confirms that he wants an eight o'clock meeting. I know enough not to take too much of his time, so ask in leaving if I can bring him coffee.

"No. I have had enough for now. But thanks for asking."

Upon entering the main cabin I find Roger in the galley.

"Good morning."

"Good morning, Bob. How are you?"

"Very well thanks. Did you have a pleasant evening?"

"I did," he responds. "My friends and I met at a restaurant in the old section where we often go for dinner."

He goes on in a light and easy manner to tell me about his three buddies and how they had met several months ago. They apparently are of the same age and social backgrounds with many common interests. All are single and wish to remain so, in that they can continue to wander and explore before settling down. He reminds me a little of myself at his age.

"I'm making scramble eggs. Can I make a couple for you?" he asks.

"Yes. I would appreciate that," I respond. "What can I do to help?"

"Make your own toast, if you wish."

I put two slices of bread in the toaster, pour myself fresh coffee and sit at the dining room table. The hot coffee tastes good, stimulating my taste buds for the eggs and toast. The eggs are fluffy and firm, done by someone with experience and knowledge of cooking.

"Where did you learn to cook eggs so well," I ask.

"In the service and my mom," he explains. I learned he had spent four years in the service as a Navy Seal, that his father is a Navy career officer presently assigned to the Pentagon and his mother is a career diplomat presently serving in the Far East. The Seal training certainly explains his excellent physical condition.

Finished with breakfast, we wash and put away our dishes and clean the galley. He excuses himself to go to his cabin, while I refill my coffee mug and settle into the forward bench of the crew table in the cockpit. I open one of the many magazines laying about the area and casually page through its contents. There is no shortage of reading material onboard, from magazines to paperbacks and hard cover.

Roger, immediately upon entering his cabin closes and locks the door. Hurriedly he washes his face and hands and vigorously brushes his teeth, all part of a long-standing habit of personal hygiene. He then reaches up to open one of the storage cabinets located above his bunk to remove the package. Carefully he examines it, turning it over and over while giving it a mild shaking before returning it to the space above. ' I wish I knew what is in there' he says to himself 'and what have I got myself into.' He unlocks the door and heads for the meeting.

I catch Paco out of the corner of my eye as he makes his way onto the dock loaded down with gear. I slide out, cross the width of the cockpit and enter the early morning heat and humidity to meet him at the lifeline gate.

"Hola. Buenos días," I say reaching for some of his bags to bring aboard.

"Hola, Roberto."

I take a duffel bag and one other bag. He comes aboard with his remaining items without need of assistance. We make our way into the cockpit and down to his cabin where I place the bags on his bunk.

"Thank you, Roberto. That is a big help." He is wet with perspiration from the apparent long walk to the boat. I know he has no car, so probably came by bus or a taxi from home.

"De nada." I respond before returning to the cockpit. Allen and Roger are seated, looking at the latest weather fax. Paco joins up quickly.

"The weather continues to hold nicely. The high pressure system to our west has moved our way a few hundred miles, but it will continue to dominate with good weather for at least the next three days," starts Allen. "I listened to the weather net earlier this morning where good weather is reported from Acapulco south to Ensenada north. Our window of opportunity is now and we need to make the most of it.

The watch schedule will be three hours on, nine hours off. I will take the watch from six to nine. Who wants the nine to twelve?"

Before either Paco or Roger can respond, I answer, "Me."

"Very well. Who takes twelve to three?"

Roger volunteers, leaving Paco with the three to six.

"I want to cast off no later than nine forty five for the fuel dock where we have a ten o'clock appointment. By my watch, that is one hour and fifteen minutes from now. Are there any questions?"

I can think of nothing, nor can either of my two shipmates.

"Let's get busy," says Allen rising from the table.

I take my mug below and rinse it out. Exiting outside via the sliding cockpit door, I start to unsnap the sun covers. They provide some help in filtering out the strong sunrays and in part helps keep the boats interior cooler. Each cover is custom fit to its respective window, so consequently is numbered accordingly. I find that many of the snaps are difficult to get to to release because of their age and the length of time they have been in place. With care I remove the twelve or so covers, brushing each clean, folding each and placing them in their designated locker located on the aft deck.

Next I gather together a plastic pail with a sponge and squeegee, adding a small amount of liquid soap with water. With the water hose I wash and rinse the windows removing months of dirt and grime. I then squeegee them dry, coil the hose and I store my equipment before stepping into the cockpit to cool off. Allen has the sail covers off and neatly folded.

These go into the same locker as the window covers.

Paco enters the cockpit from one of the engine rooms below. He is ready to start the engines in preparation of our moving to the fuel dock. He asks for permission of Allen who gives him an affirmative hand sign from his position on the aft deck. As the two engine ignition keys are in place, a red buoy on a key chain for the port and a green buoy on a key chain for the starboard, Paco chooses to turn the port engine first. It comes to life after a few seconds with a cloud of blue smoke from the below water exhaust pipe. I watch as the oil pressure gauge registers sixty pounds and the tachometer reads 1200 Rpms. After several minutes, he starts the starboard engine with identical results.

"Bob, can you stand by while I go below to check for oil leaks?"

"Sure," I answer.

He ducks down the aft passageway leading to the engine rooms. I take note that the port engine oil pressure is fluctuating slightly. I would describe it as "nervous". Both water temperature gauges show a slow but steady rise in heat.

We are beginning to draw a crowd of people on the dock in anticipation of our departure now that the engines are turning. Many have watched the preparation, or lack of, for months. Most are well-wishers who know the history of the boat and are here to give Allen and his crew their best.

Paco reports that both engines have passed his inspection and they therefore are ready to go.

"Ok gang," announces Allen, "let's go to the fuel dock. Paco you are the deck manager, I'll take my signals from you."

"Bob, you handle the forward lines. Roger takes the aft. I'll do the mid-ship," instructs Paco.

We are starboard side-tied to the dock requiring that we back away before Allen has the maneuvering room necessary to take us out to mid channel. The aft and mid lines come free first with the help of several of the folks on the dock. Paco uses the boat hook to shove the stern away while I hold secure with the bowline. Once satisfied with our position, he hand signals to reverse engines and for me to release my line. We float free of the dock to the waves and cheers of our gathered crowd.

I coil the bow line on the foredeck for use later and go aft to help get fenders (hard rubber devises to protect the side of the boat) ready as needed at the fuel dock.

Allen has powered us into the main channel that leads from our position at the back of the marina to the fuel dock at the repair facility, known as Opequimar. We make a hard left turn at the marinas western boundary and proceed up a narrow channel. The yacht club that I had visited is clearly visible to the right followed by a newly opened high rise hotel. To our left are several large homes built to the water's edge, their red tile roofs and sparkling white stucco walls reflecting the late morning sun. Each property has a ramp leading down to a dock with a sizable yacht. It is hard to believe that less than fifteen years ago, that this entire area was little more than a swamp with this as a shallow creek. Now, vessels in excess of one hundred feet and drawing twenty feet in depth come and go on a regular basis.

Athena's twenty five-foot beam (width) seems to engulf the entire span of the channel as we approach the fuel docks to our right and the commercial sport fishing docks to our left. It is here that the channel pinches down to its narrowest point.

Allen brings us to a virtual stop opposite the fuel dock, which is vacant. There is little in the way of a tide running and no wind that aids maneuverability. He and Paco elect to enter the dock bow in, thereby utilizing the existing fenders and tie down line configuration.

Allen spins the boat on its axis by applying opposing engine thrust before easing us forward to where we tie off to the dock with the help of Allen's son Fred who has come over from his sail loft shop to wish us well and assist in fueling.

' Allen shuts down the two engines before coming forward from the cockpit.

"Hello son," he says. "Are they ready for us?"

"Yup, the boys should be right along."

"Good."

Within minutes, the two gas attendants come lumbering down the ramp onto the floating dock to the diesel gas pump.

Paco, in charge of fueling, has the two fuel caps off; one each located aft, port and starboard.

One attendant hauls the fuel nozzle under the lifeline while the second feeds the hose out to him.

Fueling goes swiftly and without incident. Upon completion, Allen goes to the office for payment while we make final preparations for leaving. Meanwhile I spend a few minutes with Fred who brings me up to date on his activities. His business is doing very well he tells me and I learn he is engaged to his high school sweetheart although no wedding date has been set. He is a hard working lad who will do well. I like him very much.

Allen returns joined by Kate. There are rounds of hugs and kisses before Allen restarts the two engines. With little fanfare, the mooring lines are released, the engines reversed taking us back to mid channel where Allen turns us 90 degrees and sets a course leading to the open waters of Banderas Bay.

The mooring lines are removed from their cleats and taken aft to their storage locker for future use. Roger and I release the four fenders from their respective tie downs and remove them aft as well.

With tasks completed for the moment, I give a long distant wave from the fantail (back of boat) to Fred and Kate as they fad from view. We have an armada of small boats escorting us down the channel, filled with waving, cheering boating friends. It is quite a sight.

The Puerto Vallarta cruise ship terminal, now to our left, has two luxury liners in port. The bow of one is perpendicular to us, towers over the harbor entrance. It puts in perspective the size of these floating palaces of the sea.

Entering Banderas Bay, our armada leaves us with final waves of goodbye and air horn blasts.

I check my watch. It is just minutes before 11:00. I make a mental note in order to record our times and other activities in the log.

Allen brings the engine speeds to 2150 rpm's and to a course of 270 degrees. The sea is nearly flat as the afternoon wind has yet to pick up. Athena responds nicely by coming up to six knots of speed with ease and an apparent willingness to get underway.

"Bob, it is your watch. She is yours," says Allen offering me the wheel.

"Paco lets you, Roger and I shake out some sails."

I elect to hand steer for the time being in order to get the feel of Athena as well as my anticipating the course change necessary to setting sails.

With her large wheel, thirty-six inches in diameter, Athena answers quickly to small corrections. I find that a ten-degree course change can be easily accomplished with a quarter turn of the wheel. Located with the wheel is the ship's magnetic compass, easily readable from my steering position. It is eight to ten inches in diameter with large letters displaying the four points of the earth, the smaller letters for the intermediate points, all quickly identifiable at a glance.

On each side of the compass are two additional important instruments. To the left is the depth finder; to the right is the speed through the water indicator. I notice that the speed indicator is at zero suggesting that the paddle wheel on the boats bottom may be fouled. The depth finder seems fine as it registers the varying irregularities to the bottom as we pass over them. We are in 100 feet of water and holding steady. A check overhead and to my right is the Global Position System (GPS) unit. Among many pieces of information it provides, it is displaying our ground speed at six knots, also holding steady.

The guys now have the sail ties off the mainsail with the up haul attached. Allen sticks his head into the cockpit.

"Slow down to steerage and bring her up into the wind."

Acknowledging, I reduce engine power together with a turn of the wheel of fifteen degrees to starboard. As our boat speed slows, we come up nicely into the light breeze. Immediately I hear the electric winch start to carry the heavy mainsail up the mast. Allen controls it from his position forward of the cockpit while Roger and Paco, standing on the cabin roof make certain that the sail runs out properly. Within a few minutes, satisfied with the fit and shape, Allen secures the controls and has Paco set the boom on a close haul. They then roll out the foresail. This is a one hundred and fifty percent Genoa, set on roller furling and controlled by electric winches. Allen sets a port tack on a close haul and now signals for me to return to course and speed. The sails fill, adding a half-knot to our speed.

"Hey guys," says Allen once everyone is back inside, "I have a few quick items I'd like to review in order to avoid any misunderstandings later."

I engage the autopilot so as not to wander off course while listening.

"First, I think it is important for me to say that as the Captain, I want and need to know what is happening at all times. I expect to be notified no matter what time of day or night for anything that you consider abnormal. Understood?" he asks looking at each of us.

I nod in the affirmative together with a, "yes."

He continues, "I want latitude/longitude entries into the logbook and these coordinates plotted on the chart every three hours at watch change. Also recordings in the ships log book of engine oil pressures, temperatures and rpm's. We will do a visual inspection into each engine room as well. We will use this time zone, Central Standard Time (CST) for all of our recordings. OK?"

Again I respond in the affirmative.

"Good, then let's have a good, safe trip while enjoying ourselves. By my watch it is twelve hundred hours, time for a watch change and I am hungry." With that he goes below into the main cabin and galley.

Roger, my relief, slides in behind the wheel. I brief him on course, speed, our position and engine operations. I record each of the items required into the log together with the inoperative analog speed indicator and mark our first chart location. I then check each engine room for oil/ water leaks and general conditions. Finally I confirm with Roger that

I am relieved and the watch is his.

I go below to my cabin where I am greeted by the hum and vibration of the port engine drive shaft and propeller as it runs through the space below the cabin floor. Admittedly, this is something I had not anticipated. Feeling that there is little else to do but move back to the cabin of the first night, I decide to remain here. It is cozy and comfortably cool with just adequate space for my gear and me. I'll find out soon enough how smart this choice will be.

I wash and head up to the galley for lunch. It is clear that both Allen and Paco have eaten because of the clutter and unwashed dishes/utensils. At least they put them in the sink. I make Roger and myself a ham and cheese sandwich with chips and a Fresca. Afterwards I wash the dishes and do a cursory cleanup of the galley.

I rejoin Roger in the cockpit where I find Paco comfortably settled into the aft settee of the eating area. He is working in a log, recording figures and maintenance duties performed on the two engines and generators. I've seen him before on prior trips keeping track of maintenance & repair schedules in this type of log.

He momentarily looks up. "Hola, Bob," he says quickly returning to his columns and notations.

It is obvious that he is absorbed in his work, so I quietly slip into the opposite settee. Through the windshield I have a broad vista of the sparkling sea before us. It is a royal blue, cheerful and inviting. A steady breeze of eight to ten knots has come up creating swells of one foot. The sails draw well driving the boat through the chop from the quartering sea.

We are paralleling the southern shore of this large body of water known as Banderas Bay or the Bay of Flags. From its entrance to the Pacific Ocean to its eastern terminal at the city of Puerto Vallarta the bay is some twenty-five miles long and ten miles wide. Looking aft, the Sierra Madre Mountains form a beautiful backdrop to the city that was once known as Puerto Las Peñas. In 1918, during the Mexican Revolution, it was renamed in honor of the governor of the State of Jalisco who greatly contributed to the modernization of the state and of the village itself.

"My village, Chimo, is just ahead," says Paco breaking the silence. "This is where my family came from before moving to Vallarta many years ago. I still have cousins, aunts & uncles living there."

I remember a similar conversation with him on a previous trip. He comes from a very large family. He has, I believe, fifteen or sixteen brothers and sisters, all from the same father but two mothers. His father and stepmother are alive and live not far from he and his family. Between aunts, uncles, cousins, nephews, children, grandchildren and great grandchildren, Paco estimates that the clan numbers around one thousand. Most of them live in and near Puerto Vallarta with very few ever having moved away. One exception is an older brother who lives in Washington State and who Paco went to live with after high school. He refined his English while there and learned how to pick apples during his six-month stay.

He and I have shared some interesting experiences. One was on the delivery of a thirty-one foot Islander sailboat from Puerto Vallarta to San Diego. Over time I have met his wife, two children and their German shepherd dog. There is a bond between us that transcends our personal and business lives.

The remainder of the afternoon is spent reading and lounging, enjoying the smooth ride of Athena as she steps blithely along at six and one half knots.

At 1500 hours, the next watch change occurs without incident. Cabo Corrientes is programmed as our first waypoint on the GPS instrument. The estimated time of arrival is 1900 hours.

Allen prepares dinner of hamburger steak, mashed potatoes and buttered carrots. We eat at the large table on the bridge where Paco can have his meal while remaining vigil to the ship's safety. No booze is allowed while we are underway, another of Allen's iron clad rules.

Allen relieves Paco at 1800 hours while Roger and I wash dishes and clean the galley. By 1930 the evening sun has slipped below the horizon in a fiery ball of brilliant colors that streak the deep blue sky. The sails flap to the roll of the boat as the wind diminishes to a whisper whereupon Allen gives the order to store them away. Afterwards we do a quick inspection for loose equipment and general safety as we prepare for night operations.

As darkness descends the Cabo Corrientes lighthouse, on our port side, is perched high upon a rocky bluff where its sweeping white light is a sentinel to the southern entrance to Banderas Bay. Nautical charts warn of rocky out-cropping's two miles into the bay as well as extremely rough water caused by the confluence of the two bodies of water (the Bay of Banderas and the Pacific Ocean) running against one another. I have heard many stories also of how nasty this section can be when the tide and wind fight each other.

Tonight is not the case. The sea is smooth and tranquil. There is a halo effect brought about by the end of sunlight and the start of darkness. A gentle off shore wind brings the smells of land where a few lights twinkle in the darkness. In the heavens above, the first stars become visible where they watch as we round the headland to take up our new heading of 150 degrees. Allen lays a rumb line (a straight pencil line drawn on a nautical chart that is referenced to by plotting actual locations en route) directly to Acapulco, a distance of 445km.

Before my watch, I slip below to freshen up and relax. I find that the noise and vibration of the port engine is tolerable, so I feel comfortable with my decision and will remain here.

At 20:45 I go above. I duck into the galley for a bottle of water and give Roger a quick hello. He is in the midst of a movie, seated on the floor.

"I'll see you at midnight," I say. "Do you need a wakeup call?"

"No. I do not plan on going to bed. I prefer staying up."

"Ok, see you then."

I inform Allen that I am ready to take the watch. He slides out from behind the wheel meeting me at the chart station. We plot the lat/lon figures on the chart and into the ship's log. Our position is abeam (90 degrees) of Punta Ipala, a small spit of land jutting out from the mainland. Our course remains at 150 degrees magnetic with a boat speed of six knots while our ground speed is over seven knots.

"We appear to be getting a little help from a southerly current," says Allen.

"As much as one knot," I respond.

We do seem to be getting a bit of a push probably from the outgoing tide.

Allen leaves to perform engine room checks as I slip in behind the wheel. Now in complete darkness, there is no horizon, only ink blackness surrounding the boat. Radar shows we are five miles off shore with no obstacles within a ten-mile range. The depth finder shows a water depth of three hundred feet over a smooth bottom. GPS shows a ground speed of seven knots. Our ETA (estimated time of arrival) in Acapulco is in sixty-eight hours, somewhat faster than the original estimate because of the favorable current. Engine instruments read normal.

Allen completes his entries and retreats to his stateroom. Paco has long ago retired to his bunk. Now alone, I feel a little overwhelmed when considering the responsibilities associated with the watch. In all my years on the water I have never completely overcome the adrenaline rush. It is not so much a fear factor as it is the excitement and thrill of the trust placed upon me either by others or by myself.

The three hours pass quickly without incident. Roger arrives on time and as expected ready to take over. We discuss our progress and position, after which I inspect the engine rooms, make my log entries and officially turn over the watch. Tired, I go below to my quarters. I don't attempt to read, just slip into bed and switch off the lights. The rhythm and beat of the drive train put me to sleep in very little time.

CHAPTER ELEVEN

Tenacatita to Acapulco

Day 2 Wednesday

Mendoza, alone in his office is seated at his desk toying with a small instrument no larger than a deck of cards. He extends an antenna before activating the on/off switch on its side. Instantly the display window illuminates followed in a few seconds by two rows of characters.

He reclines in his overstuffed leather chair, staring at the display as the series of numbers and letters stabilize. "Perfecto," he exclaims after a few minutes before bouncing out of his chair. With the instrument, he moves to a corner of his office where a navigation chart of western Mexico and the Central Americas hangs. Using information from the instrument he plots a latitude and longitude position for Athena. Stepping back, he studies where this tiny dot relates to a similar mark made last evening. A broad smile covers his face. "Yes," he says to no one. "This is going to work just fine."

08:15. I awaken in disbelief that I have slept so late. I hustle to wash and dress. I barely have time for coffee before reporting for the 09:00 watch.

"Buenos días," I say to Allen upon entering the cockpit.

"Buenos días," he replies. "I have decided to go into Tenacatita for a few hours. (Tenacatita is a small village en route) I feel we should do engine and transmission checks as well as there are a couple of other things that are best done now rather than later."

"I understand," I say. "What is our new heading?"

"Ninety-five degrees. GPS says we will be there at 11:00 hours."

The weather remains clear and bright. The sun, well above the horizon, is making for another hot and humid day. There is a slight sea breeze from the west. The sea is virtually calm. Athena slides smoothly through the water with a boat speed of six knots.

Within an hour I can clearly make out the entrance leading into the bay where the village of Tenacatita is located. I have been here on several occasions with our boat, so expect to find things familiar. I mentally record 10:30 hours as the time we pass in between the two headlands that protect and shelter the bay.

"Bob, I'd like you to help Paco change engine oil and filters," says Allen.

"Roger is going overboard to determine the boat speed paddle wheel difficulty and I have a clogged toilet in my head to fix."

"That's fine," I respond.

"I'll take her the final distance," he advises, slipping in behind the wheel. He reduces power, disengages the autopilot before starting a turn to port. Paco and Roger are forward readying the anchor. I step outside into the intense sunlight and heat where even with a hat and sunglasses it takes several minutes for my eyes to fully adjust to the glare.

I join the guys who are now in readiness with the anchor and ground tackle waiting for Allen's command from the cockpit. This is an exercise we will repeat many times before our final destination.

We are approaching a high sweeping white sandy beach, stretching from left to right for several miles in each direction. Coconut palms line the beach evenly spaced, all having attained the same height indicating they were planted at the same time. The village, now directly ahead, sits beyond and behind the beach where it is sheltered from the many tropical storms that visit this area. On the crest of the beach are ten or so tiendas, the majority of them serving seafood dishes, fajitas and beer.

There is a road from the main highway into the village from which visitors come, but more importantly for the economy there is a body of water beyond our present position where the cruisers hang out. On several occasions in our boat, we rode the anchor there for a week or more in the company of ten to fifteen other gypsy boaters. Often we would dinghy over here to have lunch or simply come for late afternoon snacks and beer. Generally we found the food good, plentiful and inexpensive.

Allen gives the command to drop anchor. It is a sixty-five pound brut that requires skill to get it overboard without causing personal injury. It falls free from its perch, entering the clear water with a generous splash. Paco then signals to backup Athena in order to run out one hundred feet of chain. Satisfied that we are securely in place Allen shuts down the engines. I return inside to record in the log that it is 11:00 hours. We are 200 yards from the beach in thirty-five feet of crystal clear water.

Without delay we go to work. Paco and I have the oil and filters changed in less than thirty minutes. Afterwards we do pressure checks on the oil system and check transmission fluids. Everything checks out well.

I find Allen who has his toilet dissembled in what best can be described as a stinky mess. He feels he has the situation under control and needs no help.

I am able to help Roger replace a lower batten on the mainsail and replace a bulb in one of the deck spreader lamps. He had earlier found that the paddle wheel on the speed indicator was fouled with seaweed, which he cleaned.

As it is nearing 13:00 hours, I make sandwiches for what I know will be a hungry group. I put out chips and cold drinks for the taking.

"I believe we all need a swim," announces Allen emerging from his cabin in his bathing suit. We join him in the delightfully refreshing bay water. It is a great treat as the four of us act like little kids on vacation.

All too soon it is time to turn our attention to getting ready to leave. On the dive platform, we soap up and rinse off with hot water. We towel off, dress and make final preparations to get underway.

The anchor comes off the bottom at 14:15 hours. We make a sweeping turn to port and head towards the open ocean. The wind at fifteen knots is on our nose from the west as we clear the headlands. There are intermittent white caps with two-foot swells, under a cloudless cobalt blue sky.

Once satisfied that we are out of danger of rocks and shoals, Allen has us shake out and raise the mainsail followed by the big genoa. Easing to port, the wind fills the two sails producing a surprising two-knot increase in boat speed. He brings us to our 150-degree bearing and sets the autopilot. And yes, we now have a working speed indicator that when compared to GPS there is only a slight variation between their two readings.

Paco assumes the watch at 15:00 hours.

The remainder of the afternoon and evening are uneventful. I relax and read on the aft deck in a lounge chair. Dinner consists of an Irish stew by Allen and an apple pie by Roger with vanilla ice cream.

As the wind dies off at 20:00 hours, we bring in the sails and prepare for night operations. Another of Allen's iron clad rules is that you must wear a harness and be tethered to the boat if outside after dusk or in bad weather.

At 21:00 hours I assume my watch. At 22:30 hours, I note shipping traffic on our starboard beam, five miles distance moving in a northerly direction. I listen for any voice communication on the Very High Frequency radio (VHF), but hear none. Aside from that, it is a quiet watch as I find myself falling into a pattern of routine activity. The first evening's butterflies are gone.

At midnight, Roger relieves me. I stand outside in the comfortable night air to stare at the blanket of stars above. With no interference from artificial light, the sensation of closeness to the heavens is eerie.

Returning inside I say goodnight to Roger and retire below. My little compartment feels cozy and familiar. The swim earlier together with the hot shower, a good dinner and the late hour have relaxed and tired me. I manage to read a few pages from a book from the boat's library before shutting off the light and drifting off to sleep.

Day 3. Thursday.

07:30. I have been awake since 06:30, but too comfortable to get up. I've enjoyed watching the early morning sunshine reflected off the water playing games in my cabin with different shadows and shapes. I have let my imagination entertain me until now.

I briefly look in on Paco curled up in his bunk sleeping soundly as I stop in the galley to where I find the coffeepot near empty. I empty it, rinse it out and start a new pot. I pour orange juice and go into the cockpit to where I find Allen at the wheel.

"Good morning skipper."

"Hi Bob. How are you?"

"I feel well and slept very soundly. I think the swim and the other days activities wore me out."

I take note that our course remains at 150 degrees magnetic and that we remain close to the rhumb line. We are offshore by several miles following the landmass as we run in a southeasterly direction.

09:00 With my coffee from below, I relieve Allen of the watch. He completes the log entries and does his last engine room inspections before going below to look for a weather fax and perhaps to raise Kate on the SSB (single side band radio).

Because of our favorable ground speed at six knots, our ETA into Acapulco is calculated at 12:00 hours. With the following sea, it has been a comfortable and enjoyable ride.

Visibility remains very good so that I am able to pick out many landmarks along the coast. The section we are now abeam is familiar from when my wife and I had our boat here. I can identify Cabeza Negra, Punta Lazarardo and Bufadero Bluff. In particular, I shall not forget Bufadero Bluff, a small town where we stopped to buy a block of ice (our refrigerator was ailing) and make a landline telephone call to wish a son a happy birthday. Once anchored in the tiny harbor, we took the dinghy to shore where we encountered light to moderate surf. Although we got a little wet going ashore, it was considered "no big deal" because we knew we would dry out in short order in the ninety-degree heat. After securing the dinghy high above the surf line to a coconut tree we walked up the dirt road to the village perched upon the bluff. We located the single pay telephone only to realize that based on the number of folks in line, we had over an hour to wait. Deciding not to wait, we had a quick bite to eat and purchased a ten pound block of ice that I carried on a shoulder back down the road. What was startling to us as we prepared our return through the surf was the height and power of the breakers. In the time that we were in town, the surf had risen dramatically and become angry. I can remember us standing waist deep in the turbulent water, each on either side of the dinghy, attempting to judge which incoming wave looked the least ominous. The plan was to both climb aboard in unison after which I would start the engine and motor out. Well, as it turned out, I managed to get onboard and did get the engine started but my wife was unable to pull herself into the boat and remained behind. I did get through the surf and deliver the ice to the boat but then came the problem of how to get Pat off of the beach. I returned to the surf line in the dinghy where it was apparent that I would be foolish to attempt a landing and even if I did make it safely, what made me think I could get her in the boat and back out. Returning to our boat I could do little but wait until the surf subsided.

As this was a Sunday, the beach was crowded with families, many having come by panga. I felt that if there was anything capable of getting through the now pounding surf, it was one of those large, heavy, high prow boats. I kept hoping that my wife would ask one of the owners to be brought out. Ultimately she did approach the sons of an owner. With some Spanish together with lots of sign language she managed to convey her needs.

They in turn went after "Papa" their father, a short, stout, muscular man who took charge of the rescue operation. It took four strong young men to slide their panga (boat) into the water where my wife was ordered by papa "to get in." While the young men steadied the panga into the oncoming waves, Papa nimbly jumped aboard and in three pulls brought the outboard motor to life. The two sons came on board as Papa shifted into forward gear, gave gas to the engine and plunged into the breaking surf. In less time than it takes to describe the scene, Papa had the panga and his passenger beyond the wild water and headed out my way. He brought his boat alongside ours where my wife was able to come safely aboard.

We have told this tale on many occasions since then in a light hearted, humorous way. Quietly we both agree that it was much more serious at the time. Both of us could easily have drowned in the undertow at the beach or been pitch poled (rolled end to end) by any of the four foot high swells or been hurt in a number of other ways. We are lucky and indeed fortunate that a Mexican family took pity and was willing to interrupt their day on the beach to help us out.

Today, through binoculars, I can view the still sleepy village and the tiny harbor of Bufadero Bluff and wonder what might have been.

Allen brings up the latest weather fax.

"Our high pressure system is weakening, moving to the east. The forecast is for low clouds, fog and light rain moving in within the next twenty-four to thirty-six hours. It should not bother us, I don't believe."

"With any luck we should be in Acapulco before it arrives," I say.

He gives a nod of agreement.

My three-hour watch is quickly over as Roger takes the wheel at noon. I make my security checks and log entries before making lunch and stepping outside to join Paco on the fantail. He has a fishing line in the water, enjoying the thrill of the catch.

The weather remains clear and bright. The early afternoon sun beats down on the awning where underneath the temperature is above ninety degrees. There is a sufficient breeze to make it feel comfortable enough if you do not need to move around too much. I stretch out on one of the lounges under the sun awning, relaxed as I eat my lunch before dozing off for a quick siesta.

I am startled by the singing sound of a fishing reel as it plays out line from a strike. Paco leaps to the aft rail from his seat to tighten the break on the reel and slow down the fast escaping line. I hear him say that it is a big one as he fights to gain control of the situation. In the wink of an eye, two hundred feet off the stern, there is a flash of blue and silver as the large fish dances and twists on the water's surface.

"Marlin," yells Paco. "Ask to slow the boat."

I run to the cockpit, passing a startled Roger at the wheel and duck my head into Allen's cabin where he is sitting at his desk.

Paco asks to slow the boat. It appears he has hooked a good size Marlin."

Rising from his chair, he comes up into the cockpit and looks aft to find Paco still fighting the fish.

"Roger, reduce rpms to six hundred. Keep the same heading if you can."

Outside we ask if there is anything we can do to help.

"Someone get the gaff. I am going to try to bring it alongside and will need help in landing it."

"Let's lower the starboard swim platform and bring it onboard there," says Allen looking at me.

I raise the deck hatch and scramble down the stairwell leading to the controls that lower the platform. Once down I am able to step out at water level on the platform, four feet beyond the starboard pontoon's end. Allen hands down the eight-foot gaff that I stow for later use.

The reduction in boat speed helps Paco. Even so he has a fight on his hands. The fish has surfaced several more times after which it dives in an effort to shake loose the hook. Sweat rolls off of Paco's head, the salt from perspiration stinging his eyes. The muscles and veins in his arms bulge as he works the pole, reeling in line only to have the fish take it all back. It has been thirty minutes since the strike with no signs of fatigue from the other end.

"Let me take over." says Allen. "You need a break."

Reluctantly, Paco hands the rod and reel to Allen. I know he wants to continue but realizes he needs a break. He falls into a deck chair, exhausted.

The fight continues now with Allen's strong, fresh arms and back. I run below to my cabin for the camera, returning to capture the battle. Allen after a fifteen-minute interval, transfers the pole back to a refreshed Paco.

Allen descends below to the swim platform where he prepares to bring aboard the tiring fish.

After several more minutes, Paco is able to bring it to the side of the platform, where we realize that the hook and line was not swallowed but rather only hooked to his jaw. The decision is made to release the fish.

Allen fashions a length of line with a slipknot on one end that he manages to slide over its tail and up to the gill area pulling it snug before tying it off to the platform. He hollers up to Paco to ease off tension on the pole and come below.

"Bob, ask Roger to stop the boat."

I scurry up the ladder, slide the cockpit door open and inform Roger.

From above on the fantail I can see the beautiful fish tethered to us in the clear water. I estimate it to be five to six feet in length and one hundred pounds. It's blue and silver markings are striking, magnified by the transparent water. Allen and Paco, on their knees, stretch out from the platform to examine how to remove the hook without further injury. They have rolled the fish to a degree that its one eye appears to be watching them. I snap away as the drama unfolds. Several times there is a thrashing about, indicating it is still very much alive. With Paco holding on as best he can, Allen takes a large pair of pliers and somehow, avoiding injury to himself, twists the hook free. He holds it up high above his head as a symbol of success.

"You will have a sore mouth for a few days, but I think you'll be OK," he says to the watchful eye.

"Let it go," he instructs Paco.

With a quick tug, the tether comes loose and slowly the fish starts to drift away from the dive platform. Realizing that it is free it takes two or three powerful strokes with its tail before disappearing into the depth of the Pacific.

Allen and Paco bear hug one another over their success in setting it free without injury. Both, exhausted and sweaty from the ordeal, dive into the cool water for a well-deserved "time out."

From my perspective I am pleased the way it turned out. It was too large a fish to try to filet and eat. We certainly have enough on board. It may have made a good trophy, but where and how would we been able to get it to a taxidermist? *No, he is better off in the water where hopefully he is a smarter fish than before.*

Allen and Paco hose each other off with fresh water while cleaning up the platform and securing the area. Roger engages the drive train and we are once again under way. Paco secures his pole and retires to his bunk while Allen returns to his desk, the excitement for the moment, over.

The late afternoon sun is not as intense as before because of a high thin layer of stratus clouds moving in from the west, the indication of declining weather conditions ahead.

Remaining outside, I take up my earlier position on the lounge chair and relax. Although we remain several miles off shore, I can through the binoculars continue to pick out many familiar points of interest. The smoke stacks of Lazaro Cardenas are easily identifiable. It is there that we spent a very quiet night in the inner harbor of this very busy industrial port en route back north from Ixtapa to Puerto Vallarta.

Allen works his magic again in the galley, preparing stuffed pork chops, baked potatoes and vegetables. We have the left over pie and ice cream for dessert.

I assume the watch at 2100 as the glow of lights from Ixtapa appears on the horizon.

Again I reflect on a prior visit here where we spent two enjoyable months at the Ixtapa marina. We met many interesting and fun folks; two in particular were a brother/sister team, Jim and Shirley on their sailboat, Pelican. It was with them that we took a bus trip to Oaxaca via Acapulco and Huatulco. We were gone for a ten day period and saw parts of the country we would most likely never had seen, including Monte Alban, one of the most important and spectacular pre-Hispanic ruins in Mexico. Additionally we visited Teotitlan del Valle, where magnificent hand-dyed and hand-stitched carpets are made on foot pedal looms and where exquisite black pottery is made in San Bartolo.

On one other occasion, Jim and I went alone by bus to Acapulco. Pat had flown to Houston for a grandson's first birthday and Shirley was not interested in going. We stayed in an older hotel in the old section where I had the opportunity to visit and see up close many of the original parts of the city.

The watch goes quickly without problems. Roger relieves at 24:00 hours. GPS says we have one hundred miles to Acapulco.

I waste little time in getting below and ready for bed. I read for a short time before shutting of the light. Tomorrow should be an interesting and busy day.

Day four. Friday

0700. There is no sun as a heavy over cast covers the sky causing the cabin to be darker than prior mornings. I clean up, get dressed and head for the galley for coffee and toast.

Relieving Allen, I see we have made good progress overnight as our ETA in Acapulco is now 1400 hours. The logbook indicates nothing unusual or abnormal during the last three watches. Our ground speed remains at six knots without aid of the sails. There is little or no wind, only a low layer of moist marine clouds.

1000. We are now less than a mile off shore as we approach the western headland that protects Acapulco Bay from the open waters of the Pacific Ocean. To port I can identify the cliffs in front of the Hotel El Mirador that the Acapulco Divers use for their spectacular plunges into the surf, fifty feet below. There is no activity from what I can see this morning. Later it will be teaming with spectators seated and lined along the viewing stands, as well as a swarm of private and charter boats standing outside the surf line.

The coastline is jagged and rocky, vertically rising from the sea to a height of sixty to one hundred feet. On the top is low brush or tree vegetation. A few shacks and tarpaper houses can be seen overlooking the long drop into the sea. Mostly undeveloped, except for the hotel, its barren look provides little evidence of the glitter and glitz that lies inside the bay, out of sight.

1200. I turn the watch to Roger. My lat/lon readings show us mid channel of the mainland and Roqueta Island. We are steering manually, remaining several hundred feet off shore as we turn easterly. This part of the southwestern headland is low in height and not as rocky or jagged. There are several attractive homes built into the side of the hill with what must be wonderful open vistas of the Pacific Ocean.

Realizing how hungry I am, I go below to the galley where earlier Roger had made ham sandwiches together with potatoes chips and an assortment of raw vegetables. I fill up a plate; grab a Fresca and go back above to watch the landscape unfold as we enter Acapulco Bay. I slide into the aft settee. The clouds are thinning, allowing hazy sunshine to brighten the day.

1300. Far ahead I am able to see the distant eastern shore of Acapulco Bay only as a silhouette, the jagged outline of the many resort hotels that line the beach for many blocks. As we proceed in a more northerly direction, I sense the length and sweep of the white sandy crescent shaped beach of this fabled tourist resort.

I go outside on the port rail to get a better view and take pictures of the peninsula, now abeam, known as Punta Griffo. This landmass protrudes into Acapulco Bay to create the commercial port and fishing center, our destination.

We pass Playa Caletilla, a densely populated local beach community and are approaching its sister, Playa Caleta. Both are known for their "morning beaches" because of their eastern exposure. Playa Caleta features a lighthouse at the entrance to its tiny harbor with numerous condos, homes and shore front buildings lining the beach. There is, I believe, an amusement park on the beach where I can see two waterslides. The beach is crowded on this warm overcast day.

Continuing to turn to port, we round the eastern end of Punta Griffo that features a rocky shoreline and a bluff. A partially completed resort hotel or condo sits high up overlooking Boca Grande. It appears to be abandoned; work having stopped some time ago. Above it at the top of the bluff is an attractive two story white wall, red tile roof building appearing well maintained and luxurious.

Proceeding, we follow the curve of the land until we come under the lee of Peninsula de las Playas and enter the protected harbor. Condos, private homes and hotels crowd the terraced side of the hilly peninsula. This is part of the old section, or Colonial section of the city, considered by many as the best part of the city in which to live.

Several of the private homes display the grandeur of what living was like in the early twentieth century. One in particular, built half way up the steep slope has a private cable car to transport you down to the boathouse or up to the luxurious house.

There are two marinas here. The older and more well know is Club de Yates de Acapulco or The Acapulco Yacht Club. It is now visible tucked away at the extreme west-end of the bay. The newer one is La Marina de Acapulco. It is several hundred feet to the right of the yacht club, identified by a majestic lighthouse. Here is where we will stay. The limited space for transit boats at the yacht club prohibit us from mooring there.

15:30 We pass between the entry markers into the marina and starboard side tie at the transit dock. Allen, from past experience, knows where he wants to tie down.

Acapulco is our first stop. It has taken us 68 hours to travel 445 miles from Puerto Vallarta. We have achieved an average boat speed of six and one half knots. We will fuel here as well as perform some maintenance tasks. Our goal is to be back underway, Sunday morning.

16:00 I tag along with Allen to the marina office, a lengthy hike.

"What is the age of this marina?" I ask.

"I believe five years."

"It is beat up for being so new."

"They suffered severe hurricane damage one year ago," he explains.

Many of the floating docks are missing, having been torn loose of their attachment fittings while others have boards missing or are loose.

We check in, pay a two-night fee and ask about fuel. We are told that the only diesel fuel available is from the yacht club, by appointment. The office manager suggests we call on a landline and offers her telephone.

Allen dials and speaks to someone in his best Spanish.

"There is an open time at 08:00 tomorrow. I took it," he says after hanging up.

"You are very lucky, Senor Allen. I have heard where people have waited for days for fuel," says the manager.

"Apparently we are doing some things right. Thank you for your help," he says as we leave the office.

As we approach Athena, Allen recognizes Larry standing with Paco.

"Hello, old friend," he says as they embrace in a bear hug.

"Captain Daniels, it is good to see you."

Larry turns out to be an old friend who worked at Opequimar in Puerto Vallarta before coming here as dock master. He explains that the marina owners promise many things, but little gets done. He admits to being very disappointed in the way things have developed since his arrival and fears he will be jobless soon.

Allen prepares spaghetti and meatballs for the three of us as Roger has gone into town without explanation. Strangely he wasted little time after we docked to leave. After dinner I clean the galley and make a pot of coffee as I work on a picture puzzle. Allen, aroused by the fresh smell of coffee, joins me at the big table in the main salon after pouring himself a mug.

"I haven't worked on a puzzle for years," he says taking a big swallow of the hot coffee.

"Neither had I, until we found several of them under the sofa."

There is silence as we both find several pieces and place them in their respective places.

"Do you know where Roger was going this evening?" he asks.

"No. He said nothing to me before leaving," I respond.

"Quite frankly, I'm a little worried about him. He hasn't been the same carefree individual I knew before we left Puerto Vallarta. He seems to have something on his mind. Have you noticed anything?"

"No, not really," I reply. "Partly I suppose because I haven't known him for that long a period of time."

"Well, he's a big boy. He knows how to handle himself. Leave the cockpit door unlocked for him. Good night," he says heading off to his cabin.

At 22:00 I call it quits on the puzzle, secure the coffeepot and shut off the cabin lights, leaving only the night light on. I look in on Paco who is fast asleep. I read for a time before dowsing the reading light. It is unusually quiet without the drive shaft noise. I almost miss it.

CHAPTER TWELVE

Acapulco

Day 5. Saturday

I become aware of activity on the deck directly above me. The darkness of the cabin makes it difficult to see the time on my watch before I am able to switch on my reading light. It is two-fifteen. *What can be going on at this hour?* I ask myself as I slide out of bed and slip into a pair of jeans. Reaching the cockpit door, I decide to remain concealed, out of sight where it becomes quickly apparent that Allen is upset and is expressing his displeasure at Roger. "I do not appreciate your being out until this hour of the morning."

"I lost track of the time," replies Roger.

"As Captain, I have the right to know where you go and what you are doing while in my employment. Understood?"

"Understood," replies Roger.

"And, there is something else. There is no reason to lock your cabin door unless you are hiding something inside. Are you hiding anything you don't want to be found?"

"No, of course not. It is a habit I have had for years."

"I'd like it stopped. If for a number of reasons we need to get into that space for emergency purposes, we would have to break down the door. Understood?"

"Yes, understood."

I ease my way back down the passageway to my cabin feeling I had heard enough, perhaps too much. I slip out of the jeans and climb back into bed. Switching off the light, I lay in the darkness thinking of the day's activities.

06:15 Despite a restless night, I am up and about. While the coffee perks, I go up to the cockpit where I find Allen and Paco discussing how they want to move the boat to the yacht club fuel dock.

"I believe that when we leave here, we should be able to pick up the channel markers for the club without any trouble," says Allen. "Once we get inside the basin, we will need to feel our way to the fuel dock. I know our wide beam is going to make it close to some of the boats on the end of the dock."

Paco nods his head in understanding.

"Good morning, Bob. How are you?" they ask.

"Very well," I answer.

"Did you hear Roger and I at two o'clock this morning?" asks Allen.

"Yes, I did," I say without thinking of the consequences of ease dropping.

"I don't know how much you heard, but …."

"I probably heard too much," I interrupt.

"I hope I made my point. Even Paco has sensed a change in his attitude."

"He is not the same guy," offers Paco.

"Let's be ready to leave at 07:30," says Allen as he stands to leave us.

I go below for my coffee that I bring up on deck. It is a pretty morning with the temperature in the eighties although the humidity feels lower than yesterday, making a comfortable combination.

I take a picture of the whitewashed lighthouse set against a cloudless deep blue sky. Behind it and on either side are a number of multistoried buildings, also colorfully reflecting the early morning sun. A gentle breeze sends light ripples across the water.

My solitude is broken by the rumble of the port engine coming to life accompanied by its cloud of blue smoke. A minute later the starboard engine starts. Paco informs me that I will be responsible for the stern lines while Roger, who has appeared from below, will be at the bow. After a brief engine warm up, we cast off.

Allen backs us down in order to clear the dock before turning 180 degrees to port, lining us up with the marina exit. Now he powers us out into the open water, busy with traffic from fishing, sightseeing and pleasure boats.

We make a slight turn to starboard, before picking up the channel buoy that will take us to the yacht club's entrance.

Of the several times I have visited the club, this is my first time to arrive by water. I snap numerous pictures as we pass several outward-bound boats as well as numerous ones anchored in a random pattern. The club's entrance, now seen ahead, is a narrow opening between two non-floating concrete pilings. Behind them are the crowded docks with numerous boats each med-moored, stern to the dock and anchored forward. (a favorite method used in the Mediterranean Sea.)

Allen negotiates the turn to starboard with skill to bring us inside. The fuel dock is visible by its green canopy and PEMEX sign to port. It is vacant with the exception of a small ski boat that will not interfere with our docking. As we draw near, Paco hops onto the dock where I pass him the stern line, which he secures. One of the attendants handles the bowline. Paco further secures us with two spring lines before Allen shuts down the engines. I note by my watch that it is a few minutes before eight AM.

Fueling begins almost immediately with Paco in charge. He begins by filling a one gallon plastic bucket with soapy water that he places on the deck nearby in the event of a spill. Soapy water he knows helps disperse diesel.

Feeling not needed, I ask permission to go up to the club to look around. Allen nods in the affirmative.

I grab my camera and step off onto the dock. It is a good distance to the club that gives me a chance to stretch my legs. I pass all shapes and sizes of boats; all look to be well cared for and used on a frequent basis. Electricity, water and telephone service is available at all of the slips.

At the docks end stands the club's majestic metal flagpole standing fifty feet tall, the base of it I estimate at twelve inches in circumference capable of sustaining hurricane winds. It flies the lone Mexican flag.

The clubhouse is a handsome two-story structure appearing to be relatively new, although the club dates back to 1920. It is considered by many to be the most handsome and best-managed yacht club in the world. It has many facilities and amenities needed and sought after by traveling yachtsmen including hot showers and restrooms, bar and restaurant, laundry and dry cleaning services. The members are mostly wealthy and gracious Mexicans who live in Mexico City, a short jet flight away. It has been suggested that a more accurate name for the club would be The Mexico City Yacht Club. Not likely...

The ground floor consists of an open-air dining room with clusters of tables adorned by blue table clothes with bamboo wicker chairs scattered about the spacious room. To the back is a well-stocked bar, created by a semi-circle counter and perhaps two dozen high backed bar stools.

It was here that I, together with Jim from Pelican (mentioned earlier), came to have a drink and escape the heat. Our hotel was a short walk from here. The club was having an awards ceremony following a sponsored race. As we entered, the race committee chairman stopped his presentation to welcome us with a "please feel at home." It was a wonderful gesture of the clubs renowned hospitality.

I walk through the empty lounge to the dining room where breakfast is being served, buffet style. There is a fair size group of people eating, which for Mexico is unusual. Mexicans, like their Spanish cousins, usually skip this meal in favor of large afternoon affairs. The dining room faces the Olympic size outdoor swimming pool that is surrounded with colorful blue and white striped lounges and umbrellas.

I wander about admiring the scores of photographs depicting the clubs history, past commodores and awards/trophies. There are several meeting rooms and a full size gym for working out. Finally I make my way back outside where I am greeted by the heat and humidity of the day. I notice that our bright, clear sky has given way to high, thin clouds.

I decide that I have enough time to walk to the rear of the building where here, as I remember, are the administrative offices. They offer a wide range of services from check in and out of the club, making long distant telephone calls, repair services and providing general information. In an adjoining building is a well-stocked marine parts store.

I leave the club grounds through a well-used rod-iron gate to cross the street where there is a palapa restaurant. To me it reflects the atmosphere of the real Mexico. It is a lushly landscaped patio garden, where if you look closely into the trees you'll find an iguana or two. I remember the food as good and inexpensive and the beer ice cold. All crumbs are wiped to the ground where they are immediately consumed by one of the many chickens that roam freely.

Realizing the time, I hustle back. The boat has attracted several onlookers; curious I suppose as to our size, shape (a catamaran) and destination. Paco is still fueling much to my relief. Allen is standing at the lifeline talking with one of the inquiring members.

Fueling is completed at 09:30. Allen pays the older attendant; a chap who I've been told has been here forever. We free ourselves from the dock and carefully make our way back out into the bay. Boat traffic remains heavy, so we take our time in returning to the marina.

Safely secured at 10:00, we tackle the remaining repairs and duties assigned by Allen. Paco with Rogers help reseal the starboard engine room deck hatch plate to prevent further water from entering the compartment. Allen stitches a tear in a corner of the aft deck awning. I know Paco will change engine oil and filters also. He has a fuel line to repair on the 20kw generator, as well.

I've been given the task of going to the super market. I've made a list of items over the past few days as I have seen them used up, mostly fresh fruit and vegetables.

Supplied with pesos, I walk up to the marina entrance and out onto the same street the yacht club is located, only it (the yacht club) is down from here. Taking this street towards the yacht club and beyond will take you out to the morning beaches that we passed yesterday. The opposite direction leads to the old commercial section of town, the way I need to go. I decide to walk, knowing that the super market is not far away.

The street I am following is Costera Miguel Aleman, named for the former Mexican President who was instrumental in bringing tourism to the city. It is more often referred to as simply, Costera. Here it is a narrow two-way street requiring cars to weave in and out of any parked vehicles, but with good-sized sidewalks on either side. The street is lined with small shops, where the locals come to shop and gossip. Many of the shops have colorful awnings to shade the sidewalks and break the heat. All are open for the day's activities and appear to be enjoying good business.

After several blocks, Costera winds down to the waterfront and the malecon. The malecon follows the curve of the beach where the commercial fishing boats bring their catch. Farther west are the docks for sightseeing yachts, smaller pleasure boats and the cruise ship terminal. Along the street is a small, tree lined promenade, a favorite spot for children.

Crossing the street, I am facing what is known as the Zocalo, the center of Old Acapulco. It is a shaded plaza in front of Nuestra Senora de la Soledad, the town's modern but unusual church. The church's stark-white exterior and blue and yellow spires, is difficult to miss. Overgrown with dense trees, the Zocalo is the hub of downtown. It is filled with vendors, shoeshine men, people lining up to use the pay phones and others sitting and relaxing on the many benches provided. There are several cafes and newsstands selling the English language Mexico City News, so tourists lodging in the area linger here, too.

I walk through the Zocalo past an attractive bandstand, where music is played on Sunday evenings. Just beyond is Sanborns, a coffee shop and bakery, par excellent. They attract locals and tourists alike; many linger for hours over the newspaper and a cup of coffee. I peek inside; thinking I might stop for coffee and a sweet, only to see how overcrowded it is, so walk on.

I pass a series of souvenir shops, silver shops, a tailor shop and a big favorite of Jim's and I, (when we visited) a fruity milk shake shop where for a dollar you get a meal. Nearby is a large flea market, a favorite destination of the cruise ship folks, and for those who need a touch of Americana, a Woolworth's.

Pleasantly I find an unoccupied pay telephone booth where I place a call to my wife. Again she picks up on the third ring with a pleasant, "Hello." We chat for several minutes, catching up on each other's activities, before I ring off with the promise to call again soon and an "I love you."

The supermarket, Gigante, is now just ahead. Much like the ones in Mazatlan and Puerto Vallarta, this also provides a one-stop shopping experience. The smallish parking lot is not crowded; because, I guess, much of their business is walkup from the neighborhoods.

Inside, I take a shopping cart and together with my list, start up and down the aisles locating much of what I need with ease. The process goes smoothly, as I leave the fruits and vegetables to last. I purchase several kilos each of bananas, oranges, apples and papaya together with ample numbers of lemons, limes, avocados, onions, tomatoes, cucumbers and several heads of lettuce. The cart is near full when I check off the last of the items. After a short wait at a checkout station, I begin to place my items on the conveyor belt.

"Would you like help?" asks a young employee, dressed in a white shirt with black tie and a nametag featuring the store logo. I am unable to read his name because of the distance.

"Yes, that would be a big help," I say.

In very little time, all of my items are scanned, bagged and placed in two separate carts. I pay the amount shown on the video screen, receive my change together with my receipt. My benefactor's name I learn is Harvey. A rather unusual name, I think for a Mexican.

"Can we take these to your car outside?" he asks.

"I will need a taxi," I explain.

"No problem." He turns and has me follow him to the outside of the store where he motions for one of the waiting taxies.

He has me loaded in quick order.

"Come see us again soon," he says closing the door behind me.

I inform the driver, who thankfully understands English, of my destination.

Exiting the parking lot, we make a series of right turns bringing us onto Costera, past the Zocalo and the Cathedral. We climb the gentle grade before the street narrows and there to our left is the marina.

I find a dock cart inside the entrance gate and with the help of the attendant, unload the taxi. I pay the driver who eagerly wastes little time departing. I think he was hoping for a larger tip, which I would have gladly given him, had he offered any help in unloading.

Allen gives a hand carrying sacks down to the galley.

"How did it go?" he asks.

"Very well," I answer. I give him a brief recap of the trip, providing the receipt and change. "It certainly helped by enlisting the aid of a store employee."

"That's an old trick I learned a long time ago," he comments while heading off to his cabin.

I busy myself with separating, labeling and putting items away. Once satisfied, I make myself a sandwich together with a Fresca and head up to the cockpit. Paco and Roger have apparently completed the hatch repair, as they are not on deck.

I go below to the port engine room where I find Paco putting his tools away.

"There are new supplies of fruit, veggies, meats and cheeses," I explain. "Can I get you anything?"

"No thanks Bob, I'll wait for dinner."

"You look like you could use a nap," I say from the tired look in his eyes.

"First a hot shower, then maybe a siesta," he responds.

"OK, then I'll see you later," I say before heading off to my cabin. Taking my own advice, I stretch out on my bunk. The air-conditioned coolness of the cabin is a real benefit in this climate at this time of the year.

It doesn't take long before I am asleep.

"All that I can tell you is that they are in Acapulco," says Carlos Mendoza. He is seated at his office desk, despite it being Saturday afternoon, a day he generally enjoys elsewhere. "By all calculations, they are on schedule," he continues to whoever is on the telephone.

He listens for a few moments before saying, "Goodbye," and hangs up the receiver. Outwardly disturbed, he rolls his eyes upward and utters a profanity under his breath.

Recovering his composure, he withdraws the instrument from his desk draw, raises the antenna and activates the on switch. The display takes a few minutes to stabilize as he walks to the chart. As he had guessed, the readings are the same as before, indicating that Athena is still in Acapulco. He switches off the instrument and returns it to his desk. He reclines in his chair to stare at the ceiling; his mind awhirl.

This is most unusual, he muses. *I have never been harassed before like this for any job I've done. This is something special. There is more in that tiny box than what meets the eye.*

🦢

17:30 I have slept very soundly. Refreshed, I shower and dress before going above to the galley where the aroma of cooking pork roast is captivating.

"Robert, fix yourself a drink and join me," bubbles a happy Allen. He is having a good time and is obviously relaxed with a rum and coke nearby.

I fix a gin and tonic with a squeeze of lime, the best of mixed drinks for a hot summer day.

"Salud," I offer stretching to touch glasses across the divider separating the galley from the dining area.

The pork roast sits on the stove top, apparently having come out of the oven within the last few minutes. It has been cooked in sauerkraut and its own juices. A large pot of potatoes is boiling nearby on a separate burner, as is a pot of fresh carrots bought earlier from the market.

"There will be just the three of us for supper. Roger has gone into town to be with his friends again."

"Oh," is about all I can think to say.

"From your expression, I can tell you are surprised."

"I guess I am; however, it is none of my business."

"I found it hard to say no to his request in spite of my dressing down this morning. As long as he is onboard for tomorrows departure, can perform his duties and not embarrass me or the boat, I told him to go ahead."

"I understand."

"He tells me that this is a group of men he served with in the Navy," Allen continues, seemingly anxious to further explain his decision. "They agreed to meet tonight to say their goodbyes."

"How many of them are there?" I ask as he sticks a fork into a boiling potato.

"I believe there are three."

"Isn't it coincidental that they were all able to meet here?" I ask.

"Good question. When I asked, he told me that is was purely coincidental that they bumped into each other. It was the reason he was so late last night."

He turns his full attention to the final preparation of the meal, apparently satisfied with his decision and the potential outcome.

I set the table in the main salon with the ships best flatware and cutlery including the Waterford crystal. I wonder if this may be its last time in use.

"Hola Amigos," says Paco entering the room, looking much refreshed from a two hour nap.

"Hey, Paco," I respond. "Can I get you something to drink before dinner?"

"A cerveza, por favor."

Like me he is surprised to learn that Roger would not be joining us. "Maybe our feet smell," he says with his big grin.

"Gentlemen, dinner is served," announces Allen as he brings the roast to the table.

The three of us make quick work of a great meal aided by a bottle of red wine. We reminisce about some of our good and bad times together. Dinner turns out to be a fun and relaxing two-hour event.

Paco and I clear the table, wash the dishes and put things back in place. I'm appreciative of his help as Allen does create a mess when cooking.

"Have you ever been to Acapulco after dark?" I ask Paco as we finish.

"No, never," he responds. "Only in day time and only to the Zocalo."

"Let's say we go this evening?"

"How about Allen? Will he join us?"

"Let's go ask him," I say as I lead the way to his cabin.

"Are you interested in joining us for a brief tour of the night life of the city?" we ask.

"No thanks guys, I'm beat. But thanks for the invitation. You go and have a good time."

"We'll be quiet when we come onboard."

Going below to my cabin I wash up, change into comfortable shoes and take sufficient money for a few rounds of drinks. I know Paco has no money, so I will need enough for the two of us.

He is ready and waiting on the fantail. We secure the port lifeline as we step onto the pier, walk up past the closed marina office and through the security gate. We notify the guard of our plans and that we expect to return in about three hours.

There are no taxis, so we walk towards the busier section of Costera where one is more likely to be found. The weather remains hot and sticky, the sea breeze of earlier now just a whisper. The walk is not uncomfortable; however, I can feel myself begin to sweat. So much for my before dinner shower.

After several attempts, we manage to get an empty taxi to stop. Paco climbs into the front passenger seat as I slip into the back. The driver, an older gentleman, speaks little English, so Paco translates. The only bar I can remember is one called Red Beard, located near the Americana Hotel.

"Ah, si, si," our driver responds as he pulls out into the evening traffic.

The taxi is an older model Nissan with no air-conditioning. The wind from the open windows provide some relief, as long as we keep moving.

We retrace my route of earlier, reaching the malecon, passing the old plaza and then the cruise ship terminal. Costera makes an S shaped turn before entering an underpass that takes us to Papagayos Park, one of the top municipal parks in the country. Named for the hotel that formerly occupied the grounds, it sits on fifty-two acres of prime real estate. There is an aviary, a roller-skating rink, a racetrack with mite-sized racecars, bumper boats in a lagoon and a replica of the space shuttle Columbia.

Driving further along on the Costera as it hugs the curve of the bay, we learn from the driver that from 1934 to 1958 the city airport occupied much of the land to our left. All of that is now gone, replaced by high-rise apartments and commercial buildings.

Costera widens to six lanes with a median strip, nicely landscaped in most instances with palms and low ground cover. Both sides of the avenue feature broad sidewalks to accommodate the throngs of pedestrians that frequent this section of the city referred to by most as the Condesa. We pass most of the name brands of clothing stores, banks and hotels from the United States, including several McDonalds and Burger Kings.

Traffic is heavy, so our progress is slow, not helped by traffic lights on each intersection, none of which are synchronized. We enter a roundabout or traffic circle, featuring in its center a sleek nude female statue known as the Diana Glorieta. Paseo del Farallon, the highway leading to Mexico City, intersects with Condesa and terminates at this point.

Several blocks later we are at our destination. I pay the driver before sliding out the curbside rear door onto the busy sidewalk. Paco precedes me and is standing looking at the mass of humanity waiting on the sidewalk to get into Red Beard.

"No way do I want to stand in that line," I tell Paco.

He shakes his head in agreement and bewilderment.

"Let's walk further up to the Americana Hotel," I offer.

We dodge in and around the waves of pedestrians as well as the window shoppers on the crowded walkway. It is an experience not to be missed, in rubbing shoulders with mankind, some well-dressed while others could care less how they look.

At last, we are at the hotel, The Fiesta Americana Condesa Acapulco, its proper name. Built back to the early seventies, it has been a favorite for North American visitors over the years. Located in the thick of the Condesa main activity, as well as right on the beach, it remains much as I remember it from my first trip here in 1975.

We enter the open-air lobby, where room registration is to our right while a cocktail lounge, bar and restaurant are to the left and to the rear of the lobby.

"This is a proper place for a beer," I say referring to the lounge.

We are seated in the middle of the room where we can enjoy a piano being played from a distance as well as the ocean breeze from the bay below. Looking about, I calculate the majority of patrons are North Americans, not unusual I guess.

"May I help you?" asks a tall, slender waitress.

We both order Coronas. "Tall and cold," I add.

"You got it," she says with a slight smile and twinkle in her eye.

She leaves us each a cocktail napkin before winding her way through the cluster of tables towards the bar. I'm taken by her agility and balance.

"What do you think of this place?" I ask.

"Nice. I've never been in such a place," answers Paco still taking in all the surroundings.

I've known him long enough to know that he does not fib. He and his family for the most part have lived a quiet, sheltered life as middle class Mexicans. Until he met Allen, he probably hadn't traveled more than a few hundred miles from his home except for the six months with a brother in Washington State, many years ago.

"Here you are, gentleman. Two of the coldest beers I could find," says our long legged waitress. "Shall I run a tab?"

"Sure," I answer. "But tell me, are you from the states?"

"A California girl."

"Can we know your name?"

"Sure, it's Cindy. I'll be back to check on you." Cindy I guess to be in her middle to late twenties, five feet ten and blond hair.

"Salud," I say as we toast each other. The cold beer tastes good after the long excursion to get here.

We relax to enjoy the atmosphere while speculating what lies ahead in the trip and when we will reach the canal. I ask if he feels the engines are holding up ok.

"I think so. I don't see anything going wrong," he answers, "but they are old and tired. Anything can happen."

I excuse myself to visit the rest room, located to the back of the lobby area. Returning to our table, my attention is drawn to a group of men seated at a back table of the lounge. One of the men in particular looks like Roger from this distance. Instinctively I walk towards them, thinking it would be great to meet his buddies. The closer I get to them the more I realize that it is Roger and that they are in a heated discussion. Although

I am unable to understand what is being said, their body language tells me that Roger is the focus of the other's anger. It is quickly evident that these are not service buddies. These are older, middle aged Hispanic men. I instinctively shy away from any further advance, hoping not to be detected and embarrass Roger.

"I think I have just seen Roger at a table in the back with a group of men," I say upon returning to Paco.

"Did you say hello?"

"No, they were having an argument with Roger as the focus of their frustrations."

"He said he was meeting with buddies."

"Yes, I know. But these fellows appeared to be older Hispanic businessmen in suits and ties."

"I'm going to go look."

He heads off in the direction I have indicated, while I try to make sense out of what I had seen.

"Another round," asks Cindy.

"Please." I respond. "Question? Is that your station over in the far corner?"

"No, but I know whose it is. Shall I ask her to come over here?"

"That's not necessary. I was somewhat interested in who a group of men are that are seated there."

"I'll find out," she says with a little grin.

I can do little else but sit back and try to relax. Before long, I see Paco making his way back. Once seated, he indicates that he saw no one looking like Roger. Yes, there are five men in business suits at a table, but no one resembling him.

"Did you ask them?"

"No, I felt out of place approaching them."

"I understand," I say knowing the culture of his country.

Our drinks arrive.

"You look upset?" Cindy says looking at me.

"No, I'm ok. I thought I recognized a friend, but apparently not," I say deciding the least said, the best.

"I know the men you are inquiring about. They come here often, always to that table. They are careful not to speak while being served. Management tells us not to speak to them unless asked. They always order a bottle of tequila. They stay for maybe an hour."

"Is it always the same four or five?" I ask.

"Generally yes, but sometimes there is one other, a younger man."

"Thanks. I appreciate the information."

Before she leaves I pay the bill with a handsome gratuity.

"Well Paco, my imagination must be working overtime. I swear that that was Roger there at the table."

"If so, he slipped away very quickly."

"Perhaps he did see me after all and didn't want to be confronted."

"Maybe so."

We drink up and walk out onto the Condesa. The sidewalk remains busy as does traffic on the street. We agree that it is time to head for the boat. Although it is early by Acapulco time, some of the discos are just now opening, neither of us seems interested in further drinking or eating.

Crossing Condesa, we walk for several blocks window-shopping and people dodging. We are making better time walking than in a taxi. After eight or so blocks, we tire and find an empty taxi. At first, progress is slow but finally we move along at a decent rate of speed, passing the earlier landmarks until arriving at the marina. I pay the driver, offer a greeting to the guard and walk the long pier to the quietly awaiting Athena.

Stepping into the cockpit we are met by Allen who, rested and relaxed, wants to know how our evening went. We offer a brief recap of our wanderings as well as my seemingly sighting of Roger.

"Well, he is onboard. He preceded you by twenty minutes. He had very little to say to me and went immediately to his cabin complaining of not feeling well."

"Are our plans to be underway by 10:00 hours," asks Paco.

"Yes, although I'm a little concerned about a low pressure system moving our way from the west. It is a considerable distance out in the Pacific, so it's difficult to predict where it will finally go. It could influence my decision regarding our next port of call. Presently we are cleared to Puerto Madero."

We discuss the pros and cons of remaining here until the system decides what it is going to do. We decide to wait until tomorrows weather report to make our final decision.

"Well I'm off to bed," I announce. "It sounds like we have several full days ahead of us. Goodnight."

I go below to my cabin, ready myself for bed and try to read; however, I am bothered by what I had seen earlier. I cannot convince myself that it was not Roger. Finally, I fall asleep. Sometime during the night, I switch off the reading light.

What is happening to me? asks Roger of himself now confined to the safety and solitude of his cabin as he sits on his bunk, his head in his hands staring at the floor. *How stupid could I possibly have been to believe those three so called buddies just happened to be passing through from Puerto Vallarta and wanted to say hello? And then to leave me in the clutches of the Acapulco Mafia who insist that I am the one responsible for our scheduled delivery date is unbelievable. As I sit here tonight, I'm not even sure where I am to deliver the package. This is crazy.*

CHAPTER THIRTEEN

Blanco

Day 6. Sunday.

07:00 I am awake but not feeling too spry. Shaved, washed and dressed, I start above to see what may be happening. I peek in at Paco who remains fast asleep. The cockpit is empty, but Allen is at his desk.

"Good morning," I offer, trying not to surprise him from behind.

"Good morning, Bob. Did you sleep well?"

"No, not surprisingly after all I drank last night."

"I'm sorry I didn't feel up to going with you last night. It was best for me to stay here and relax."

"We understand," I offer. "Can I get you anything from the galley?"

"Not just now. I'm afraid that what is left of the coffee is old and strong."

"If I make pancakes, bacon and scrambled eggs, will you have some?"

"You bet. Let me know if I can help in any way."

I make my way to the galley where I start a fresh pot of coffee brewing while I fry bacon and mix pancake batter. I give a few sharp knocks on Rogers's cabin door announcing that breakfast is near ready. He responds by saying that he will be right along. Next I roust out Paco. He reluctantly opens an eye to confirm that he will be there.

"Chow in five minutes," I say passing Allen's cabin.

"On my way," he responds.

By the time I finish with the eggs and pancakes, Allen has the big table in the salon set. I put out the items buffet style on the counter top that separates the galley from the salon. Roger and Paco join in for what turns out to be a fun and relaxed meal. There is no indication from Roger of 'not feeling well' as he consumes a healthy amount of food.

"That was great," says Allen leaning back in his chair.

"Thanks Bob. I enjoyed it," says Roger.

"I must be becoming a gringo," says Paco with a grin. "I never eat this at home."

I am pleased with their compliments.

"Before we go," says Allen; "I have a couple of things to say. So far I feel that everything has gone very well. My thanks go to each of you. This next leg of the trip may be uncomfortable. We have a tropical depression tracking in an easterly direction, which we will encounter as we move south and east. From this morning's weather fax I've learned it has winds of from twenty to thirty miles per hour with rain and sea heights of three to five feet. So, rather than plot a course directly to the Mexican/Guatemala border, I have decided to follow the coast line remaining two miles off shore to hopefully help minimize the problems Athena has with high seas.

"Perhaps it would be best to remain here until the system clears then head straight line to Madero," I offer.

"Yes, I've considered that; however, I believe by leaving now we can be well down the coast before the storm hits and if need be we can duck into one of several harbors to take refuse."

"Then let's get underway," quips Roger, seemingly eager to get going.

"I'll take care of the galley," I announce.

At 09:30 we slip our mooring lines as Allen takes us out of the marina and into the calm waters of the bay. The weather is ideal with bright, clear sky, with little to no wind and unlimited visibility. There are no indications of any weather problems lurking to our south.

We stow our mooring lines and fenders in preparation of their non-use for the next several days. Paco busies himself with engine room checks while Roger double checks safety and deck gear.

I join Allen in the cockpit. It is my watch, but until he relinquishes control, I stand by.

There is very little boat traffic, it being Sunday. Allen kicks up our boat speed to five and a half knots. Our course follows the western headland of the bay, passing the many older homes of early Acapulco perched on the rugged terrain. Once clear, we establish a southeasterly heading that takes us out into open water.

"It's yours," announces Allen at 10:00 as he sets the autopilot and slides out from behind the wheel. He makes his log entries before joining Paco and Roger on the fore deck. We pick up a gentle ocean swell from the west, as we pull further away from the shelter of the headland. To port is Punta Brujo while to starboard is Isla la Roqueta. Behind us, fading into the azure haze, is the outline of the hotels and high-rises of La Costera. I ask myself whether I will ever return to this fabled spot.

11:00 On the port side we are abeam an open body of water, Bahia de Puerto Marques famous for its new hotel development. One in particular is the Acapulco Princess, built in the shape of a pyramid flanked by two towers, surrounded by lush gardens and a championship eighteen-hole golf course.

It was here that the billionaire Howard Hughes was air evacuated out to Houston before his death. Many historians speculate that he was dead before ever leaving.

The boys run out the genoa to take advantage of the now fresh sea breeze, generating an additional half-knot of boat speed. GPS shows our ground speed at six knots.

I stand relieved of the watch by Roger at noon. He is in a remarkably cheerful mood.

The afternoon is spent under the awning of the aft deck in a lounge chair. In spite of the heat and humidity, it is very comfortable. The awning cuts the suns intensity coupled with the afternoon sea breeze and forward boat speed. I read; catch up on my log book notes between dozing on and off. Paco joins me for a time, trying his luck by setting out a pair of fishing poles.

By 16:00, there is the beginning of a high thin cloud cover from the south. Too far in the distance to bother us now, but first signs of changing weather ahead. Our progress remains good with a fresh westerly wind driving us along under the big genny.

The landscape is changing from a rugged, rock bound coastline to long sweeping white sandy beaches. Scrub brush and cactus's dominate the ground behind where the rolling waves crash. It is as remote an area of the country, of the world for that matter, as I have ever seen.

17:00 I fold and stow my chair. The interior is cool from the ships refrigeration system, almost cold at first encounter. I peek in at Allen, only to learn he is in the galley making dinner. The navigation chart shows us as two miles off shore, paralleling the coast. GPS shows we have traveled fifty-two miles, averaging just under six knots of speed.

17:30 Allen serves a tuna casserole, salad and garlic bread. Roger and I clean the galley before settling in to watch a movie. I want to ask him about what I thought I saw last evening, but decide to leave it alone.

21:00 My watch. Our forward progress remains good with all systems normal. Allen makes his logbook entries before saying good night and going below.

24:00 The watch passes quickly without incident. Relieved by Roger

I make my entries and inspections. Retiring below I ready for bed, make notes to my log, read a few pages and extinguish the light. I am little disturbed by the drive train noise or vibration. My worries of earlier seem unimportant as I slip off to a deep and restful sleep.

Day 7. Monday

06:30 My first waking sensation is that the boat is being buffeted about by high seas. Through my porthole I see wave heights of two to three feet with an occasional white cap. The sky is overcast with low gray clouds. It is clear that we have encountered the low-pressure system as predicted. Not particularly anxious to go above, I go back to bed where I listen to Athena's displeasure.

At 07:45, I roll out of bed and prepare myself for the day.

Allen is at the helm, looking a bit tired. We exchange good mornings, but little more. 'The coffee is old,' he says as I go below. I make a fresh pot, eat a bowl of cereal with juice and toast. My coffee with me, I go above to wait for my watch by sliding into the aft settee.

"I'm afraid we are in for a rough twenty-four hours," says Allen. "The weather map shows the storm intensifying to the degree that it has been upgraded to a tropical depression and been given the name Blanco."

"I could tell from below that we were being bounced around pretty well," I say.

"Is everything secure below?" he asks.

I secure all items that I feel may come loose and get broken. Even the coffee pot is put away in a cupboard, its contents emptied and placed in a thermos.

I take the watch at 09:00. From the log I see that our forward progress has been severely reduced. Since midnight we have come thirty-two miles averaging only 4.0 knots an hour.

I find that the boat has to be hand steered. The autopilot is incapable of handling the wild gyrations caused by the rolling furrows of water coming in upon us. The wind has kicked up as well, registering twenty-five mph with gusts to thirty-five.

10:00 Allen has me reduce engine rpms to 2000 to help ease the pounding we are taking. He spells me for fifteen minutes so that I may rest from the constant battle with the wheel in controlling the boat.

12:00 Relieved by Roger. Allen further reduces engine speed to 1800 rpms. I make my log notations and perform my inspections before going below to hunker down for the afternoon. The boats gyrations are felt less down here. I literally stow away.

18:00 Dinner consists of cold sandwiches, chips and soda. We are getting the stuffing kicked out of us. It is difficult to move about without being knocked off of your feet and thrown about. None of us are in much of a mood to eat or speak.

21:00 I take the watch. Conditions have not improved. We are like a cork in a large tub of water, pushed one way then to another. It has been raining for several hours now, making visibility at times impossible. Allen remains in the cockpit, seated at the aft settee, unwilling to go below. He has little to say with the exception of a word of advice now and then.

22:00 The watch is tiring by the constant course corrections. In addition, it is frustrating to build up speed only to have it stopped by a large wave trapped below.

22:30 Allen spells me for a fifteen-minute break. I am able to go below and relax for a few minutes. My arms ache from the constant turning of the wheel.

24:00 Exhausted, I make my rounds and plot our position as best as possible. I tell Roger to call me if needed. I go below and fall asleep fully clothed.

Day 8. Tuesday.

02:30 Awaken by premonition, I relieve Roger. Allen has finally gone to bed. Despite Rogers good physical condition, he is I believe glad to get a few minutes reprieve.

0730. It continues bumpy despite our reduced speed. In the morning light I can still see a very angry sea under fast moving low gray clouds.

I manage a bowl of cereal and milk before reporting to the bridge. Allen is at the wheel looking tired after a long watch of manually steering. I check the log to learn that our progress has been a meager twenty-five miles since midnight.

09:00 I find that it remains difficult to keep a steady heading. Our forward progress is constantly impaired by the hydraulic effect of water being trapped under the boats superstructure.

1030. Allen brings up the latest weather fax that shows the center of Blanco is passing to the East and we should be seeing improved weather conditions within the next few hours. He also states that boats to our south are reporting clearing conditions on the VHF.

1100. I note that we are abeam the light house at Puerto Angel. Our progress remains slow and wet. The rain continues to be whipped by the wind. The windshield wipers are just barely able to keep our vision clear.

Allen briefly considers ducking into Puerto Angel to "catch our breath", but decides against it after looking closer at the wind swept conditions inside the small inlet.

At mid-day I turn the watch over to Roger who appears tired and somewhat aggravated.

"Can I make you lunch?" I ask.

"No, I am not hungry," he responds in a sharp tone.

"If you need anything, please let me know," I say before going below to the galley. *I wonder what has him so disturbed,* I ask myself. *I'm sure it is this rough weather and lack of sleep. We are all that way'*

I take my lunch up to the cockpit area and slide into the aft settee. Like Allen and me before, Roger fights to keep the boat on course. The rain seems to have tapered off some but the wind has not.

1300. I decide to remain in the cockpit. My mind wanders as I focus on the nearby shoreline. It remains a low sandy solitary beach where the tree line is set well back from the pounding surf. There is a certain kind of mystique, conjuring up the feeling of being on a deserted island, isolated from the outside world. I feel that at any minute a bearded, rag torn soul will appear waving his arms for help.

Suddenly without warning, the boat makes a radical change in course to starboard and points out to sea. I look over to Roger who says to no one in particular; "I've had enough of this. This is where we were yesterday. I'm going to find smoother water."

Astonished, I slid from the settee and approach him. "Roger, you cannot make this course change without Allen's approval," I nearly yell at him.

There is no response. It is as if he has not heard me.

Before I can say or do anything else, Allen bolts from his cabin, demanding to know why we have changed course.

"We have not moved in twenty-four hours," wails Roger, using hand signs pointing to the coastline.

"What makes you think that we have not made forward progress?" asks Allen in a calm voice.

"I recognize the same beach from yesterday."

"Did you check our position on the chart before taking the watch?"

"Yes, but I know this as the same beach."

"Tell you what, let Bob take the helm while you and I plot our present position for verification. Bob, take the helm please."

I slide behind the wheel. Without asking, I resume the old heading.

Allen and Roger move to the settee together with the chart, logbook and present GPS reading.

Paco joins us with a questioned expression upon his face. In looking at Allen, he knows from experience that it is best to not ask questions. He goes below to the galley to get ready for his fast approaching watch. I do my best to maintain the heading and forward speed.

1500. Paco takes the watch. I make engine rounds and sign off on the log for Roger before going below. I feel tired and in need of a few minutes to myself. The events of the past hour have me perplexed and a little worried. I doze off briefly, awaking feeling somewhat refreshed and relaxed. A splash of water on my face helps revitalize me as well.

In the galley refrigerator I find a Fresca before making my way up to the cockpit. Paco is at the wheel and Allen is sitting alone at the settee.

"May I join you?"

"Yes," answers Allen, waving me to sit opposite him.

"How is Roger?" I ask.

"OK, I hope. He has gone below to rest and get some sleep."

"Any ideas as to what caused his unusual behavior?"

"He appears to be under a great deal of pressure. I was unable to determine from what and why. He was confused and disorientated when we first sat down but quickly recovered after a few minutes. He had no trouble comprehending our present position from yesterday's location. He was very apologetic and hopeful of making restitution."

"I felt he looked tired and irritable at the start of the watch," I offer.

Allen continues," We three need to help him by keeping a close eye on his behavior. I have come to realize that he is a loner, so that may prove difficult. There may be resentment towards the three of us because of our previous relations whereupon he feels left out. We should make him more a part of our conversations and engage him in discussions."

I decide to keep my thoughts to myself.

1700. Miraculously, the sun is making brief but positive appearances as the cloud cover is breaking up. Visibility, rapidly improving, allows us to see the headland to Huatulco Bay.

"Paco, we'll spend the night. Take us inside and up close to the beach. We all need a good night's sleep."

It is welcome news to me. I know it is to Paco from the look on his face.

1730. The continuing splashes of sun come and go as we make the gradual turn into the protected bay created by the natural headland to our port and the manmade rock breakwater to our starboard. We pass a large rusting buoy apparently belonging to the Navy. Tied to it this evening is an equally rusted shrimper, two men and a woman wave from onboard as we pass. They have ridden the storm out here, I guess. A white sandy beach is nestled to the back of the bay with a hotel directly behind.

1800. Paco anchors us in thirty feet of water just off the two jetties that form the entrance into the marina on the south end of the beach. Allen and I handle the ground tackle and secure us for the night.

With little hesitation after securing the engines, Paco and Allen go ashore to check in with the port captain. I remain onboard to clean up the boat and check on Roger.

Knocking on his cabin door, I call his name. I hear him move about before answering in a sleepy voice. Without offering to open the door I advise him of the evenings plan to go ashore for dinner. He replies saying that he prefers to stay aboard.

"Are you sure? We really think it is best that you join us," I say.

"No thanks, I'm fine."

With that I leave and go about a cursory pickup of loose items. Not much in the way of cleaning has been able to be performed over the past two days. The dirty dishes will have to wait until later. I go below to my cabin to clean up and take my camera before returning to the cockpit.

It is not long before I hear the dingy coming along side. Once onboard I advise Allen of Rogers decision. Not happy he goes below to speak with him.

"How did it go at the port captain's office?" I ask Paco while we wait.

"He was not there. We left a message saying that we would be back in the morning."

"Isn't that unusual, that no one was around for check in?"

"Not really. This is a small port of entry and policies are not taken as seriously as in larger places like Puerto Vallarta," he says with a smile.

I understand that, I guess. What has always troubled me is the Mexican policy that requires a vessel to check in and out of each state in the country. Of course it means extra revenues to that state and that is more the reason for the policy than anything else.

Allen returns and announces that Roger will be joining us.

"He maintains that he is feeling ok and all he needs is time and space to be back to his old self."

20:00 The four of us load into the dinghy headed for shore. Paco motors us to the dinghy dock inside the marina. After tying off and unloading we walk up past the port captain's office, across a portion of the beach towards the restaurant in front of the hotel. The sun, long gone into the Pacific, leaves a glow in the western sky as a promise of good weather for tomorrow.

Flood lights from the hotel light our way along the beach to the restaurant where we find a table and seat ourselves. Quickly, I count a total of ten tables scattered about with red and white-checkered tablecloths and a small flower arrangement in the center. A thatch roof provides cover above while the sandy beach is the floor. To the rear is a bar with what appears a well-stocked assortment of alcohol, wines and beer. The kitchen, I guess, must be in the hotel or at least it is out of sight.

"Señores, Hola, my name is Pedro. May I get you something from the bar?" asks a young man appearing with menus. He is dressed in white long pants, a flower lei shirt and is barefoot.

We wait for Allen to order. If he orders an alcoholic drink, we will also.

"Rum and coke," is his answer.

Paco asks for a beer, Roger a screwdriver and I a frozen margarita. Pedro thanks us and departs for the bar where he appears to be the bartender also.

The conversation is light while we wait for drinks. Roger seems at ease and joins in the banter without signs of anything troubling him. Allen tells one of his many sea stories while drinks arrive.

"Salud," offers Allen as a toast. My margarita tastes especially good after the past three days of sobriety.

"I want to offer my apology to each of you for my behavior this afternoon," says Roger after a brief silence. "I want to assure you that it will not happen again." It is clear that he is embarrassed and not use to having to make apologies. "Thanks to each of you for your understanding." he concludes.

"Nothing more need be said," says Allen, summarizing all of our feelings.

During dinner we discuss our plans for tomorrow. It is Allen's wish to be under way as soon as our paperwork is complete. Each of us has items to accomplish before then, but for now we relax and generally have some fun. A second round of drinks helps to further take our minds off the past days experiences and prepare us for what may lie ahead.

The restaurant is becoming busy. Two families with small children are seated behind us; vacationers I guess, although summer is not the time most folks come here to visit. Further back towards the bar is a young couple I sense are honeymooning, several other older couples who I bet are here for an anniversary and at a table by himself is a gentleman who looks to be on business.

My meal completed, I excuse myself and take my unfinished margarita and plastic chair down to the water's edge. Barefoot, I place the chair in the water and sit at ankle depth. The water is warm while the fine white sand feels good between my toes. I dig them deep below the sandy surface. I smile as I can recall doing this as a kid.

The bay water is smooth and tranquil. Athena's masthead anchor light reflection is unbroken in the calmness of the water. Further out in the bay I can see the flashing red harbor entrance light on the southern jetty, clear and sharp in the clean, rain-washed air. Above is a canopy of stars, so close that I feel I can touch them. The big and small dippers are as clear and near as I can ever recall, as is Orion and the North Star. The moon in its near full stage is rising behind me and is just now peeking through the palm trees to the back of the hotel. It is a magic moment. I try to hold onto it for as long as possible.

Too soon it is time to head back. Allen has paid the bill and is starting to walk back towards the dinghy dock. Returning the chair to the restaurant, I hustle to catch up. We load up and are quickly underway to the awaiting boat. We tether the dinghy to the port side for use tomorrow morning.

The remainder of the evening passes quickly as we individually work on tasks assigned. I clean the galley, set the coffee pot up for morning use, and remove a pound of bacon from the freezer to defrost as well as a loaf of bread.

Retiring to my cabin, I shower and make entries into my log. It has been an interesting few days and I want to make sure I have recorded the events accurately.

I slip into bed hoping to read several pages from my book. Rather than the port engine drive train rhythm while under way, I have the fifteen KW Genset generator, to keep me company.

I find I am too tired to read. I switch the reading light off, unable to concentrate. Sleep comes very fast.

CHAPTER FOURTEEN

The Tehuantepec

Day 9 Wednesday.

03:30 I awaken from a sour stomach, caused I'm sure by the two margaritas and the Mexican food. After taking two antacids I go topside and step out on deck into the warm, still night air. The moon now high overhead bathes the deck in sufficient light to allow me to go forward to check the anchor rode. Satisfied that we remain secure, I peer forward to see that the shrimp boat is gone. The large buoy is empty. To our south I can see the glow of the hotel lights that form the major tourist attraction to this coastal city. Returning below I sleep in short, fitful spells.

06:30 By my calculations I suspect my three companions are already up and about. Dressed, I go to the galley, make a fresh pot of coffee and take two aspirins with tomato juice in an effort to settle my head and stomach. No one seems interested in breakfast, including myself.

07:30 Allen suggests that we take a quick look at a new marina located in the next bay to our south. He reasons that we cannot leave before 09:00 after visiting the port captain so we'll do some sightseeing. The four of us pile into the dinghy with Paco at the helm. It is a pretty morning; Blanco having cleared the air leaving a clear blue sky. I can see a line of white cumulus clouds well out to sea.

Paco takes out of the bay, around the jetty and down the coast to where a marker for the new marina sits atop a manmade stone jetty extending a quarter mile out from the beach. He throttles back as we enter the narrow channel created by the two parallel stone jetties. Inside we find it is well protected from surge and wave action; however, the marina is small and undeveloped. There are three boats med-tied (similar to the Acapulco Yacht Club), grouped together at the only working dock. One of the three boats is a catamaran, a party/tour boat named The Tequila. We learn from a crewmember on board that business is very slow. Perhaps they go out three times a week with maybe twenty to thirty people.

After thanking him for the information we motor further up the channel only to find it a dead end. All around us are signs of neglect and lack of interest on behalf of the owners. Soil erosion caused by bulkhead collapse is the biggest issue. I feel that it could be something of value if taken care of soon.

08:30 Back on board. We continue with chores in preparation for departure. Allen surprisingly asks me to go with him. He explains that I will do small errands while he handles paperwork with the port captain. Luckily, I find a taxi driver near the port captain's office that speaks decent English who takes me into the town of Santa Cruz, located three kilometers north of the marina.

Here I am able to send several faxes, a market for a small grocery list, a pharmacy, a music store (I expand the cassette library), post office (cards for wife and kids) and a marine supply store. I return to the marina at 11:30 where I pay the driver, thanking him for his help and patience. We are by now good buddies.

Carrying the purchases, I walk along the malecon leading to the waiting dinghy. Nearing the port captain's office, Allen steps from within and motions for me to follow him back inside. It takes my eyes several seconds to adjust from the brightness of the outside. The coolness of the building is noticeable. I become aware that there are at least two other individuals with Allen, who now takes my packages and offers me a chair. As my eyes adjust, I can see the uniform of the port captain as one, the other is only a silhouette.

"Bob, let me introduce you to these two gentlemen. First is the Huatulco Port Captain, Mr. Juan Rodriquez." The uniformed officer steps forward to shake my hand.

"The second is Special Officer John Weber from the Federal Bureau of Investigation." Stepping forward and extending his hand I recognize him as the lone man in the restaurant last night. Speechless, I can do little more than shake his hand and take a big swallow. He asks me to be reseated.

"This has nothing to do with Pat or home, they are fine," starts Allen. "I do want you to listen to what Mr. Weber has to say," motioning to him to take over. I sense that Allen is somewhat disturbed over whatever is going on.

"Please call me John," he says as he drags a chair towards me and sits on it backwards, resting his arms on the back. He looks at me at eye level before continuing through deep brown eyes. He has a ruddy complexion, is clean shaven with thinning brown hair.

"We suspect that your boat is carrying stolen merchandise," he begins. I sense he is monitoring my reaction as it takes me a few seconds to fully comprehend what he has said. Seeing my distress, he says, "Let me put your mind at ease. The Bureau does not believe that you, Allen or Paco are involved or that you have any knowledge of what I am about to tell you." I look toward Allen who has his back towards us, offering little comfort. "Let me be brief and to the point," agent Weber continues. "Indications are that your boat is being used to transport a stolen gem to a source in Panama. Our informants tell us that the gem is in the possession of the young man known as Roger who has been hired to deliver it. He picked it up in Puerto Vallarta from a businessman with known links to the Mexican/Columbian underworld."

"It explains to some degree Roger's erratic behavior," says Allen walking towards us. "He has been nervous and on edge since we started."

"We suspect that he was contacted in Acapulco and told that there was now a deadline for the goods to be in Panama, something he obviously has no control over. Additionally, we are of the opinion that he has been imbedded with a signaling device that monitors your whereabouts."

I am stunned, unable to speak.

Agent Weber continues. "We could have allowed you to continue on; however, it was decided to alert Captain Daniels of our information. He in turn asked that you be included as well." I nod in understanding. "We could seize the boat here, but we want to attempt to apprehend the individuals that are waiting for the gem. They are the real catch in our opinion. We would like you and Captain Daniels's cooperation."

"I understand," I am able to say.

"The Bureau has the full cooperation of the Mexican and Panamanian authorities. What we want to do is create a sting with your help. We think we know who will be the pickup person and we believe it will occur in Colon." Again he stops for effect.

Allen now pulls up a chair and joins in the discussion. The port captain moves to the open door where he can watch outside activity and act as a sentry. I find myself thinking that this is surreal, something I must be watching on TV.

"Basically we would have you go about your business of delivering the boat in a normal manner. We would have you be extra vigilant with Roger, watching him as closely as possible without raising his suspicion. If you leave the boat, make certain he leaves with you. If he is required to remain on board, have someone stay with him. We do not believe that any effort will be made to contact him again as in Acapulco, but we don't know that as a fact."

So, I was right. I did see him at the hotel," I say relieved.

"Yes, you did. We are not certain why the individuals risked being seen. We do think it was a scare tactic to make certain Roger understood that he and the boat were being closely watched."

"How did Roger know that they wanted to meet?" asks Allen.

"We believe it was Larry, the dock master, who passed on the information."

"How do we reach you if we have a need?" asks Allen.

Agent Weber stands to go get a paper bag from near the port captain's desk. "By activating this," he says.

"It looks like an EPIRB."

"It is exactly that, but it transmits on a special frequency monitored twenty-four seven by the Bureau using the GPS system. If there is a problem, you should trigger the on switch here. Once activated, you can expect all hell to break loose shortly thereafter."

"What specifically do you anticipate will happen in Colon/" asks Allen.

"We think the exchange will take place onshore, soon after you transit the Canal. Our thoughts are that because you will need to clear customs before continuing, you will anchor off the Caribbean Yacht Club to come ashore there. Are we correct?"

"Yes, that is how I have done it on previous trips."

"Good. Then we will be there when you arrive." Thinking for a minute, he continues. "We plan to closely monitor your movement. When you reach Panamanian waters, if something is to happen at Balboa, we will be handy there as well."

Satisfied that he has covered all bases, Weber stands and replaces his chair.

"Are we free to go?" asks Allen of both men.

"Good luck," Weber says as he nods his approval. The port captain asks Allen to complete the check out papers.

Collecting my packages I step out into the bright sunlight. I squint against the glare of the midday sun before my eyes can adjust. I am taken aback also by the heat and humidity.

I make my way to the ramp and onto the dinghy dock where I place my packages inside the waiting tender. I am careful not to sit on the fiberglass seat without first covering it with a towel as protection against the very hot surface.

After several minutes Allen arrives. He takes care in getting in and seated. "I prefer for the time being to keep all of this just between us," he says. "I hate to keep anything from Paco, but for now I think it best to have it stay with us."

He cranks the big Yamaha engine to life before I release us from the dock. Shifting into forward we slowly make our way out into mid channel where with increased power we speed to the waiting Athena.

Paco waits for us at the port lifeline opening with a questioned look. "Hola," he says from above while taking the dinghy's painter from me. "I thought I might have to swim in to get you two."

"Sorry for the long wait," answers Allen as we both scramble onboard. "I had trouble with checking us out, How are things here? Are we ready to get underway?"

"Everything is ready," answers Paco now joined by Roger. "It will take a few minutes to stow the dinghy."

"Good. Let's do it. I'll give you a hand."

I go below to put groceries and the other purchases away. I find the galley is clean and that the laundry is folded and put away. In my cabin I wash and change my shirt. I sit on my bunk before going topside to think awhile on the morning's events, concluding that at least for the moment there is little else I can do but go about my normal activities.

From above deck I hear the whine from the electric windlass as the dinghy is being brought on board and stowed, followed by the rumble and vibration of the port engine coming to life.

I gather myself together and go above. In the cockpit I find Allen at the wheel while Roger and Paco are positioned forward preparing to bring the anchor on board. Paco signals Allen to move Athena forward over the anchor where he and Roger bring chain and anchor aboard by the windlass. The locker cover is then secured as part of the deck.

15:20 We proceed out of the bay to take up a southeasterly heading. Our next GPS waypoint is at Salina Cruz, thirty miles distance.

With unlimited visibility, I am able to see into Huatulco Bay where I identify the five mega size hotels that occupy this lovely spot. They are strung out along the rocky coastline immediately east of where we had been anchored. Included are a Sheridan, The Royal Maeva, a Club Med, The Royal Caribbean and The Club Plaza.

It was here at the Royal Caribbean that my wife and I, together with Jim & Shirley from Pelican, spent a day waiting for the bus to take us up to the mountain town of Oaxaca. We were free to explore the hotel grounds, use the facilities while he had lunch and drinks around one of several swimming pools on the property. It was a great way to spend twelve hours rather than in the bus terminal. I would someday hope to revisit this place with more time to explore.

Dinner is a meatball stir fry by Allen with lots of vegetables included. Roger chips in with a banana flambé for desert.

21:00 My watch. We are ten miles northwest of the busy industrial port of Salina Cruz and ten miles offshore to avoid the heavy shipping traffic. The lights from the city cast a bright glow in the eastern sky signifying its large size.

22:00 Allen joins me as a second set of eyes while we cross directly through the shipping lane. Radar provides us with the location of two container ships, both outbound, which we give a wide berth. They are heavily laden and create quite a good size wake requiring us to reduce speed. Otherwise we pass through without further incident leaving the bright lights of Salina Cruz in our wake.

23:00 We now enter the westerly boundary of the Gulf of Tehuantepec. The town from which it derives its name is located some twelve kilometers inland from the water. Why this gulf of two hundred miles in length received its name from a relatively small inland town, only the Mexicans know.

Allen provides a new magnetic compass heading and GPS waypoint taking us in a more southerly direction towards the coastal town of La Soledad. We are now beginning to follow the gentle curve of the gulf.

24:00 I turn the watch over to Roger. He is in a seemly good mood, relaxed and cheerful. I remain in the cockpit after my engine room checks and recordings where we make small talk about the good weather we are experiencing and how it may affect the transit of this most infamous body of water. I can sense nothing is bothering him at this point in time. I retire to my cabin where I record notes to my journal, read before turning out the lights. Sleep is slow in coming. I have too much on my mind.

Day 10 Thursday

06:30 I am aroused by the suns brightness dancing about off my cabin walls. It has risen over the Sierra Madres in a clear, cloudless sky. The sea is flat and must have remained so all night. A look out of my window indicates that we have moved in closer to shore. I estimate we are about two miles out from a low sandy white beach. I leisurely shower, shave and dress in shorts and tee shirt with lots of sunscreen. Coffee I find is freshly made in the galley.

"Good morning," I offer to Allen as I enter the cockpit.

"And a good morning to you Bob. How are you this fine day?"

"Overall, good. A lot on my mind after yesterday, but feeling well. Have you spoken to Paco?"

"No. I have not had the opportunity."

Sensing that he did not wish to carry the conversation further, I excuse myself to return to the galley for a light breakfast. Afterwards I slide into the back seat of the crew table to wait for the start of my watch.

We are well on our way into this most notorious body of water. Here the winds can blow at gale force depending on atmospheric conditions both here on the Pacific side of the Sierras as well as on the Caribbean side. When a high pressure system forms on either side of this narrow strip of land (one hundred miles wide) with a corresponding low on the other side, the resulting winds moving between the two, particularly east to west over and through the Sierras can cause towering waves up to two hundred miles off shore. From my reading experiences of boaters caught in either situation, the best that one can do is stay as close to the shoreline as possible. An old saying goes, 'one foot on the boat, the other foot on the beach.'

09:00 My watch. I relieve Allen who goes below to monitor the single side band radio mornings 'boaters net' (by mutual consent of a time, every day boaters up and down the west coast gather on VHF to discuss a variety of topics including weather, mail, sick call and items of interest to the fleet) and to receive the latest weather fax. The sea is flat with a gentle off shore breeze of two to three knots. We are getting a nice push from a two knot current giving us an over the bottom speed of seven knots. The autopilot requires a one to two degree correction each hour as we continue to follow the crescent shape of the bay

"Buenos días, Roberto," says Paco as he comes into the cockpit with his coffee and sits at the crew table.

"Buenos días, Paco. How are you?"

"Very good, very good. We are getting a good ride, I am glad. It could be much different."

Allen pops up from his cabin with the latest weather fax, laying it on the table.

"Our luck seems to be back," he says. "High pressure is in control on both sides of the peninsula and the forecast is calling for more of the same. There is always the threat of an isolated thunder storm, but otherwise no one is reporting any bad weather anywhere between Costa Rica to San Diego."

Folding the fax, Allen motions Paco to follow him to his cabin. The two disappear below to what I guess will be a briefing on yesterday's events in the port captain's office.

12:00 The remainder of the watch is routine. The hourly engine room checks reveal nothing abnormal as I turn things over to Roger. Earlier he had been out on deck exercising and sun bathing. Now, after a hot shower and dry clothes, he is in the best of moods.

13:00 We gather for lunch at the settee where we discuss our progress. It is Allen's feelings that we should reduce engine power sufficient to bring boat speed to five knots. At our present rate we will arrive at Puerto Madero at 03:00, where he would be reluctant to enter the harbor under cover of darkness. All agreeing, he orders Roger to reduce engine RPM's to 2100. The boat speed drops to just over three knots but with the two knot current assist, we show five knots over the bottom.

13:30 I gather my camera, sunscreen and sunglasses to retire on the fantail. I stretch out on a lounge chair under the awning where I find it quite comfortable. I watch a large thunderhead that has formed off of our starboard bow. It towers as high as ten thousand feet and spreads out over a distance of several miles. It is five miles away and appears stationary. Lightning plays about its base with the slate color of rain highlighted by the afternoon sun.

The sun at its near apex is drenching the landscaping to my right (port side) with incredible colors. The Sierra Madres is dressed in a deep purple, silhouetted against a cobalt sky while the foreground of white sand and green palms create a painter's pallet.

A low point in the jagged mountain range reminds me from my earlier readings that it was here that the roots to the beginning planning process of the Panama Canal occurred. President Ulysses S. Grant instructed Admiral Ammen to organize a series of expeditions in order to do a "practical investigation" of this section of Mexico, together with Nicaragua and Panama. If there was to be a water corridor, he wanted it to be in the proper place, as determined by civil engineers and naval authorities. Captain Robert Shufeldt would lead the Tehuantepec expedition in 1870 aboard the USS Kansas. Their main point of exploration centered at the entrance to the San Juan River, now directly off of our port beam.

The most convincing place expected to see a canal built at that time was at Nicaragua, through Lake Nicaragua. If not there, then probably at Panama. Tehuantepec had the virtue of being much closer to the United States; however that was about all the survey team could provide in the way of favorable findings. Tehuantepec was thereafter labeled as too wide (sea to sea) and too mountainous. Years earlier in 1811, the German born naturalist and explorer Alexander Von Humboldt, had decreed that the best that could be done at Tehuantepec would be to build good roads for camels. Interestingly, he said the same for Panama.

18:00 Paco has made an interesting fish stew, Mexican style. He uses one of the Bonita caught earlier. After kitchen detail, I join Roger on the fore deck to watch the setting sun. The earlier thunderstorm has completely dissipated leaving behind a long low cloud formation on the far horizon in an otherwise clear sky. The early evening night air feels comforting to the bare skin. We sit on the cabin sole facing forward. "This thank goodness, has been an uneventful transit," I say in an attempt to start a conversation."

"Yes our luck seems to be holding up well since Blanco," he responds.

"What are your plans after this trip?" I ask after a prolonged silence.

"I'm not sure. I have buddies in Vallarta who I like. I'll probably stay there for a while longer."

"You remind me a great deal of myself when I was about your age," I comment. "I was single, living in Los Angeles and traveled quite a bit whenever I wished. Of course it helped that I worked for an airline."

"When was that?"

"The mid nineteen fifties."

"The beginning of the end of propeller driven aircraft."

"You are right. Are you a student of aviation?"

"Somewhat. At one time I thought I would become an aeronautical engineer. I took a few introductory classes in high school and college."

"What changed your mind?"

"I soon realized that I was not college material. With my parents blessing, I joined the Navy."

"I believe that I was told you became a Navy Seal?"

"Yes."

"Tough duty I understand," I say in attempting to keep the conversation alive.

"I loved it," he says turning first away, then directly towards me. "I should never have left the service."

"Then why did you?"

I got pissed off because I was overlooked for a promotion."

"How long had you been in the service at that time?"

"Eight years. I was ready to re-up within a few months."

He suddenly stands and takes several steps towards the bow but returns and reseats himself besides me.

"I have never told as much about myself to anyone as I have with you this evening," he says. "For some reason I feel comfortable in your company."

"Thank you. I hope that I continue to hold your trust. But tell me more of your navy life and the events leading up to your separation."

"Well as I said, I went into the service rather than embarrass myself in the pursuit of a higher education. I scored well on the entrance exams and was in good physical condition, so was offered Seal school after boot camp. For reasons that I didn't fully understand, I applied myself beyond any expectation I thought I was capable of achieving. I rapidly advanced to the rank of second class petty officer and never thought twice about not reenlisting after four years." He pauses, and then continues. "I made first class within a year and seemed sure of chief within twenty-four months. My unit saw lots of action where I had the opportunity to utilize the training and discipline I had been taught.

When I was eligible to take the chief's test, I passed the exam only to be notified that there were no openings available. On the fourth attempt and denial, I decided to leave the service. It was a huge mistake and one that I will always regret. Since then I have bounced from job to job, country to country, never feeling happy or content with myself."

"How long ago has it been since you got out?"

"Almost three years."

"Have you given any thought about seeing if the Navy will take you back?"

"Not really. I am too pig headed and stubborn."

"I don't believe you are either," I say. "From what I have observed, you are good at boat handling, follow directions well and are a real asset to this delivery."

Standing, I excuse myself explaining it is near my watch time. "I like to continue this conversation whenever possible, if agreeable with you."

"Sure, I'd like that also."

"See you at midnight," I say as I leave to enter the cockpit.

"That looked like an interesting conversation," says Allen from the ship's wheel. "Did you learn anything of interest?"

"I am not sure. We talked out his Navy days and how much he regrets leaving the service."

"Did he tell you that he was dishonorably discharged?"

"No. I got the impression that he left voluntarily. How did you aware of this?"

"A fax from the FBI giving me that and other facts about him. It seems he has had several brushes with the law over the past few years. Nothing serious, but none the less he has not been an exemplary citizen either."

"Nothing of that nature," I respond. " I did get the impression that he considers himself somewhat of a failure in life. We plan to talk further."

21:00 I take over the watch. I note in the log that we are abeam the small village of Barra de Zacapulco, proceeding in a southerly direction. Our over the bottom speed is a steady five knots. Our ETA at the entrance to Puerto Madero harbor is 06:00. The weather remains clear with the exception of a thunderstorm cell five miles directly ahead. I put on my radio head phones and slip in the newly purchased Frank Sinatra tape.

22:30 The storm produces short periods of rain and several bright flashes of lightning. It is interesting to watch on radar as we literally drive through it.

24:00 Roger relieves me promptly at the appointed hour as has been his habit from the beginning of the trip. We exchange the basic of information regarding our position and ETA at Madero. I note that we are well beyond the southern extremes of the Gulf of Tehuantepec. Although he has not slept during my watch having spent the time out on deck or below in the TV lounge, he appears fresh and alert.

"Whenever you are ready to sit down again, let me know," I say.

"Thanks Bob. I will."

I am tired and wish only to go below to my cabin. I try to read but crash within a few minutes. The rhythm and vibration of the boat I now find soothing to a mindfull of questions and very few answers. Sleep comes quickly.

CHAPTER FIFTEEN

Maria

Day 11. Friday.

05:00 Semi-conscience, I realize that we have reduced rpm's and have slowed down. I suspect that we must be close to the entrance to Puerto Madero but know that Allen will wait for daylight before entering. As it remains dark outside, I see no reason to get up just now.

07:00 I join Allen and Paco in the cockpit with my coffee. I slide into the settee to watch the show. We are at the harbor entrance in the early morning light. Visibility is reduced because of patchy fog, so Allen proceeds slowly with the aid of radar and Paco's keen eyes.

Two parallel stone jetties stretch several hundred feet into the open water forming a narrow channel leading to the harbor. Each jetty has a steel light tower at the seaward end with their respective red and green flashing beacons. Off of our starboard stern lies a Mexican warship hidden now again in the fog bank. It appears to be a destroyer, but it is hard to determine.

Cautiously, Allen eases Athena into the channel and proceeds to its end. Here we enter a large turning basin where the main channel continues ahead while another runs off to starboard at a ninety degree angle. "If I remember correctly," says Allen, "the port captain and fuel docks are straight ahead."

Paco agrees as they peer into the dull grayness surrounding Athena.

From out of the fog on the port side appears a rowboat occupied by two men. One is rowing while the other stands in the stern waving his arms to gain our attention. Allen shifts into neutral to allow our boat to come to a stop while Paco and I step outside to determine what they want. As the rowboat draws near, we can see that the two occupants are young Mexicans. Remaining several yards away, the standing man shouts, "Hola, we are offering services for the buying of gasoline, water and port captain. May we be of help?"

119

Allen steps outside and asks that I take the wheel while he and Paco decide whether to accept their offer. I keep Athena centered in the channel as the rowboat comes along side. One young man comes aboard to present Allen with a business card. I estimate him to be in his mid-twenties, clean shaven, wearing clean shorts and deck shoes. He is muscular on a six foot frame. I can see but not hear the conversation; however, after several minutes it is apparent that we have accepted their services.

Allen returns to the cockpit and hands me the business card. It has simply printed, John y Sam.

"I believe that they can save us time. They seem to know where everything is, so I hired them. The on deck is John and he will take us to the transit dock. There is no longer a fuel dock and the port captain's office location has changed."

"How do we get fuel?" I ask.

"In fifty gallon drums from the Pemex station located in town."

"Oh, ok," I say thinking that this should be an interesting experience. Taking the wheel, Allen moves us into the right hand tributary while Paco joined by Roger and John prepare for a port side tie down. Proceeding up the waterway we pass fifty or more haphazardly moored shrimp boats. They are badly rusted from lack of maintenance, showing years of neglect.

Just beyond them we approach a concrete pier that John indicates is where we tie up. Allen, after several maneuvers, manages to bring Athena parallel to the pier where several eager bystanders offer their assistance to secure us. Paco in control of the situation has us quickly tied down and secure. Allen shuts down the engines. I note in the logbook that the time is 08:15 hours.

The weather has and is improving rapidly. The fog has burned off to reveal a barren, flat landscape of marshland. In the far distance towards the ocean is what I learn is a Mexican Navy facility. Its gray single story building is barely identifiable against the sunless sky. To our stern are two rows of corrugated metal buildings, facing onto the concrete pier.

All appear to be in use, but for what is unclear. Beyond them stands a large two story building that houses a cannery. It also looks in good condition, well maintained from the exterior.

Sam arrives driving a red Nissan flatbed truck. Immediately Allen, Paco, John and he leave for the port captain's office. Roger and I are left to do maintenance and keep an eye on the boat.

Athena is drawing a great amount of attention from the locals. They have come to look, inspect and discuss. Several offer their service for a price to wash the topside or to dive to clean the bottom. Most just stand

and look perhaps not having seen a private boat for quite some time. They form circles of discussion, men with little else to do with their time.

Roger and I wash the deck, clean windows and do general pickup chores. We both keep a watchful eye on our ever increasing size audience. It is hard for me to feel sorry or compassionate towards most of them. They are badly overweight and show little effort good hygiene. Many must have the crabs because of the way they are constantly scratching at their private parts. One in particular seems to enjoy rubbing is large belly as if it were a ripe watermelon.

12:00 The guys are back. Allen explains that he was able to both check us in and out with the port captain. "Once fueling is complete, we are free to leave," he explains to Roger and me.

Under Paco's supervision, the first of six fifty gallon oil drums is readied to be relieved of its contents. It has been fitted with an on/off valve together with a fifty foot length of two-inch in diameter neoprene hose. The hose is then fed to Paco, now onboard, who places it into the port side fuel intake. The oil drum is tipped on its side the valve opened allowing fuel to be gravity fed into the boat's tank. It is not the most sophisticated methods of fueling, but it seems to be working. It will require one more trip to the Pemex station to satisfy Athena's needs.

With Allen's approval, I seize the opportunity to explore the area. I grab my camera and walk towards where I believe I should find the center of commerce. The dirt street between the metal buildings is rutted, filled with standing pools of water from recent rains. I'm still unable to determine what if anything may be housed inside. Reaching the cannery, it is quiet and shuttered. The building fronts on the main street where an office is located. It is closed and locked as well.

Looking both to the left and right there is only signs of poverty and neglect along the street. Several ramshackle single story homes stand across the street under the hot noonday sun. Junk cars seem to be the item of choice for front yard décor.

On my left a short distance stands what appears to be a small grocery store. I walk along the side of the dusty street towards it, although I may as well walk down the center for these is no traffic. A mangy dog comes to sniff at me but quickly leaves. An elderly woman is hanging out her wash on a clothesline strung between her house and a falling down shed. She waves momentarily. The clothes flutter in the early afternoon breeze.

I climb the three steps to the shaded porch of the store where a number of rocking chairs stand idly by. I sense this is the place where one can sit with a neighbor or friend and get the latest news and gossip. Entering through the screen door I step into a well-stocked, clean grocery store.

Four busy ceiling fans above make a noticeable difference from the outside heat. Passing to the rear I find a refrigerated cabinet where I locate a cold Fresca. Without thinking of paying I open it and take several long swallows.

"May I help you?" asks a female voice from the front.

"I hope I didn't alarm you," she says in perfect English as I join her at the stores front counter.

She is petite with coal black short cropped hair, beautiful white even teeth and big brown eyes.

"No…," I say. "Well, actually yes. I didn't expect to hear English spoken here and I failed to see you when I came in."

"I understand," she says with a smile.

"I'm impressed by this store, located in the middle of nowhere. Are you the owner?" I uncharacteristically blurt out. This is I know is rude of me.

"No. It belongs to my Uncle. I am here to help him for a few weeks before returning home to Miami."

"Is Miami your home?" Again I am prying into another's personal affairs.

"Yes, although I spend a lot of time here. This is where I was born and raised. And you sir, where is home for you?"

"I live in northern New England. I am here today on a sailboat en route to the Panama Canal."

She slides off the stool and comes out from behind the counter extending her hand. "Welcome to Puerto Madero. My name is Maria."

"Thank you Maria, my name is Bob."

"I knew you are from the boat."

"How so," I ask.

"Word travels fast in our little community. Besides the port captain told me."

We are distracted as a young man enters the store. Maria puts a finger on her lips to signify that I should be silent. The man wastes little time gathering a few lunch items, pays and exits.

"It is best that we not speak English as there is still much unrest among my people regarding our economy. As a gringo my people would not think twice of capturing you and holding you for ransom as well as for the national publicity."

"I have read about how your people have risen up in protest over the lack of government funding, but I thought under President Fox many of the demands have been met."

"He has done much. However we continue to be an impoverished region economically."

"The cannery appears to be shut down. Is it temporary?"

"It operates only for short periods of time during the shrimping season. It is an example of misappropriation of government money to process a harvest from the sea that has been declining for years. Many of the boats in the harbor have not moved in over ten years due to depleted shrimp quantities," she says cynically. "That money spent to build the cannery would have been much better utilized to develop our tourist trade by dredging the harbor and building a marina to accommodate the many pleasure boats that ply our waters. When I look at what is happening just a few miles away on the Yucatan peninsula and at Vera Cruz, I become very angry."

Movement at the screen door interrupts our conversation. A small child enters going directly to the dairy display to bring a liter of milk to the counter. Maria motions that she may leave after recording the purchase on a tablet.

"I should be getting back," I say as I give ten pesos for my drink.

"I'll walk with you if you don't mind. Just give me a minute to close. It is nearly siesta time and I'd like to see the boat."

I push open the screen door entering the heat and glare of the afternoon. The street remains quiet in both directions.

Maria is soon to join me on the porch, closing the inside flimsy wood door before allowing the screen door to close. She wears a large brim straw hat and oversized sun glasses for protection from the intense sun. I realize just how attractive she is in a pair of denim jeans and shirt. A pair of sandals protects her feet.

"Let's walk on the other side of the street," she says reaching to take my hand. "It is less dusty and rocky."

I follow her lead as we cross over. Her hand feels soft but firm in mine. She releases it to walk in front of me. I cannot help but notice how well she fills out the jeans. At the cannery we turn right towards the boat. I catch up and walk next to her as we approach the pier. John, Sam and Paco are back with the second load of fuel. As we approach the pickup truck, the many observers turn their attention towards Maria and become quiet, retreating away from the area. Even John and Sam stop what they are doing.

"It is OK," speaks Maria in Spanish. "I only come to look at the boat."

Allen comes forward to greet us. I'm certain he is wondering what this is all about. I introduce him to Maria as they shake hands.

"I didn't want Bob wandering around alone so I escorted him back. Besides I want to see the boat like everyone else."

"You are welcome to visit," says Allen. "But tell me why has your presence caused such a stir?"

"I am known as an outspoken female which is generally not considered proper for a Mexican woman. Also my uncle is a wealthy and well known businessman in Madero and I fall in his shadow."

Allen nods in understanding.

"Bob can show you around. I need to remain here."

Maria and I watch the fueling operation for a few minutes before I invite her to come onboard. We stand on the fantail under the sun awning while I explain some of the boats physical characteristics. She listens well, asking good questions that indicate her interest and understanding.

"I'm hungry," I say. How about you? Can I fix us lunch?"

"Yes, that would be nice."

I slide open the cockpit door allowing her to step inside. The cool air of the boats interior greets us as Maria gives a tiny squeal of delight.

"This is wonderful," she exclaims.

I briefly explain the inner workings of the cockpit/bridge, the navigation station and the ships log. We then go below to the main cabin and TV lounge. I allow her to look over the spaces as I start lunch.

"Which would you like," I ask, "Ham and cheese or turkey and cheese on white, wheat or rye bread?"

Coming into the galley she moves me aside. "Let me do this. Tell me what you want and where things are," she says with a determined look. We make turkey, cheese, tomato, lettuce and mayonnaise sandwiches together with pickle slices and potato chips. She moves about the galley with the sureness and confidence of someone familiar with taking charge. Soft drinks and glasses are placed with the sandwiches on a tray and taken topside to the settee. From here we are able to watch the deck activities while we eat our lunch. As we finish the last oil drum is drained. Allen pays John and Sam and they in their pickup depart.

I remove our plates to the galley while Maria relaxes.

"Would you care to see the rest of Athena?" I ask upon returning.

"Yes, by all means,"

Good let's start here. Come this way. Step down, this is Allen's cabin."

I show her his cabin, the starboard engine room, Paco's cabin, our shared head before entering my cabin.

"This is tiny but nice," she says in looking around.

"It works well for me," I say. "Thank goodness I made up my bunk this morning and straightened up a few things."

"It looks fine."

Her closeness is over powering as we stand in silence. Her brown eyes look up at me in searching ways that speak of sadness and loneliness. She comes to me and wraps her arms around my neck, pulling me towards her. Her mouth is sweet and tender. Her body is firm, her breasts hard as I wrap my arms around her waist. The embrace lasts but for a few seconds before she withdraws from me.

"I am so sorry. Please forgive me," she says turning away. It is clear that she is embarrassed and uncomfortable.

"There is nothing to be sorry about," I say as I attempt to comfort her. "It was spontaneous and innocent."

I encourage her to sit on the edge of the bunk to help regain her self-composure. "Let's remain here for a while," I say. "I think we both need time to settle our emotions."

She nods in agreement.

I step into the head to wet a face cloth and bring it to her. She dabs her eyes and cheeks before patting the bunk for me to come sit next to her. She lays her head on my shoulder. "Thank you. You are a good person." She raises her head and looks at me. "I am so ashamed for the way I am acting. Can you possible forgive me?"

"Of course," I say kissing her forehead.

"What would your wife say if she knew?"

"How do you know I am married?"

"Oh, I can tell a married man," she answers looking at me through her deep brown eyes.

"Of course you are right," I respond.

Once again we are silent. I enjoy her closeness.

"Are you married?" I ask after several minutes.

"No. Anytime someone starts to get close in a relationship I break it off. Now at age forty-five, my biological clock is telling me that it is too late," she says with a sigh. "Besides I am too busy with my business in Miami and the need to be here with my uncle."

"I cannot agree with you that you are beyond the point of falling in love and having a meaningful relationship. I believe you just have not met the right person yet. He will come along one day and when he does you will know right away."

I indicate it is time for me to see if I am needed on deck as it must be close to our departure time. "Please feel free to use the restroom and I'll meet you topside."

"Thank you," she says squeezing my hand.

On deck I find Roger completing the washing down of the deck of diesel fuel spills. The earlier gathering of on lookers has dwindled down to only a few. It is very hot even under the sun awning. The afternoon breeze feels like a blast furnace.

Maria steps out on deck looking refreshed.

"May I walk you to the store?" I ask.

"No, that is not necessary. I will be fine."

"Ok," I say disappointedly.

"It has been a pleasure spending time with you. I wish you all the best of luck and be careful."

Before I can respond she steps nimbly through the lifeline onto the pier. Without looking back she walks down the rutted road towards the main street. I have a sudden urge to follow, but quickly realize that would be foolish. I can only watch as she disappears at the cannery.

Allen emerges from the cockpit wiping his hands on a towel. "As soon as Paco completes the oil and filter change on the port engine we need to be underway," he tells Roger and I. "I half expect a visit from the Navy and would like to avoid that if possible."

"Is there a reason for a visit?" asks Roger.

"Just a routine inspection. I was told that there has been an accidental death of an enlisted man and today is his funeral. Apparently the activities associated with the funeral have taken priority over a visit, at least for now."

15:30 We are away from the pier. Allen slowly eases Athena out of the small tributary before making a left hand turn into the main channel. Paco, Roger and I stow fenders and all loose gear in preparation of several days at sea. Allen now powers us out into the open water. The naval vessel here this morning is gone. There is no activity in the immediate area, only empty open ocean.

We set a southwesterly course to a waypoint twenty one miles to sea in international waters. Allen's wish is to be outside the jurisdiction of Guatemala and Nicaragua, two countries known for their high jacking of pleasure vessels.

Dinner consists of leftovers from previous meals. There is a somber mood at the table. My companions are tired from a long day of activity in the hot sun.

17:00 We reach our established waypoint and begin a gradual turn southeastward to pick up a course of 114 degrees. GPS gives our distance to the Papagayos of Costa Rica as 475 miles. Out ETA based on historical information is 73 hours.

21:00 I relieve Allen of the watch who does not linger for long before saying goodnight. Paco has long before turned in while Roger watches a movie below.

Radar is alive with echoes from shrimpers working along our route.

Even though they are well lighted, it is difficult to judge their speed and direction. I give them all a wide berth.

To the north over the Guatemala Mountains I observe lightning flashes dancing within the clouds of a thunderstorm. The flashes look like artillery explosions in a military exercise.

22:00 GPS shows that we remain twenty-one miles off shore proceeding at six knots through the water, but only four and one half over the bottom. Our heading remains at 114 degrees magnetic.

24:00 At change over to Roger I notify him and note in the log that it appears we now have a two-knot current running against us. We exchange basic information but little else.

I retire below to my cabin where I lie awake on my bunk in the darkness listening to the hum and steady vibration from the port engine drive train while thinking over the day's events. I smell Maria's fragrance.

CHAPTER SIXTEEN

Baby Allen

Day 12. Saturday.

0630. Sunlight dances about in my cabin. A good night's rest has me refreshed; eager to face the day's activities. Leisurely, I wash and dress before making my way topside. Allen and I exchange good morning greeting before I make my way to the galley where I start a fresh pot of coffee. While waiting for my morning "kick start", I have a bowl of cereal and make a couple pieces of toast generously smeared with peanut butter. I take my fresh brewed coffee and toast above to the cockpit and slide into the aft settee.

The weather in a word is "spectacular". The sky is clear and cloudless with unlimited visibility. A slight off shore breeze of five knots produces little in the way of wave action. The outside air temperature is eighty degrees; relative humidity is seventy percent and a steady barometer at thirty inches of mercury. Our forward progress would seem unimpeded; however, Allen points out that we have a two-knot current running against us. Our over the ground speed is five-knots. GPS shows we are twenty miles off the coast of Guatemala on a southeast heading of 114 degrees.

"I spoke earlier with Kate," says Allen from behind the ship's wheel. "She has had a telephone call from Pat in which she asks that you call home at your first opportunity. It is not an emergency; however, Kate said Pat sounded distraught. I thought, if you wanted, we would try a patch through KMI on the Single Side Band radio for a land line to home."

Rather stunned, I answer in the affirmative, attempting to determine what is happening at home to cause her to call.

I take the wheel while Allen goes below to his cabin. I hear him call

KMI, the marine operator located north of San Francisco. After several attempts, the operator answers, asking for a telephone number and billing instructions.

"Hold on one minute please," asks Allen. "I'll get the party making the call." He comes above to relieve me.

"Good morning," I start after getting seated and orientated at the desk. I provide the operator with the necessary information and sit back to wait for the connection. Within thirty seconds there comes the familiar ring of the house telephone. One, two, three rings before I hear Pat's, "Hello."

"Good morning from Guatemala. How are you?" I start.

"Oh honey, I'm glad to hear your voice. I think I'm OK but I wanted to speak with you about a visitor I had yesterday."

"Who was that?" I ask.

"His business card and identification shows him as Ronald Pears from the Boston office of the FBI. He was very polite indicating that he was simply doing a background check on the two of us but refused to say for what or why. He stayed for only a few minutes, asking perhaps five or so questions."

I try to remain calm when asking, "What were his questions?"

"When were we last out of the country, for how long and where did we visit. Another had to do with where we spent most of the year as our primary residence. When we travel, do we usually go alone? They were crazy questions which I wished you had been here to answer."

"Did he ask where I was?"

"No. He seemed to know that you were not here."

"Anything else?"

No, that was about it. He was alone in a white car with Maine license plates. After thanking me for my time, he drove away."

"Did he leave his business card?"

"Yes. I have it here."

"Let me have his telephone number, please."

She provides the number, an area code in Boston that I recognize. We talk for another two or three minutes in which I try to assure her that there is nothing to worry about and that I would call him at my first opportunity. I say goodbye with the usual "I love you."

Gathering my thoughts I return to the cockpit.

"Were you able to hear the conversation?" I ask Allen.

"Enough to hear that the Feds paid Pat a visit."

"I don't understand why?"

"I think they wanted to assure themselves that you are who you say you are. Remember you were brought into the loop at my insistence before they could do security and background checks."

"That makes sense," I say trying to calm my nerves. I realize that the events of the past few days are having a wide spread rippling effect.

At 09:00 I assume the watch as Allen retires to his cabin. He assures me that there is nothing to worry about. The visit to Pat was routine.

Our course remains at 114 degrees.

An hour into my 09:00 watch, I observe an open panga off the starboard bow. First as a tiny speck on the horizon, it grows in size. It is not moving, appearing to be dead in the water. Through the binoculars I can see two men, but it is difficult to see what they are doing. I yell below for Allen and/or Paco. Paco is the first to emerge. I point to the boat and give a brief explanation of what I've observed. They are now mid-ship as we pass.

"They are trying to get our attention," says Paco.

Allen joins us, training the binoculars on the bobbing boat now well aft of us. "Reduce power to engine idle, but maintain this course," he instructs me. "Paco, get on the bull horn to see what they may need."

With our forward momentum stopped, Paco steps out onto the fantail and hails them.

"It appears that there are three of them. An older male in the stern at the outboard engine, a young male seated just forward of mid-ship and the third, I am unable to be sure, may be a woman seated on the floor with her head in the lap of the younger male," says Allen watching through the binoculars.

After several voice exchanges Paco returns to the cockpit. "They are out of fuel with a pregnant woman who is very sick. They are asking for our help."

"What are they doing out here?" asks Allen as he considers the risks in stopping to help.

Roger, aroused by the boats sudden stop has joined us on the bridge.

Turning the situation over in his mind, Allen makes his decision.

"OK, we'll see what we can do. Bob; turn us around so Paco can bring them alongside. Once secured, Roger you go onboard and access the situation. Bob, you stay at the helm. I will monitor from the deck with the loaded flare guns. Any signs of foul play, we will cut them loose."

I spin the wheel to starboard, apply engine power to make a wide circle around them. Roger removes the first aid kit from its holder, checking its contents before joining Paco at the port lifeline opening awaiting the panga to come along side. Athena is now stopped, rising and dipping in the mid-morning light swells. Allen is positioned mid-ship at the port rail to watch the events unfold.

Taking the panga's line, Paco secures it to a deck cleat. He then informs the occupants that Roger is coming onboard. Roger with little effort descends into the smaller boat before knelling beside the prone woman, now out of my line of my sight. Several minutes pass before he informs Paco that he is ready to return to Athena. Coming aboard he goes directly to Allen.

"The woman is badly dehydrated and weak from lack of nourishment. I estimate she is in the last trimester of the pregnancy. She needs rest, food and water, but I do not believe she is in any danger of having the baby."

"Paco, try and find out what they are doing out here," asks Allen. "Roger, in your opinion, what can we do to help them without getting too involved?"

"Give them food and water enough for several days."

Considering Roger's answer, he says, "Let's at least do that then. Put together a 'care package' with whatever you think will best help them."

Roger leaves for the galley.

"I hate to leave them but I have little choice," says Allen. "We have a schedule to keep and quite frankly this is not a good place to be benevolent with the number of hijackings reported in these waters. We'll do what we can. Bob keep an eye to the horizon for any signs of an accomplice."

Paco reports from his interrogation. "They have been on the water for ten days. The old man, his son and daughter in law got caught up with tropical storm Blanca that pushed them out to sea where they ran out of fuel. We are the first to stop and offer help. They are very appreciative for anything we can give them."

Roger delivers two bags of food and water to the panga. He steps down into the boat while Paco hands the bags down to him. Roger pays particular attention to the woman making certain that she takes nourishment. It is clear that they are ravished from hunger.

"Paco, ask if they have a compass? Find out what the name is of their destination and I'll give them a course and bearing from GPS."

Roger returns from the panga. "Is it possible to bring the woman onboard for a short period of time? She needs to use a rest room, walk a little and clean up."

"I have no problem with that," answers Allen. "Just make it fast."

"I'll get right to it."

Allen looks nervously at his watch. We have been delayed for a half-hour. He scans the horizon for signs of any activity.

"Here is where they need to go. The old man does have a compass," informs Paco.

"Give them what we can for fuel. I'll run some numbers for a course."

The boat becomes a beehive of activity. The woman, under Rogers's care has been brought on board and taken below. I estimate she is in her mid-thirties, in seemingly good health in spite of her appearance.

Paco with the younger man start to fill two of their fuel cans and all of their water jugs. The elder man remains in the panga, seemingly content but ever watchful of the events unfolding around him.

Several minutes pass when unexpectedly Roger yells from below, "Bob, I need help. Get Allen down here right away." Having heard Roger anxious voice, Allen bounds out from his cabin and down the ladder into the main salon. Almost immediately from below he calls to me to get Paco without delay. Fortunately, I find him on the aft deck where I convey the urgent message. Immediately, he bolts through the cockpit and disappears below. After what seems like an eternity, Allen sticks his head up from below to announce that, "We are going to have a baby. Get the father down here right away."

To my relief the young man understands sufficient English and rushes below.

Not wanting to leave my station at the ships wheel and the only person to monitor our surroundings, I am unable to see completely into the main salon as to what is happening. What I am able to see is that the big dining table has been cleared and covered with a white sheet where Allen has the young lady lying with her head towards me on a pillow.

I search the horizon through my binoculars for anything suspicious as well as keeping the boat as stable from the rolling swells as possible.

"Señor, what is happening?"

I am startled by the voice coming from behind me. My heart skips several beats as I spin around and come to the realization that the voice is from the elderly man who I last saw in the stern of the small panga tied to our side.

"You speak English," I blurt out.

"Yes, not well but enough. I am the young lady's father. May I ask where she and my son in law may be?"

"Below, right down that ladder," I point with little concern for security.

The wait is not long before I hear the sharp slap on bare skin and the cry of new life from below. "It is a boy," announces Paco from the stairwell, a huge smile on his face.

"Good show," I say to no one in particular, except perhaps to myself.

Allen is the first to appear from below looking tired, but with a smile.

He promptly slides into the aft settee. "I never thought I'd see a day like this," he exclaims. "Thank goodness for Roger being there. He did a great job as did Paco."

"Is the baby and family all Ok?' I ask.

"Yes, everyone is fine."

"May I join you?" asks the older man emerging from below.

"Yes, please do. Have a seat," answers Allen.

"We owe you a debt of gratitude for all that you have done," he starts after settling in across from Allen. "Bless you all and thank you."

"You're welcome," answers Allen.

"I also owe you an apology and an explanation. My family and I are not what we appear. We may very well have put you and your boat in a dangerous situation. You see sir, I am a fugitive from justice."

"How so and just who are you?" asks Allen, now fully engaged.

"My name is Gaston de la Hoya. I am a native of Cuba having lived the past twenty-five years in Guatemala where I am or was a high government official. Factions within the government have wrongly accused me of spying and passing classified information to Cuba. My family and I have been ridiculed, harassed and most recently our lives have been threatened."

"How did you manage to get here?" asks Allen.

"One evening there was a knock on the door of our house. It was an old friend and trusted colleague. He apologized for the intrusion but quickly stated that he was conveying an urgent message, a warning that my life was in eminent danger and that I must leave the country that night. I would be given safe passage if I left immediately. A boat for my use was at the local marina with sufficient food and fuel to take me to Mexico. Without further explanation he departed, hardly saying good-bye. My daughter and son-in-law refused to allow me to go alone."

"How long ago did all this happen?" asks Allen.

"Ten days," answers the old man.

"And we are the first to stop to offer assistance?"

"Yes. Several large ships passed us but none stopped."

"Do you have any idea where your present location is?" asks Allen.

"No. A big storm came upon us and I think blew us out to sea."

"You are correct. You are over twenty miles from any part of Guatemala."

"I see. Again I cannot thank you enough," replies Gaston.

Standing now, Allen paces the width of the cabin, lost in thought.

"It is clear that we cannot put you back in that boat and leave you here, nor can we take you with us," says Allen. "Our only course of action is to find someone to come get you." He turns to me and instructs me to resume our previous course and speed while he descends into his cabin.

The elderly gentleman remains seated, seemingly in a state of disbelief. My offer of something to eat or drink is politely declined.

Our course is 114 degrees and boat speed remains unchanged. A check of GPS indicates that we actually drifted backward one and one half miles due to the current over the two-hour delay. Paco reports that the baby, mother and father are resting comfortably in a starboard cabin and that Roger has gone to clean up before his noon watch. He secures the panga for towing.

11:30 Allen calls for Gaston to join him below.

The weather remains beautiful, now with a freshening south wind of five knots causing the sea to kick up a bit. It is a comfortable ride. Our two knot head current remains however, as Roger relieves me of the watch. He appears to be in good spirits after a rather bazaar morning. After my engine room rounds and logbook notations, I remain in the cockpit.

Allen and Gaston return with the news that they are to remain with us for the time being, perhaps all the way to Costa Rica. Allen explains that as long as they or we are in no eminent danger, they are to remain in our care.

"Agent Weber will try to determine what should be done with Gaston. He is under house arrest and has agreed to comply with my wishes," states Allen while Gaston nods his approval. "For now, it is business as usual. Paco, show Gaston where his berth is located "

I go below for lunch. The balance of the day is spent relaxing and reading in the settee. Again by midafternoon there is a string of towering thunderclouds across the horizon running east to west off our starboard beam. Their flat bottoms form an interesting straight line above the ocean's horizon as lightning and rain are easily seen together.

Paco creates one of his interesting and tasty fish casseroles for dinner. Our guests eat hardy, still hungry from the long ordeal behind them. Cake and ice cream for dessert. They retire almost immediately after helping clear the table. The woman seems surprisingly strong, the baby content to sleep in a make shift basket that was found somewhere aboard.

After kitchen cleanup, I watch the ending of the movie Amadeus that Roger and I had started earlier in the week.

2100 My watch. I note, very little activity, with no boat traffic. I find a Mexican FM radio station playing partial English music to help pass the time.

2400. Relieved, I make my rounds and entries. I hang out for a time with Roger, but he now seems distant and non-commutative. I suspect he is tired. I head for my cabin where I ready for bed to read. The light goes out as I fall asleep to the rhythm and beat of the port engine's drive train while thinking that this was yet another unusual day. I fall asleep wondering what they will name the boy.

Day 13. Sunday.

07:30. I awake to the enjoyment of sunlight in the cabin. The sea is flat with a thin overcast sky.

08:15 Allen is on watch as I enter the cockpit from the galley with coffee and orange juice. A quick check of the logbook confirms that the current remains. Our over the bottom speed is down to four and one-half knots.

09:00 My watch. GPS has us as 260 kilometers to Coco. Our course is 115 degrees. ETA now is projected for Tuesday afternoon, some forty-eight plus hours to go. Paco cooks breakfast of eggs ranchero, flour tortillas and refried beans. Surprisingly, the reclusive Roger joins us, as do our four passengers. The meal is delicious, one of Paco's best efforts. The woman's name we learn is Emilia and the young man's is Ricardo. The baby they are thinking will be called Allen, for Captain Allen. Emilia, we soon learn is not bashful. She pitches in to do the dishes and cleans the galley to a degree that it has not seen in years. We learn that she is a homemaker and he an automobile mechanic. Their English is very good, the results of a good education.

After eating, Allen asks Paco, Roger and I to meet him in the cockpit. "I want to say how well I felt each of us handled the situation yesterday," he starts. "I thought we took every precaution to protect the boat and ourselves. I have read of numerous cases where similar situations have led to hijackings and deaths. Yesterday could easily have been an attempt through disguise to capture and take us over." He pauses before continuing. "Our passengers could be off loaded later today by helicopter according to information I have just received."

"That is quicker than I had expected," I say.

"Yes and I'm not sure why. We need to remain diligent, after all we know very little about these folks."

Paco speaks, "I need to shut down each of the engines for routine maintenance. Ten to fifteen minutes each I would estimate."

"OK," says Allen. "We need to keep in mind how far behind schedule we are and that this current against us is not helping."

Allen retires to his cabin while I resume full attention to the watch.

10:15 Paco asks that I shut down the port engine. He is joined by Ricardo who explains that it is the least he can do in exchange for our help.

A large thunderstorm is developing directly ahead and to a point two miles southwest of our position. The storm blossoms rapidly before us, now sending bands of light rain in our direction. Visibility reduces to less than a quarter mile. Paco hurriedly enters the cockpit to restart the port engine but leaves it at idle RPM while he vanishes below to check for oil leaks.

"Reduce power on the starboard engine," instructs Allen seeing how difficult it is for me to maintain course. "That should make her easier to handle."

Of course he is correct. I am now able to maintain our 115-degree course with very little effort. Boat speed is now under one knot.

We are now in a torrential downpour where the visibility is zero. The windshield wipers are ineffective and radar becomes my eyes in this envelope of darkness. Although it is mid-day with brilliant sunshine outside, inside there is limited sunlight, suggesting days end and twilight. Intense flashes of lightning followed by the crash of thunder break the subdued light.

Paco returns to the cockpit giving thumbs up hand signal indicating "no leaks." I engage the port engine's transmission and bring both engines' rpm's to 2000. Athena moves smartly ahead towards the outer wall of the storm cell. In a short time we begin to emerge into the brightness of the day. Within five minutes we are in full sunshine as we begin to dry out from the soaking. Water steadily streams from off the cabin roof and awning before collecting in the gunnels and running overboard. Steam rises from the deck as the standing water evaporates in the hot noonday sun.

Paco asks to cut the starboard engine. In doing so, I reduce power on the port engine for ease of handling. He completes his task in fifteen minutes before asking for a restart and leak check. Once given the OK, I bring both engines to power and set the autopilot to our 115-degree course.

12:00 Relieved by Roger, I make my engine room inspections and final log book notations. Emilia who is fast becoming a valuable asset to all of our wellbeing has prepared a lunch of sandwiches, chips and fresh fruits.

As is becoming my customary routine, I return to the fantail with book, camera and sunscreen to while-away the afternoon hours.

Relaxed in my favorite deck chair, I scan the far horizon where under a blue cloudless sky, lies the country of Nicaragua. I think back to my only visit there to the city of Managua in 1975. It occurred nearly two and one half years (December 31, 1972) after a massive earthquake that virtually destroyed the entire ten or twelve square block area of downtown.

The destruction was absolute. Concrete foundations, sidewalks and pot-holed asphalt roadways were the only remains of what was the center of commerce. The only exception was a slender ten-story concrete office building standing virtually undisturbed in the center of the leveled city. A Bank of America sign sat prominently on the top floor.

Lake Managua lay peacefully in the distance, a huge body of water stretching out as far as the eye could see, its waters lapping at the foot of the now largely abandoned city. From this image I can understand the early feelings that this body of water represented the most valued asset for a canal to connect the Atlantic and Pacific Oceans. But of course this never happened, as every survey made by the midcentury was flawed by bad assumptions or inadequate data.

The rest of what I remember of the country is now sketchy. My host, the McDonald's licensee, drove me around to show me several neighbor-hoods and centers of business including where his restaurant was still located. I vividly recall a large (huge) Coca-Cola billboard, located in one of the suburbs with the local time displayed in hours, minutes and sec-onds. That and the recollection of the tragic death of the Pittsburgh Pirate baseball great Roberto Clemente who perished in an airplane accident while flying relief supplies to the earthquake victims. Why these have stuck with me over the years I cannot explain. And yet I do carry visual pictures of a happy and content population in spite of their poverty and lack of basic essentials. It would be great to someday revisit.

The afternoon passes quickly between some reading and napping while allowing my mind to drift in and out of the last few days' activities.

My solace is interrupted by Allen who calls me inside. "The evacua-tion of our passengers has been postponed indefinitely," he informs Paco, Roger, Gaston and I as we assemble at the cockpit table. "I'm guessing that it will occur tomorrow, but I'm not certain."

Dinner consists of steak, potatoes and fresh veggies with ice cream for dessert. Emilia insists on serving us and performing the galley cleanup, after which she vacuums the main saloons carpet and dusts everything in sight. Roger, Richardo & I work on a picture puzzle of a New Eng-land lighthouse. We work well together and enjoy each other's company. I attempt to learn more of Ricardo's background as it was evident to Paco that he has had extensive engine experience from the way he knew what needed to be done with changing oil filters, etc. He offered little else than to say his training came from the school of hard knocks.

21:00 I take the watch. Our forward progress remains slow, impeded by the insistent current directly on our nose. Our course remains at 115 degrees; GPS shows we have 200 miles to target.

"It appears we have a change in the weather ahead," says Allen carrying a weather fax from below. He points to a low-pressure cell that is causing the disturbance. Our steady barometer earlier, I note, has dropped slightly confirming the information. "I don't think it is anything to worry about. Tomorrow morning's forecast will tell us what to expect." He makes the notation in the log when I ask if there is any news on what to expect of our passengers. "No, nothing," he replies before saying goodnight and retiring below.

The next hour of the watch passes without incident. I am able to find a news talk AM radio station from Los Angeles, California that entertains and helps pass the time.

22:00 "May I join you?" asks Gaston as he ascends from the cabin below.

"Yes, of course," I answer, anxious for any company. He seats himself in the aft settee before speaking, "May I call you Bob or do you prefer Robert?"

"Either one, although I do prefer Bob."

"Good, then it shall be Bob," he continues. "I have been observing you since my arrival onboard and it is you that I have decided to entrust something of extreme importance." Sliding out from the settee, he approaches and hands me a plain white envelope. "Please take this and I will explain." The envelope is light to my feel, suggesting it has but one or two sheets of paper as its contents. Gaston remains in my immediate vicinity as he lowers his voice to say, "Inside that envelope is the location of several floppy disks that contain vital information to the security of America. I am asking that you and only you see to it that the envelope is given to your FBI agent, Mr. Weber. Can I depend on you for this?"

"But why me?" I ask. "This needs to go to Captain Daniels."

"No, you are the best person to have it."

He steps to the passageway and returns without further comment to the cabin below despite my attempts to ask him to remain. Bewildered and shaken, I can do little else but slip the envelope into my back pocket and resume the watch.

Roger relieves at midnight. I notify him of the anticipated weather change, perform my checks, make my log entries and say good night. For a change I am not interested in anything but getting to my cabin. I examine the sealed envelope before putting it away. I slip into bed where I read for thirty minutes before turning out the light. Sleep comes slowly, my mind awhirl.

CHAPTER SEVENTEEN

Land Fall

Day 14. Monday.

It is a typical summer morning in southeast Texas. The heat and humidity of the day is bearable only because of the early hour. The cloudless sky will undoubtedly give way to late afternoon clouds and rain.

Matt steps from his car to cross the parking lot to his office. He pulls open the heavy glass door entering the cool air of the lobby, passes through the security check before giving the police officer his customary morning greeting. His small office is to the rear and to the right of the lobby.

The waiting room has several seated individuals, which is not unusual. His secretary greets him with a concerned expression as he stops for messages.

"There is a man here waiting for you from the FBI."

"Oh, where is he?" Matt asks.

"He is the man in the dark suit."

"Did he give you his business card?"

"Yes. Here it is," she nervously answers.

Matt, taking the card walks toward him. "May I help you?"

"Is it possible that we can use your office for privacy?" he says rising from his chair to shake Matt's hand.

"Of course. Please follow me," says Matt leading the way.

"Thank you for seeing me with no notice."

"What is this all about?" asks Matt seated from behind his desk.

"I'll speak plainly and come directly to the point. What is your relationship with a Mexican man by the name of Carlos Mendoza?"

Surprised by the question, Matt carefully considers his answer. "I don't know him. I met him for the first time last week. Why?"

"What was the purpose of your meeting with him?" asks the man, ignoring Matt's question.

"He was introduced to me as a member of a fund raising committee for a children's hospital in Puerto Vallarta, Mexico. They are looking for a charitable grant from my parent's foundation."

The man peers across the desk.

"What is your relationship with the sailboat called Athena?"

Matt, now becoming annoyed, answers "What possibly can Athena have to do with Mendoza?"

"Please answer my question."

"I know the boat from a casual meeting with one of the crew who is taking her to Florida."

"Nothing beyond that?"

"Only that she has been in Mexico for several years and is owned by a British bank."

"Why were you seen onboard her just before she left?"

"Visiting the captain. I was in hopes of seeing the gentleman who I spoke of earlier; however, when I learned that he and the captain were ready to leave, I decided to postpone my visit."

"Do you know a Roger Andrew?"

"No, that is a name I do not know?"

"What is the name of the man you do know?"

"Bob."

"He visited your home, correct?"

Realizing that the man knows a great deal, Matt answers simply, "Yes."

"For what purpose?"

"It was social."

"I realize your hesitancy to answer more thoroughly. Let me assure you that neither you nor your family are under any form of investigation."

"It certainly feels that way. What is this all about?"

"It is believed that Mendoza is involved in a smuggling scheme. We know him as a shadowy figure with ties to one of the Colombian cartels."

"Are you implying that Athena is carrying stolen goods?"

"Yes. We believe that a young man by the name of Roger Andrew is being paid to carry a package to Panama. He is unaware that he is carrying a valuable gem."

"Is the captain or Bob aware of this?"

"Yes. I met to alert them of the possibility after they left Puerto Vallarta."

Matt leans back in his chair. He closes his eyes for a few seconds to think. The man remains silent, watching.

"How do I fit into the equation?" asks Matt.

"We are asking that you attempt to learn as much of Mr. Mendoza's business dealings as possible."

"How?"

"Through the interview and qualifying process you ask of your grant applicants."

"We concern ourselves more with the organization than the individuals."

"He is not aware of that."

"You want me to be a sleuth?"

"I suppose you can say that. We believe you would be the last person he would be suspicious of for any questions asked."

"I would need to arrange for a meeting quickly, correct?"

"Yes, within the next several days."

"I'll see what I can do," says Matt as Special Agent Weber stands to leave.

07:00 I awake to a different ride. Athena is pounding and hobby horsing along rather than the smooth roll of the past few days. Through my porthole I see white caps against a low overcast cloud cover. It is apparent that we have reached the disturbance forecast last night.

I wash, dress and head to the bridge where Allen has the watch. The log indicates that the weather started to deteriorate just after 5:00 AM. Forward progress remains impaired by the ever-present current and now the difficulty with the wave heights.

I go below for coffee and a light breakfast prepared by Emilia, returning afterward to the relative comfort of the settee. Allen informs me that, weather permitting, we can expect our passengers will be picked up by midafternoon. More details will come later.

09:00 I take the watch. GPS shows we are 155km from target. With any luck we will make landfall tomorrow at midday.

On one of my rounds of engine checks, I note a small water leak on the port engine at the raw water pump. Together with noting it in the log, I alert Paco who with Richardo make a repair. The balance of the watch goes smoothly. We run in and out of rainsqualls and gusting winds. I find that hand steering is more effective than the autopilot.

12:00 Roger relieves.

Fortunately, the weather starts to improve with breaks in the clouds and periods of sun. We try various combinations of sail configurations attempting to maximize boat speed and comfort. I hang out on the fantail, mostly reading. Paco has the port engine shut down as the water leak has returned. He soon explains that it will require a welder in Costa Rica.

13:00 Allen alerts us that the rescue helicopter has a 14:00 ETA. He assigns me to the wheel while Paco and Roger are to handle lines leaving him to coordinate the loading of our passengers. Meanwhile, he assembles the family in the cockpit and readies them for departure.

13:50 "I believe I see it," exclaims Roger, pointing to the northwest.

All eyes concentrate on what quickly becomes the familiar orange and white colors of a United States Coast Guard helicopter. It swoops down upon us like a giant bird of prey.

"Sailing vessel Athena, how do you read?" asks a crisp, clear male voice over Athena's VHF radio.

"Loud and clear," answers Allen.

"Captain Allen Daniels?" asks the voice.

"Roger that," replies Allen.

The helicopter now positions itself directly overhead. Its powerful rotating blade whips the sea into a froth of confusion. The engines high pitch whine makes it nearly impossible to hear or be heard.

"Captain Daniels, this is air-rescue 6037, United States Coast Guard. My instructions are to evacuate a party of four. Is this correct?"

"Affirmative," answers Allen.

"Captain Daniels, please bring your boat to a full stop and prepare passengers for evacuation."

I have reduced power and now disengage the transmissions.

"We will send you the mother and baby first," informs Allen.

"No one told us of a child."

"A two day old boy," answers Allen with a noticeable grin.

A lone figure clad in a bright orange life vest descends gracefully onto Athena's foredeck. His descent is monitored above by another individual utilizing a crane and winch controlling the rappelling rope and the rescue basket. He signals for the first passenger to come forward. Allen, with help from Roger, brings Emilia and the baby out on deck and to the Coast Guardsman. Much to my surprise, Emilia is told that she and baby Allen will not be allowed to ride together. Emilia's body language displays her unhappiness and fear of harm to her newborn son. Skillfully the guardsman separates them and places the tiny bundle of new life into the basket and straps him in. He then signals to those above that all is in readiness. Baby Allen ascends smoothly upward before being guided into the aircraft's interior. Next goes Emilia followed by Richardo with the same ease of ascent as the son before them. Lastly, it is Gaston's time. He looks unsure of himself. He stumbles twice crossing the deck even with assistance from Roger. Once secured in the basket Gaston gives a sign of the cross while looking to the heavens. He together with the guardsman ascends up and into the safety of the cabin's interior. With the aircraft's door closed it rises and banks smoothly away from Athena before turning back towards us. "Good luck Captain, air rescue 6037 is clear." And with that, the Sirkorsky Jayhawk HH-60 aircraft and its occupants rapidly depart to quickly become a tiny spot on the horizon.

"Where do you suppose their destination may be?" I ask Allen.

"Probably to a Coast Guard Cutter located off the southern California coast. Typically that is from where a rescue helicopter will dispatch. I doubt that they will take Gaston directly to San Diego."

"Why is that?"

Allen now calls for the four of us to gather in the cockpit. Paco has the helm.

"Based on what I have been told by agent Weber, this has not been a completely legal operation. The United States, under international and maritime laws, have no authority to come and get Gaston and his family other than for humanitarian reasons. If Emilia had not had the baby, the state department would not have agreed to interfere in what is a Guatemalan problem. Because of the unexpected birth and because I think the state department would like the opportunity to speak to Gaston, I believe a decision was made to bend the rules. We will not read about this in any publication, I dare say."

"What about Gaston? Is he who he says he is?" I ask.

" I have no reason to believe otherwise. Why do you ask?"

"He left me with an envelope and asked that if anything where to happen to him that I have the envelope delivered to agent Weber. He told me that the content describes where two floppy discs can be found. He would not tell me anything more."

"Where is the envelope?"

"In my cabin."

"Better go get it and I'll put it away in the safe. I'll also notify Weber."

Allen serves another of his world famous "one-pot" dinners. Actually, it is a repeat of several nights ago.(kind of an Irish stew without dumplings) It seems none of us are hungry. Following dinner cleanup, we stand outside at the port rail enjoying the beautiful sunset that is accentuated by a string of thunderclouds on the far horizon. It is a very pleasant evening, the wind and sea having moderated. Paco entertains us with several of his fishing tales.

21:00 I take the watch. Radar shows storm activity surrounding us, one in particular has moved directly into our path. On the six-mile range, it completely fills the radar screen. Roger rechecks the lightning grounding system. Paco stows all loose gear. We could be in for a wild ride.

21:30 Entering the leading edge of the storm it is unlike yesterday as there is not the sensation of entering darkness, the sun having set an hour ago. There is the eerie feeling of being inside a dome or bowl; illuminated by the rapid succession of lightning flashes from every direction, much like the strobe lights that entertainers use.

Rain swirls around the cockpit windows, beating down on us with vengeance. The wipers are of no use because of the volumes of water. Visibility is zero anyway. The wind creates a whining/singing sound as it whistles through the rigging and around the boat.

I see wave heights of one to two feet, shaped like candy kisses as the wind whips them skyward. We step over them causing a rocking, side-to-side motion. Our boat speed drops to 3 knots.

21:45 Radar shows us approximately at the center. The storm intensity has not diminished. It remains a swirling mix of rain, wind, lightning and claps (booms) of thunder. Several lightning flashes are so close that there is no time lapse between it and the thunderclap.

We are all in the cockpit area, speechless to the display being put on by Mother Nature. There is little any one of us can do except watch and hope we survive the torrent.

22:30 The storm moves away, as quickly as it came upon us, leaving us under a clear, star studded sky. Rainwater streams down the scuppers from the boats super structure. A quick survey outside and inside reveals no damage.

24:00 I turn the watch over to Roger. I make my rounds and log my notations. Before turning in, I go outside to enjoy the night air. The night is like velvet, the stars so bright with a quarter-moon. It seems difficult to believe the roughing up we got an hour before. I think back on the last few days' events and wonder where and how our little family may be.

Going below to my cabin, I fall into bed where I have little difficulty falling asleep.

Day 15 Tuesday

06:20 My porthole reveals a gray, cloud swept sky and a white-capped sea. It is too early to get up I figure, so I try going back to sleep. With little success at 06:45 I dress and go above to the cockpit. Allen has the watch. We are in a quartering sea with two to three foot waves. He is flying the genoa. It together with the two engines is producing a forward speed of seven knots through the water, six and one half knots over the ground.

Spray from the hull crashing into the swells and aided by the wind, fly over the deck and cabin.

I go below for breakfast, bringing it up to the settee.

"If you look sharply about eleven o'clock you can see the thin outline of land. Punta Elena," says Allen.

With the aid of the binoculars I am able to clearly see the headland.

"Punta Elena is the northern portion of the Gulf of Papagayos," he explains.

08:45 We furl the genoa and set out the cutter staysail. With the wind increasing, the smaller sail places less strain on the ships rigging with equally good results.

09:00 My watch. GPS shows thirty nautical miles to Playa del Coco, our destination. The errant current that has plagued our forward progress for three days is gone. Our through the water speed is equal to our over the bottom speed. We are making very good time.

10:00 I am able to see clearly the most Eastern Shore of the bay. The deep black silhouette of Punta Elena against the white and grey clouds stretching behind it on our port beam.

10:30 I sight a sail several miles off our starboard bow. After several tries on the VHF, we raise the occupants and learn the boat is named "Just Imagine" out of San Francisco. We exchange weather, fueling and general information. They are headed north to the Sea of Cortez to summer before returning home. We wish each other well.

The sea is moderating as we continue to come under the lee of the headland. Wave heights are down as the wind has decreased. The cloud cover thins as the sun burns through. We furl the cutter.

11:00 The suns reflection dances off the ocean's surface, sparkling against a cobalt blue sky. A symbolic welcome to what I have experienced as a warm and friendly country.

"Phantom, Phantom. Do you read me?" calls Allen on the VHF. "This is the sailing vessel Athena approaching you from the north. Do you read me?" Information from Just Imagine tells us that Phantom is anchored at Bahia del Coco, our destination and port of entry.

"Hello Athena, this is Phantom. Is this Captain Allen?" comes the reply.

"Roger that. Our ETA is fourteen hundred hours. We'll come say hello on our way to the port captain. Over"

"Great. Looking forward to seeing you. Phantom out."

"Athena clear."

12:00 Relieved of watch.

I busy myself by having a light lunch and preparing to go ashore.

13:00 We round the protective headland and enter the good sized crescent shaped bay known as Bahia del Coco. There are several boats randomly anchored inside, some pleasure some commercial. The village is partially visible through the dense growth of palm trees and shrubs. A long pier extends from what would appear the center of town, out into the bay sixty to seventy-five feet. A closer look indicates that a further extension of the pier has been destroyed. A thatched palm canopy covers the first twenty feet of the remaining pier. A wide beach of sand completes the first image.

I help Paco ready the ground tackle while Allen assists Roger at the helm.

14:00 Anchor down. We chose an open spot about one hundred feet from Phantom in thirty-five feet of water. Our coordinates from GPS are 10 33.45N 85 41.71 W. Our elapsed time was 94 hours. Distance traveled 500km at an average speed of 5.32 knots. Allen runs up the quarantine flag denoting that we have not cleared customs or immigration.

I count twenty-seven boats in the bay. Most are sports fishing boats, apparently for hire. There are five sailboats, including Phantom and seven powerboats, all privately owned.

We set about getting ready to go ashore. Under Paco's watchful eye we launch the tender from its cradle on the fantail. He tethers it at the port rail opening where we climb aboard after securing the cockpit and cabin.

It is a short ride to Phantom where we are introduced to Jerry seated in the comfort of the cockpit. It is clear that he and Allen have known one another for years. He provides us with good local information.

"Can I offer anyone a beer?" he asks.

We each decline.

"Where is your good wife?" asks Allen.

"Her mother had a heart attack on Saturday, so she flew out yesterday from San Jose to be with her."

"Sorry to hear that. Can you join us for dinner onboard tonight?"

"My pleasure," Jerry responds. "What time?"

"We'll stop by on our way back from the beach to set a time."

We decide to go ashore at the wooden pier. It is the only thing to tie off to on the entire beach. "The tide variation here is from ten to twelve feet," announces Allen as we approach the tide line. "I'd say we are at half tide and falling, so let's give ourselves a rode of six feet or more."

Roger and I jump out of the boat in a foot of water so as to prevent it from grounding on the course sand bottom. Paco raises the big outboard to its stowed position. We set a small anchor five or six feet aft before tying off forward on one piling of the pier thereby positioning the dinghy far enough out to accommodate the tide fall for the hour that we expect to be away. Satisfied with our mooring techniques, we climb a nearby ladder that takes us eight to ten feet to the top of the pier, over a handrail and onto the time worn walkway.

It is a short walk into the main square, passing a row of sport fishing tiendas, quick service establishments (no McDonald's), souvenir shops and bars. The customs office is located across the square and one half - block up the main street. We present ourselves with our papers to the officer in charge. He is very pleasant, together with his wife who handles the passport processing. The four of us are officially in the country; however, the boat is not and will have to wait until the customs officer returns tomorrow morning. Technically, it is still quarantined but we are free to move about.

Exiting the office, we decide to split up. Paco and Roger venture off in search of a welding shop while Allen and I look for a bank to exchange dollars into colones. We agree to meet in Loco Pogo, one of the bars we passed earlier, at 17:00.

Allen and I make our way up the narrow, partially blacktopped street. Although it is midafternoon, there is a considerable amount of foot and vehicle traffic; unusual, as typically this is the quiet time of day or siesta time. A road sign indicates it is 253 km to San Jose, the capital and 60 km to Liberia. From the number of busses observed, it seems clear that they are the principle means of transportation in and out of town.

After several blocks we find a bank at one end of a strip shopping center. It is a small banking facility, one teller and one officer at separate desks. You wait your turn by taking the last available chair along a wall and reseat yourself to your left as each customer is served. I count eight people ahead of Allen as he takes the end seat. Everyone is well groomed, nicely dressed, mostly in lightweight clothing because of the heat. A conversion rate sign of the world's currencies indicates that the US dollar is worth 231 colones.

Anxious to see more of the town, I excuse myself, saying that I will return shortly.

Next to the bank, actually in the same building, is a boutique. It has femininity written all over the display windows of clothing and jewelry. I step inside to the comfort of air conditioning and the scent of a woman. Although small, the space is well appointed with all items nicely displayed.

"Buenas tardes, Senor"

"Buenas tardes," I respond to a well-dressed woman.

"Let me know if I may be of help," says the voice in good English.

"Thank you. Are you the proprietor?" I ask.

Hesitating for a moment, she answers "Yes. Why do you ask?"

Realizing that I have put her on the defensive, I explain that I am surprised to find such an upscale store in such a remote part of the world. "I hope I haven't upset you."

"I did not know what to expect," she says extending her hand. "My name is Vicky."

"Bob," I answer exchanging a firm handshake.

"Are you here to go fishing?" she asks looking somewhat relieved.

"No. I am a member of a delivery crew taking a sailboat to the Panama Canal from Puerto Vallarta. We are here to clear customs for entry into the country, have an engine part repaired and do some provisioning."

"I did hear that a new pleasure boat was in the bay. Please make yourself at home, Bob. If I can be of any help, let me know."

"Would you know where I could make an international telephone call other than the public phones at the foot of the street? All of them appear to be inoperative."

"I have a phone which you are welcome to use."

I accept her offer, even being allowed to step into her rear office. I am able to dial the house directly using my calling card.

"Hi honey, how are you?" I ask after her hello.

She is thrilled to hear my voice. I am relieved to learn that she has had no further contact from the Feds. We bring each other up to date on our activities. I explain where we are and that I'll probably not be in contact again until we reach the canal. We say our good-byes and sign off with love and kisses.

Stepping out of her office, I find Vicky with her back to me busy stocking shelves with new inventory. Attractive at five foot-two, one hundred ten pounds, a size six or eight and short cropped auburn hair. She is wearing a white dress at knee length with a multi-colored sash around her slim waist and open toe tan sandals. I estimate that she is in her early forties.

Hearing me, she turns and smiles. "Were you able to get through?"

"Yes. Thank you very much. Can I pay you for the time as I'm sure there are charges?"

"No, you were not on long enough. My pleasure."

"You are very kind, thank you. I apologize again for my boldness earlier."

"Actually I am the one that needs to apologize for my reaction to your question," she responds.

We smile at one another as our eyes meet for a long moment.

"Your boat has stirred quite a bit of attention," she offers.

"Why is that?" I ask.

"I'm not sure. Rumor has it that the Federal Police are here because of it."

"That's interesting," I say trying not to look alarmed.

"Just thought I would mention it," she says.

"Well, thanks again and good luck," I say opening the door to leave when I am attracted to a colorful blouse on display. Closing the door I ask its size and price thinking it would be a nice gift for my wife. "It is a size ten and is ten US dollars," Vicky responds.

"Fine, I'll take it." She folds it professionally and places it in a bag before taking my money with a pleasant smile of thanks.

Stepping out of the shop I return to the heat and humidity of the late afternoon; all but forgotten while inside. I peek into the bank to see that Allen is still waiting. Deciding not to disturb him with my newly learned information, I remain outside reasoning that there will be time later.

The other shops in the building consist of a Mexican style restaurant, a souvenir/ postcard shop, a sport fishing/tour office and a laundry. It is all new, to the extent that the second floor is not completed.

Continuing my exploration of the town, I walk further up the street. The town consists mostly of older stucco buildings with thatched roofs dating back to the early settlement scattered along the main road. It reminds me of the many villages I have visited in Mexico over the years. Yet there are additional signs of modernization. A hotel looking very similar to a La Quinta is in the next block from the bank. I count ten new model automobiles in the hotel parking lot together with several older models and two buses, indicating good occupancy. It would seem that the reason they are here is for the deep-sea sport fishing activities. I walk several more blocks before turning back towards the beach.

17:00 I catch Allen leaving the bank. As we walk towards Poco Logo I pass along Vicky's comments. He offers little in the way of any reaction, seemingly deep in thought. We decide to keep this to ourselves as we near the bar where we find Paco and Roger who confirm they have found a welder who can repair the water pipe.

The owners of Poco Logo turn out to be an American expatriate husband and wife. She introduces herself and offers her services as a tour guide, real estate agent and rental property agent. She confirms that there are numerous North American's living and working in the area. She is a gad-about, making reference to knowing the goings and doings of the entire town. Fortunately, she makes no mention of the police and Athena, making me wonder just how plugged in she is to the local gossip. The beer is cold and the popcorn is fresh. For a short time I relax and enjoy myself, forgetting for the moment the intrigue of alleged stolen goods, a diplomat on the run and shadowy figures following us down the coast.

18:00 We walk to the grocery store where we buy needed fresh fruits and vegetables together with a few other odds and ends. In returning to the dinghy, we find her high and dry on the beach, grounded several feet from the water's edge. We stand and ponder our situation, mindful that above on the pier we are being watched by a group of interested locals. Our only choice is to try to drag her, all one thousand plus pounds. Together by two of us pushing and two pulling, we manage to get her to move. Again and again we inch her towards the water. During one break to catch our breath, I look up into the smiling faces of our audience from above. No one offers assistance.

We somehow manage to get her to the water's edge and by timing the ebb and flow of the waves, get her afloat. Exhausted, we climb aboard and motor out to Athena. Once aboard, Allen calls Jerry on the VHF while Paco prepares Dorado and sailfish for supper. Jerry accepts our invitation.

20:00 We have a fun evening. The food and his company are enjoyed by each of us. The meal is topped off by Rogers's banana flambé for dessert. I get to know Jerry well and find him interesting and entertaining. I learn that he and his wife have been cruising for three years. Their homeport is San Francisco, California. Phantom is a Kelly/Peterson 46, mid cockpit cutter sloop. They are headed for the canal where they plan on leaving Phantom in the care of a boatyard while they fly home for six months. He has two daughters, both of whom with their husbands have taken over Jerry's service station/towing business. When I ask if he was retired, he replied, "No, only on an extended leave of absence. As long as my Visa card works at the bank or ATM, I'll stay cruising."

Good man, I think.

21:30 Jerry leaves after saying his thanks and good byes. Roger and I clean the galley.

22:00 It is a beautiful evening. I stand out on the deck drinking in the night air, together with savoring the sights and sounds of the anchorage. There are many more buildings in between the palms and flora scattered along the beach than what could be seen during daylight. Tonight it is very quiet and serene. Except for a lone dogs occasion bark there is only the soft, gentle sound of the "off shore" breeze in Athena's rigging and the lapping of waves against her sides. The moon hangs just above the masthead in harmony with a thousand stars set in the heavens above. For this moment in time, I am completely at rest.

23:00 Everyone has turned in so I decide to do likewise. I lock the cabin/cockpit door, make a final entry in the log and descend to my cabin below. There will be no serenade from the engine drive train tonight; however, I will have the hum and vibration from the Genset located behind the bulkhead at the head of my bunk. I elect to sleep with my feet at the head of the bunk, my head away from the disturbance. Not surprisingly, I fall asleep quickly and sleep soundly.

CHAPTER EIGHTEEN

Tap, Tap, Tap

Day 16 Wednesday

Matt climbs the stairs leading to Carlos Mendoza's office. The appointment for 10:00 was confirmed earlier by his secretary. Without knocking he turns the brass doorknob and pushes open the solid wood door displaying only a street number. Stepping inside, he is surprised at the smallness of the room; consisting of a desk, a file cabinet and a few chairs.

"Welcome, please come in," offers Mendoza rising from his desk.

"Thank you," says Matt offering his hand.

"Please have a seat and be comfortable. May I offer coffee?"

"No, thank you. I am fine."

Matt settles into one of the leather chairs as Mendoza returns behind his desk. Matt observes two windows both looking out on the street below, a few paintings and a nautical chart for wall décor. Simple but comfortable he thinks.

"I appreciate your taking time out of a busy schedule to see me," starts Matt.

"My pleasure, I am at your disposal."

Matt takes the next few minutes to explain the grant request procedure. He tries to be careful to not exaggerate the importance of knowing as much about the applicants as the charity itself. He watches for signs in Mendoza's face that his presentation is less than truthful. Seeing none Matt presses on to ask what type of business Carlos is involved in.

"I'm an importer/exporter," he answers. He explains that his father started the business and upon his early death, Carlos took it over. He eagerly talks about how successful the company has become under his leadership and guidance.

"You must be very pleased and proud."

"I am. It has taken hard work."

"Who are some of your clients," asks Matt forging ahead. "Most are small companies within Latin America with the need for my expertise in moving goods across borders," he states.

Sensing a boastful attitude, Matt asks, "What kinds of goods do you help them with generally?"

"Everything," he says with a smile. "I have the ability to get the job done."

"Give me a recent example?"

"I was able to help a client bring several truckloads of kitchen equipment for a new restaurant into Mexico from the States without import taxes."

"I'm impressed," says Matt.

"I know the rules and how to make them work to my advantage."

"Are all your transactions legal?"

"But of course. I am not a crooked businessman," Mendoza replies with a slight air of indignity.

"I'm sure of that, otherwise you would not still be in business. Do you have any employees?"

"No."

"How do you function without people?"

"By computer. It is all I need."

Matt now sensing the need to shift gears, questions Mendoza's knowledge of the children's hospital fund-raising organization. Much to Matt's surprise he is well prepared and eager to make the case for funding. Guilt pains stabs at Matt for his subversive reason for being there as all of the grant forms and backup materials are properly and thoughtfully prepared.

"I believe I have everything," says Matt standing in preparation to leave. "Are you a sailor?" he asks of Mendoza as they walk towards the door.

"No. Why do you ask?"

"I couldn't help but notice the nautical chart on your wall."

"Oh, that. It is nothing. I should take it down." He is inwardly disturbed by his oversight in not having removed it beforehand.

They shake hands before Matt steps outside pulling the door closed. He decides to make a telephone call immediately. Upon reaching the suburban, he slips inside and starts the engine. His car cell phone comes to life with its usual cheerful melody. On the handset he plugs in a long distance number and waits while listening to the ring on the other end.

"Special agent, Weber. How are you Matt?"

"I'm fine."

"Have you met with Mendoza?"

"Yes, just now. I believe he is involved. I was able to see a nautical chart where he has been tracking the position of Athena since her departure from Vallarta."

"Anything else?"

"Nothing specific, but if I was a betting man I would say he is less than honest in his business dealings."

"Ok. Good job. I'll talk with you later." The phone goes dead.

06:45 I'm awakened by noise from the port engine room. Paco, I'm sure, is removing the raw water pipe to be taken ashore for repair.

I waste little time and roll out of bed, shower and dress. I gather my dirty clothes together for washing. After separating whites from darks I load the machine, add soap and bleach before pushing the start dial.

Allen and Paco I find are preparing to go ashore.

"I'd like you and Roger to remain on board. Get us squared away for departure as soon as we return."

"Ok," I respond.

"I have the hand held radio so we can stay in contact on channel 16."

08:30 They depart in the dinghy, making a quick stop at Phantom to say goodbye to Jerry.

I run the vacuum cleaner in the main salon while Roger cleans the cockpit windows of the accumulated salt spray. We shake out and furl the mainsail, genoa and cutter as well as mop the top of the cabin roof and main deck with clean water.

10:30 Phantom is underway from her mooring. I take a picture as she moves away carrying a mainsail only. I call Jerry on the VHF to wish him well and promise to send him a copy of the photograph. He is moving to the next bay for a few days while waiting for his wife to return.

11:45 The boys return with the repaired water hose and our boat papers. Paco goes immediately below to install the part.

Although the immigration officer did not appear, contact was made with him by telephone. His secretary apparently was very instrumental in verifying that our paperwork was correct and in order. He therefore gave her approval to allow Athena to enter the country.

"The welder took longer to repair the water pipe than expected;

otherwise, we would have been back much sooner," says Allen while we are alone in the cockpit.

"Did you see any indications of being watched by the police?" I ask.

"Hard to say. While Paco went to the welder I was inside the port captain's office, out of sight. If anyone was watching me, I didn't see them."

12:15. Following a successful pressure check of the water pipe installation, we are ready to get underway. We all pitch in to stow the dinghy back in its cradle, start the starboard engine and raise the anchor. Allen takes the wheel after making a log notation of our departure time. We move out of the bay and down the coast towards Marina Flamingo for fuel and water, a distance of twenty miles. Our course parallels the coast, as we remain a half-mile off shore in one hundred feet of water.

We pass a bay with a large hotel nestled to the back set against the mountain terrain. The chart indicates it is the Hotel Ocotal, a Couples resort.

We round Punta Zapotal, come inside Isla Brumel and head directly for Bahia Potrero where the marina and fuel dock is located.

The weather is rapidly changing as black clouds roll in from the south bringing strong gusty winds that is kicking up the sea.

13:50 We are at the entrance to the marina. Upon entering, we turn right for the fuel dock and rig for a starboard tie. Allen eases us up to the dock where we pass mooring lines to an attendant.

14:00 Secured to the dock with engines shut down. Here at last is a floating fuel dock with a proper pump and hose.

Fueling starts immediately even with the rain and wind now fully upon us. I go below for my lightweight rain slicker in an attempt to stay somewhat dry as I help Paco with the fueling operation.

"I need to stop," yells Paco above the wind. "The rain water is going to get into the fuel fill opening."

He removes the nozzle from the deck fitting while I replace the plate. None too soon as the volume of water running down the deck becomes unreal. We stand under the awning on the after deck and watch the wind drive the rain nearly sideways. Visibility is less than a quarter-mile. Even the young attendant has retreated to the shelter of his hut.

14:45 The rain subsides to little more than a shower as the sky has brightened and visibility improves. Taking the dinghy cover, we rig a tent like affair to protect Paco as he resumes fueling. He looks like a hermit peeking out from under the cover when I call his name to take his picture. His big brown eyes flash with curiosity.

While standing by to assist if needed as fueling continues, I make an accounting of the marina and its surroundings. I would start by saying that the complex looks like it was someone's grand plan or dream, now gone astray. According to Allen, that someone is an American, who with a partner established what was to be a combination resort and marina. It is evident that a lot of planning, time and money went into its original development, much of which remains, but now some twenty years later is badly neglected.

"Bob," calls Allen from the dock, "meet Jim, the owner."

Stretching over the lifeline, I extend my hand. "Nice to meet you," I say shaking hands. He is in his late forties, early fifties, five feet ten inches, one hundred sixty pounds, nearly bald but with a full beard. He has a rugged outdoors look. He doesn't stay long, explaining that he needs to get to the bank in nearby Guanacaste.

The marina is divided into two basins or bodies of water, with each having its individual entrance to the bay. A breakwater constructed of rock and stone creates the outside dimensions. Two stone towers with flashing lights, red and green/port and starboard mark the end of the breakwater and signify the openings to the two respective basins. Where we are located is the transit or visiting section; the other, much larger is designed for permanent or long term anchorage featuring floating docks with electricity and water. Only one half of the available space has been built out with docks. I quickly count fifteen boats moored where fifty slips are available, mostly powerboats.

There are several boats here with us, all badly neglected. One in particular catches my eye. She is a thirty-foot sloop; at one time some individuals pride and hope for romance and adventure I speculate. Now however it is being ravaged by the weather and "father time." Her mainsail cover is gone, exposing the sail that hangs from the boom into the water filled cockpit. Her headsail is roller furled and appears to be ok, although the two sheets (ropes) are a hopeless tangle. A green mold is inching its way over the fiberglass from stem to stern. On the several occasions when I look over, a pelican sits on the bow rail, much like a vulture, waiting for it to sink.

16:00 We complete fueling together with Roger who has been filling the fresh water tanks. We take on five hundred eighty gallons of fuel and two hundred fifty gallons of water.

While Paco and Roger change engine oil and filters, Allen and I walk up to the marina office to pay the fuel bill and send a fax. It is a challenge avoiding the potholes filled with rainwater and the mud of the dirt road. It continues to rain lightly.

"Have you been able to speak with Roger?" asks Allen once we are away from the boat.

"No, not really," I answer. "I've tried to engage him in conversation last night at watch change, but he was distant and unwilling to say anything."

Allen remains silent as we approach the hexagonal shaped marina office. We wipe our feet on a mat before entering. Inside is the counter where business is transacted. A feeling of open space greets me. Looking up I see the high pitched roof supported at the center by the hexagonal design. Eight ceiling fans provide air movement to sufficiently cool the space. I can hear the pitter patter of rain striking the sheet metal roof.

Here we meet Jim's wife. She is much younger than he, of Spanish decent with big brown eyes, high cheek bones, olive skin and cold black hair. Her white teeth flash when she smiles, which is often. She is bilingual in English and Spanish and proves to be very efficient.

"I have this to be send via fax," says Allen, handing her a sheet of hand written paper. "The contents are confidential, so I would ask that you not read anything except the telephone number to where it is being sent."

"Of course," she responds, a little indignant.

"I am sorry if I insulted your integrity," Allen says sensing her emotions. "I meant no harm. My intent is to not expose you in a matter that may cause you harm."

Her brown eyes flash as she retires towards the back of the office and the fax machine. After several minutes she returns with the sheet of paper neatly folded, handing it back with the acknowledgement of received receipt, without comment.

"Thank you. I expect a reply within the hour."

We step outside to the continuing drizzle.

"Wow," says Allen. "Talk about an attitude."

"You really ticked her off," I say.

"I don't want her knowing that I am talking to the FBI," says Allen as we walk up to the general store. Not needing anything important, he buys a few candy bars and each of us a soft drink. The store is little more than a snack shack together with a few dairy items, bread and beer. A young man takes our money and thanks us for our business.

17:30 Back on board we learn that Paco is having trouble changing engine oil. He has completed the starboard engine, but is just now starting on the port engine. It is clear that he is frustrated, spattered with used engine oil from top to bottom. "The drain hose split while I was suctioning out the crankcase and oil went everywhere. I need help cleaning up the starboard engine room and rigging a new drain line," he admits.

"Where is Roger? Why isn't he helping?" asks Allen.

"He excused himself minutes after you left and has not returned."

"I'll clean the port engine room," I say without hesitation.

Allen pitches in. In an attempt to find a solution to the drain line he first sends Paco go get cleaned up and eat one of his candy bars.

"I'll meet you in the machine shop when you're ready," he tells him.

I find the engine room messy, but not overwhelming. I gather a roll of paper towels from the storage locker, a bottle of liquid cleaner, rubber gloves and proceed to spray and wipe down section by section. The largest concentration of oil is on the floor and fortunately, in the oil pan under the engine. I manage to get the job done after several breaks to cool off in the air-conditioned spaces.

I find Allen and Paco in the starboard engine room. They have fabricated a new hose that seems to be working well. Paco is looking his self-sufficient self.

19:00 After a hot shower, I learn that we are eating on the beach. No one has had time to make dinner.

Paco and I wait in the cockpit while Allen goes for Roger who has remained sequestered in his cabin. They appear within a few minutes, ready to go. It is apparent that they have had words resulting in a chilly relationship between them.

After securing the boat, the four of us navigate the sloppy road up to the one and only restaurant in the complex, Marie's. En route, Allen excuses himself to step into the marina office. He catches up with us just before we reach our destination without comment.

Marie's is located several steps beyond the grocery store on the single road that leads in and out of the complex. Like the other buildings it is built similar in style with the high open space inside formed by the octagonal roof. There are no walls or partitions on three sides, although this evening a clear plastic material is rolled down part way to keep the rain out. The fourth side contains the kitchen together with a small four-stool bar and the scullery. Ceiling fans whirl away from above.

Upon entering, Allen comments that he remembers the food as very good. Of the ten tables, three are occupied. We choose an empty one in the center of the room and seat ourselves. The lone waitress brings menus and introduces herself as, sure enough, Marie. "I recognize you. You've been here before," she says to Allen.

"You're right, actually two or three times. How have you been?"

"Very well, thank you. Business has been slow due to the economy, but overall I'm doing OK."

"Good. We are all hungry so we'll help the economy tonight."

"I'll leave you alone for a few minutes. My specials are on the chalkboard beside the bar. I recommend the Dorado; it is fresh caught today. Anything from the bar?"

No," answers Allen for all of us. "We are underway as soon as we are done here."

We learn that Marie's has been open for thirteen and one half years. Single, she runs the business by herself with the help of a small staff. She tells us that much of her business comes from box lunches she makes for the fishing fleet.

We each order the Dorado. It is a delicious meal with great service.

There is little conversation between us, unlike times before at meals. I worry that Rogers erratic behavior will jeopardize our working relationship. Allen, although showing signs of concern, elects not to press the issue.

Finished, Allen pays the bill. We say our good-byes to Marie and trudge back down the water soaked road to the waiting Athena. The rain has stopped leaving everything soaked. The tide is at its low point leaving the ramp down to the floating dock at a treacherous forty-five degree angle. It is slick going down from the day's rain and the worn boards requiring a firm hand on the railing. I descend slowly for fear of slipping.

Once on board we make arrangements for immediate departure. Allen and I lay out our course on the chart, before starting the engines. Radar, compass and depth sounder will be our guide for tonight.

21:30. We untie and push off from the dock. Once clear, Allen backs Athena into the middle of the basin where he turns to align with the marina entrance and accelerates forward to take us out into the open bay. Fenders and lines are secured and stored.

21:45. I am given the helm and the watch. Our course of 295 degrees takes us out of Potrero Bay and to the north of Islas Santa Catalina. Once clear of it, I slowly turn to port and our new course of 178 degrees. Although overcast, visibility is good. I am able to keep visual contact with the island. We remain two miles off shore.

23:00. Excellent boat speed at six knots. Roger unfurls and sets the staysail, which gives us an added boost of half a knot and helps stabilize the roll of the boat. He then sits silently in the settee, reading and drinking coffee. Several attempts to engage him in conversation prove futile.

24:00. I turn the watch to Robin. I make my rounds and log book entries.

Our location is 2 miles abeam of Cabo Velas. GPS says that Panama is four hundred seventy-five miles away. Projected ETA is in seventy-eight hours, just over three days at six knots.

Satisfied that all is in order, I go below to my cabin. I read in bed for a half-hour before the rhythm and beat of the engine drive train serenades me to sleep.

Day 17. Thursday.

06:45. Bright sunlight streaming in through my porthole wakes me. I decide it is too early to get up, so lay in bed listening to the now familiar sounds of Athena. I doze in and out of consciousness when I hear an unusual sound. It is a rapid tap, tap, tap, lasting no more than three to five seconds. It is gone as quickly as it appeared. The noise seemed to come from the vicinity of the engine room, but I cannot be certain. I lay awake and listen for it again, but hear nothing. After a time, I put it off as my imagination.

08:00. I wash and trim my developing beard. I skirt the cockpit going directly to the galley for coffee and toast.

09:00. In relieving Allen, he has little to say, as does the log. It has been a quiet night. I want to ask him what he might have said to Roger last evening, but decide to leave it for later.

Our position is ten miles northwest of Cabo Blanco. We continue to motor-sail in a southeast direction, our course at 123 degrees. Boat speed and speed over the ground agree at seven knots. GPS estimates our ETA at 10:00 to our next waypoint. Distance is one hundred fifty miles.

10:00. My log notation is: flat sea with little wind and clear sky.

10:20. A blip on the radar six-mile range indicates a large ship on the horizon.

10:30. I note that we are directly abeam Cabo Blanco and have radar contact with a ship on our starboard bow.

11:00. I make contact with the vessel on VHF. I learn she is a cargo container, The Clipper, of Panamanian registration en route to Manzanillo, Mexico. She reports good weather to the Canal. In passing I note that she is empty as she rides high out of the water.

11:30. Roger sets the staysail. The early breeze helps our boat speed by half a knot.

12:00. I turn the watch over to Roger and complete my routine tasks.

I find Paco in the galley where I tell him about what I think I heard earlier.

We decide to report this to Allen. "You feel it may have been coming from the port engine room?" he asks.

"Yes, but I'm not sure."

"I would say you need to shut it down, do a visual inspection and check fluid levels," he tells Paco. "Inform Roger of what is happening."

I follow along to do whatever I can, like hold a flashlight, if needed.

With the engine shut down we carefully look it over for any signs of abnormality together with a check of engine, transmission and turbo charger fluids. We even look at the air filters for cleanliness. Everything checks normal. Paco has the engine restarted, transmission engaged and rpm's brought to 2150. He then takes a two foot length of half inch galvanized pipe and like a doctor's stethoscope places one end on the engine block, the other to his ear and listens.

Allen joins us and alternately listens. If this were not so serious, it would be a funny picture of them crouched down with pipe in ear. "All we can hope," says Allen raising up, "is that it was your imagination, Bob."

I eat a light lunch and retire to the aft deck for my afternoon ritual of reading and napping. Paco joins me to enjoy his favorite pastime, fishing. "Has Allen said anything to you about Roger?" he asks.

"We had a brief discussion yesterday on our way to the marina office. He asked if I had seen or sensed anything unusual from him, which I had not. Not until he abandoned you in the engine room. What was that all about?"

"I'm not sure. He simply excused himself and left without explanation. I figured that he needed to use the rest room and would return, which he never did. There is something bothering him."

I hesitate to say anything to Paco about the fax Allen sent. In fact I wonder what he received in response if anything.

Evidently satisfied, he returns to his two poles without further discussion. I return to my reading and log notations.

14:00. "Bob, take a look here," calls Paco from across the desk. He points to the first of several buoys separated by as much as a mile carrying a steel cable between them. "It is called a fish line." Plastic milk jugs located one hundred feet apart keep the cable afloat. From the cable are scores of lines with multiple fish hooks suspended at various lengths. It is strung parallel to our course. Had it been perpendicular or across our course, we could in crossing it, cut the cable and damage an engine shaft, rudder or who knows what. Many have strobe lights located on the buoys as a warning device, especially helpful at night.

17:30. Allen serves meatloaf, baked potatoes and mixed veggies together with a fresh baked apple pie for dessert. Abruptly, as we are relaxing during coffee and dessert, Allen raises his right fore finger to his mouth while making a schussing sound, calling for quiet. Silence descends as we look at Allen who now has the look of a bird dog, listening to the wind.

"I believe I heard your tapping sound, Bob."

We remain silent, each straining to hear the illusive sound. Nothing, only the beat and throb of the engines.

Paco excuses himself for an engine room check, returning with an "all's well."

We finish dessert, keeping our conversation in lower tones, each now more interested in listening than talking. Afterwards Roger and I wash dishes and clean the galley. He and I then work on our second picture puzzle on the big table in the main salon. Allen has the watch. Paco goes below to the engine rooms.

19:30. We all are astonished to hear the tapping sound. It is pronounced and lasts fully ten seconds. There is little doubt that the origin is from the port engine. Paco and Roger gather in the engine room to try to determine the source. They announce nothing abnormal.

21:00. I take the watch. The tapping now comes and goes in intervals. Paco remains in the engine room much like a doctor or nurse caring for a sick patient. Allen, returning to the cockpit from below, announces that he has decided that we need to go into Golfito, a port where he knows there is a diesel mechanic for diagnosis.

21:30. Our forward progress continues to be good. The over the bottom is just under seven knots. GPS has us at sixty-five miles to the waypoint newly established by Allen. We have an ETA of 09:00 tomorrow morning.

22:00. The watch goes well with the exception of the increased intervals of the tapping. It is becoming a steady occurrence. Engine oil pressure and temperature remain steady and normal.

There is thunderstorm activity to our southeast, but well away from our position.

24:00. I am relieved by Roger. I make my logbook notations after making my rounds. After deliberation among the four of us, Allen elects to reduce power to 2000 rpms on both engines. Unfortunately it has little effect.

Feeling unneeded, I retire below to my cabin and prepare for bed. Although noisy, the tapping does not prevent me from falling asleep.

CHAPTER NINETEEN

Golfito

Day 18. Friday

02:00. I am jarred awake by a loud bang and thump. The port engine goes silent. Remaining in my skivvies and T-shirt I leap out of bed to investigate. There is the strong smell of smoke in the passageway outside my cabin where I am nearly run over by Paco coming from his cabin. Following behind, I watch as he carefully opens the engine room door before looking inside. Allen joins him as they step inside while I remain outside ready to help.

Smoke and an acrid smell spill out, but no signs of a fire. Allen is the first out, his mouth and nose covered by a handkerchief. "It appears to be the turbo-compressor. I'm sure it is locked up," he says passing to go above.

I peek inside to see Paco kneeling at the smoking piece of machinery, still too hot to touch. "Can I do anything to help?" I ask.

"No. I'll be out soon."

I leave Paco with his promise not to remain inside for long and head towards the cockpit. Before reaching it I can hear Roger shouting at Allen. "You cannot stop. We must continue to Panama."

"I cannot risk attempting to go several hundred miles with one engine. There is a good diesel mechanic in Golfito who can possibly get us out in a few days," Allen responds.

"I don't care. We must move on."

I remain out of sight but am able to hear quite well.

"Why, Roger? What is so important that would make you want to continue with a broken engine?"

"I have an appointment."

163

"What kind of an appointment?"

"Never mind. Forget it. It's OK, let's go to Golfito."

Paco comes up from behind. I place my finger to my lips for quiet and point towards the cockpit.

"Roger, something is bothering you and has been for most of the trip. What is it? Tell me, perhaps I can help."

"Nothing that I cannot handle myself."

"Whatever it is, it is affecting your duties on board this boat and as captain I have the right to know. I have allowed this to go on for far too long." In the years that I have known Allen, I do not recall ever hearing this tone of voice.

"I am anxious to see old friends. That's all."

"Bull. You have something to deliver, don't you?"

There is a pause in the conversation. Unable to see Rogers face, it is difficult to know what is happening. "How long have you known?" Roger finally asks.

"Since Huatulco."

Again, another long pause. "I guess I'm in big trouble."

"Do you have any idea what you are carrying?"

"No. I know better than to think it is something legal."

"The authorities think it may be a stolen gem."

Feeling that the moment was right, Paco and I enter the cockpit. Roger looking dejected remains at the wheel while Allen leans on the chart table facing him. Acknowledging our presence, Allen informs Roger that Paco and I am aware of the situation. Paco and I slip into the settee.

After several long minutes of silence, Allen decides that the problem at hand, getting safely to Golfito, is the more important task. "For now it is business as usual," he states. "Once in port, we'll sort all this out and decide what needs to be done."

I return to the relative comfort and safety of my cabin where I lay on my bunk thinking of the evening's events. There is an eerie quiet that I am unaccustomed to without the beat of the drive train. I eventually drop off to sleep but do not rest well.

07:50 There are no usual sunbeams dancing about in the cabin in spite of a clear, cloudless sky. I suspect the reason is that we have changed course to a more easterly heading therefore the sun is on our bow, not mid ship.

I find Allen at the helm looking tired and concerned. The chart confirms that we are in Gulfo Dulce, the bay leading to Golfito on a 90-degree heading. GPS indicates that we have 20 miles to go to a turning waypoint for entrance into Golfito Bay. Our bottom speed is a surprising five knots as we are being helped by the incoming tide.

I visit the galley for coffee, orange juice and toast before sliding into the aft settee to watch the morning unfold until my watch.

Dense tree and flora line both sides of this large body of water where occasionally I spot a thatched roof house in a cleared space. The land is flat to the horizon with nothing to indicate any high ground.

09:00. I take the watch. I doubt that Allen will be going too far away from the cockpit. He has drawn a rumb line on the chart to help avoid known shoaled areas. Fortunately the tide is near full, so depth is not a factor as long as we remain right of center. The depth finder is our largest asset. There is a large amount of floating debris. Large logs, broken-up lumber, trash and most anything that will float is in our way in the dirty, brown water. Much of which we pass is large enough to avoid. We pass numerous fishing boats, both large and small, many gaily painted and decorated. Some are open while others have makeshift cabins made of plywood and scrap lumber.

11:00. We arrive at the waypoint needed to align ourselves with the range markers that will take us through the narrow entrance into the harbor known as Puerto Golfito. GPS has us at 8 36 25N/83 12 35W. Allen calls for reduced power together with a gradual turn to starboard to take up a course of 78 degrees. He has me bring Athena to a stop to enable him to check our position as well as determine that the way is clear.

Satisfied of no shipping and properly aligned, he takes the wheel and starts us inbound. The channel is well marked with standard red and green buoys, easily identifiable. I am surprised by the narrowness, considering the size of the ships that pass in and out. Two ships cannot possibly pass one another at any point along the quarter mile distance.

The landmass on our portside is identified on the chart as Punta Voladera, a wooded, mist shrouded jungle rising up twenty or more feet from the water's edge. The lush vegetation hides anything behind the first few feet. To our starboard is a low, flat marshland of reeds and tall grasses stretching for miles.

Once through the channel, the landmass falls away to reveal a decent size body of water. Directly ahead is a large commercial loading wharf with a container ship being loaded, each container carrying the familiar Dole logo. At two o'clock is a freighter preparing to get under way. She apparently has been at anchor as her dirty ground tackle is being washed and brought on board from a muddy bottom.

We approach two white buoys in mid channel. They are turning buoys directing us either north or south. We start a turn to starboard, passing inside the south marker and aft of the outbound freighter. Her name is Panam Christie. She flies a Panamanian flag with Panama displayed across her stern. Her propellers, partly exposed above the water line, churn and swirl the water with powerful strokes.

"Eagles Nest, Eagles Nest. This is the sailing vessel Athena. Do you read?" calls Allen on the VHF. Allen had spoken with them earlier.

"Athena, Athena. This is Eagles Nest. What is your position, Captain?"

Allen provides our location and ETA.

"Roger that. I'll meet you at the dock for a portside tie down."

"Affirmative," answers Allen. "Athena out."

Proceeding southward, the town of Golfito begins to unfold on our port side. The main road runs parallel with the shoreline while heavily forested rolling hills form a backdrop beyond the roadway, creating a narrow valley. On the water's edge are structures built upon pilings of wooden poles like stilts, allowing them to extend out over the water for several feet from the road. The buildings are irregularly shaped, framed in wood with metal/tin overhanging roofs to provide shelter from the elements. Few are painted; most have been left to weather naturally.

11:30. The more heavily populated area of the town starts to reveal itself. The valley widens here, the hills receding from the water making space for a fair sized town. In the maze of buildings, a white doomed concrete building catches my eye, a church or cemetery I think.

11:45 We stand off at the marina, an attractive single story yellow building with the typical wide overhang white roof and a large satellite dish perched on top. Two attendants stand on the floating dock signaling us to tie off where they stand. Paco and Roger have fenders rigged.

It takes Allen several tries to bring Athena parallel to the dock before lines can be thrown ashore and the attendants pull us in the remaining distance. We tie down, sandwiched in between boats fore and aft. Paco plugs in shore power while I hook up a fresh water hose. Allen shuts down the starboard engine. I note the time as 12:00 hrs.

Allen calls us together in the cockpit. He assigns various tasks to each of us while explaining that he is going ashore to use a land telephone line. "I suggest," he says, "that we keep this morning's conversation to ourselves. Later, we'll decide our next steps."

I have been assigned to empty and flush the fresh water tanks that have been dispensing brown water since our departing Puerto Madero. I slip on my bathing suit and proceed to wash down the desk and cockpit using the cloudy water to empty the tanks. I repeatedly wet myself as relief from the heat and humidity. Once empty, I run fresh water into the tanks, until they show clear water. Next, I measure several caps full of bleach, emptying them into the tanks and filling. It is not difficult work, only a bit time consuming.

Roger meanwhile has disassembled the port aft shroud turnbuckle to be taken to a welder. Allen wants it shortened by several inches. Paco has removed the steering cable assembly from the Zodiac that failed in our last use. He has also removed the starboard engine alternator to be taken to an electric shop.

13:00. Allen, returning from the marina office, suggests we walk into town for lunch. After locking the boat he takes us to a building located on the opposite end of the marina and introduces us to Kitty. She and her husband Jason, offer a variety of services including fax, phone, laundry, dive services and car rental. She is very helpful and knowledgeable, offering to telephone the best diesel mechanic in town and where to find the best welder.

Here is another case of a couple who went cruising but found a place along the way they liked and have remained. I learn they have been here for three years, originally from San Diego, California.

We thank her for her help then deciding to walk to town, a distance of a quarter of a mile. There is a wide concrete sidewalk that runs parallel to the narrow two-lane macadam road on our right while well-kept houses, many with picket fences and grassed areas, are to our left. On several occasions we are greeted with waves from folks seated on their porches.

It is an easy walk to what appears to be the geographic center of town. Here another road intersects from the right and runs off in a thirty-degree angle. The town is quiet with most shops closed for siesta. I count two meat markets, a grocery/hardware store, a bakery, the Costa Rica Hotel, several restaurants and too many bars to count. Kitty has recommended the La Dolphin to eat. We locate it easily and step inside. It is quite small, offering seating for twenty-five to thirty, mostly at a counter running around the outside wall with stools. There are only two patrons because of the late hour. We seat ourselves at one of the four tables. The place is clean and well maintained showing signs of a recent painting. A woman brings menus who we learn is the owner. An American expatriate, her name is Judy. We enjoy a light lunch consisting of sandwiches, chips and a soft drink. The conversation centers mostly on trying to get us ready to leave ASAP. Allen pays the bill with the promise that we will return, unfortunately Judy is not open for dinner. She does provide us with a large amount of local information and advice.

15:00. Back at Kitty's, she tells us that the mechanic can come at 17:00. Returning to the boat, Allen has us remove the carpeting leading into the cockpit, bridge area and down to the engine rooms. He suspects that there will be heavy traffic by the mechanic. The carpets, a beige color, need cleaning from our use. Paco, Roger and I spread them out on the dock where we scrub them with soap and hot water. Again in bathing suits we liberally spray one another with water, more like kids than adults. On one occasion Allen comes out on deck where we give him a good hosing. We have a fun time while accomplishing the cleaning task under a strong hot sun Forgotten, for the time being, are any questions or doubts about Rogers possible illegal involvement in smuggling. I sense for the first time in days that he is relieved to have this entire thing out in the open. Hanging the carpets to dry on lifelines completes the job.

16:30. I go below to my cabin for a shower and to read while waiting for the mechanic in the comfort of air-conditioning.

17:40. He comes onboard and immediately asks to be taken to the engine room. He speaks little English, requiring Paco to translate. After several minutes Paco calls for Allen to start the engine. Turning the key to the start position produces no response. "Stop, no more," calls Paco. Allen goes below while Roger and I sit at the settee in silence.

18:00. The prognosis is as we had contemplated, we need to replace the turbocompressor. The mechanic knows of no one that would have one in Costa Rica. Because of its age, he feels it is going to be difficult to find a replacement, anywhere. He wishes us well and leaves, without charge.

Allen and Paco join Roger and I at the settee. "Well, at least we have a second opinion at no cost," offers Allen reflecting on the bad news.

"Can we operate without it?" I ask.

"No, not without the possibility of seriously damaging the engine, they are designed to work as a unit, not one without the other," Allen responds. He continues, "Anticipating this, I have been in contact with an agent in San Diego whom I have used before to locate hard to find parts. If anyone can track one down, she is our person. Unfortunately our timing is bad with this being Friday but she promised to work through the weekend."

True to his character, Allen proves he is one step ahead of us. There is little that can be done I conclude until the first of next week. Our fate appears to be in the hands of a woman two thousand miles away.

19:00. We conclude that we will venture back into town for dinner. Again we walk to the town center where unlike earlier there is a beehive of human activity. All stores are open and busy as it is Friday night and pay day. The sidewalks are crowded with shoppers spilling out onto the roadway. Vehicle traffic is minimal because of pedestrian traffic.

Deciding on Chinese food, we select the Hong Kong Kitchen. Located on the diagonal street, it's narrow storefront opens directly into the food preparation area, separated from the public by a take-out pickup counter just inside. A three-foot high wall located to the left of the kitchen creates a corridor or isle leading to the seating area at the rear. We seat ourselves in the tiny, windowless room's center. My first and lasting impression of the dining area is poor because of the sticky heat and the objectionable smell from cooking food. Unlike La Dolphin, this place hasn't had a good cleaning

in ages including our waitress. I look at my companions to excuse myself. I have lost any appetite that I may have had and head for the front door.

Outdoors, in order to settle my head and stomach, I find the need to walk. I continue up the diagonal street, weaving in and out of the evening shoppers. At the Costa Rica Hotel, I see a large banner hanging from its front, advertising cold beer in the second story bar for the equivalent of one dollar. Without hesitation I climb the outside stairs to where I find a decent sized room. The bar runs along the outside wall providing a view of the street below while to the back is a nicely set dining room. A quick count says there are fifteen or sixteen stools with three occupied at the far end.

A barmaid welcomes me in English as I slide onto a stool. "You look like you can use a drink. The beer is cold."

"Wonderful. A Budweiser, Please."

"Right away." She places a cocktail napkin in front of me before going to where the beer is kept.

Still nauseated, I am in hopes that a beer will settle my churning stomach. Never a big fan of Chinese food, this was an experience I shall not easily forget. I wonder how the others are doing.

"One cold Bud, coming up," says the barmaid with bottle in hand.

"Thanks." With little hesitation I take a big swig, allowing the cold liquid to trickle down my throat. This is followed by a second and third big gulp with each easing the knotting in my stomach.

"You were dry," my barmaid exclaims after a few minutes of watching me.

"Dry and nauseated," I comment.

"How are you doing now?"

"Better, much better."

"Something to eat?" she asks.

"What do you have?"

"I'll get a menu. Be right back."

Fortunately the beer is having a soothing effect on both my head and stomach. I am actually feeling better by the minute. The menu offers a variety of finger foods together with burgers and fries. Not caring to overdo it, I order a well-done hamburger and another beer.

"What's your name?" I ask.

"Winter," she responds. "I know. It's unusual. I blame my father."

"He must have had a reason."

"He did. I reminded him of the snows of Michigan where I was born because I was so light in color."

"How long have you been living here?"

"Forty years. We came when I was six. What's your name?"

"Sorry for being impolite. I'm Bob," I say extending my hand over the counter. She responds with a firm grip and a flirtatious smile. "Glad to meet you, Bob. I'll be back with you burger." I watch as she moves towards the kitchen beyond the end of the bar before disappearing through a set of double swinging doors. She is dressed in shorts and a short sleeve light- weight blouse because of the heat.

From the bar, I am able to watch the pedestrians below. By chance I see Allen and company as they make their way up the street towards the hotel. Sliding off my stool and going to the railing, I yell down as they draw near to have them join me.

"Friends?" asks Winter upon my return.

"More like sailing companions. We are delivering a sailboat to Florida through the Panama Canal."

"You are at Eagles Nest Marina?"

"Yes."

"I had heard that a new boat had come in today."

Only Allen joins me explaining that the others want to walk around the town. I introduce him to Winter. She asks if she can serve him a drink, which he declines.

"Did you eat?" I ask.

"We did and probably will regret it," answers Allen.

"I'm sorry, but I had to get out of there. I nearly lost it."

He tells me that they talked briefly regarding Roger. "He maintains that he was assured by his buddies in Vallarta, who set this up with a man named Mendoza, that the package contained nothing illegal. He admits that the lure of big money to deliver it, clouded his mind."

"Did he tell you how much he is being paid?"

"One thousand dollars."

"Wow," I respond.

"I am going to Kitty's from here to contact Weber for advise and direction.

I want to meet at 08:00 tomorrow, so don't stay out too late." He pats me on the back while sliding off the stool and disappearing down the stairs.

"Don't forget to tell him about the envelope from Gaston," I say.

"I won't," he responds.

I watch him from my perch with his familiar gait disappear into the crowd and evening darkness.

The burger was quite good and I ate heartily, my stomach problems apparently over. I am content to remain seated while nursing my second beer to watch the ebb and flow of patrons as the bar and dining room is starting to get busy with a variety of singles and families. Winter stays busy, seemingly knowing the majority of folks and what are their drink choices. I sense that this is the eating and drinking establishment of choice by many.

Resisting temptation to have another beer, I ask for and pay the bill. I learn that the US dollar is widely accepted by most places of business, which is no exception here. "It looks as if we are here for a few days," I say in departing. "I expect I'll be back."

"Great. I'll look for you," responds Winter with a wave of good bye.

21:30. Exiting the hotel, I turn left to follow the diagonal road towards the general direction of Eagle's Nest. The crowd thins within a few blocks to become residential as the diagonal street turns south to parallel the main road. Here the buildings are constructed mostly of cider block with reinforced steel to hold them together rather than wood as seen on the waterfront. Metal (corrugated tin) is the roof material of choice. Some homes have rod iron grating covering windows and doors; none have glass or solid doors to keep the weather out.

At my first opportunity I turn right on a narrow dirt street that takes me to the main road where I find myself a few hundred feet from the marina. There is a small group of boat people on the marina dock having a party as I pass. I look for Allen thinking he may have stopped to say hello to a familiar face, but do not see him.

Onboard I learn that Allen is at Kitty's, Paco is asleep and Roger is in the TV lounge watching a movie. He asks that I join him, shutting off the set.

He explains how badly he feels and how on many occasions he had wanted to say something about his behavior, but couldn't find the words. "I am truly sorry for what I have done," he says in remorse.

"It would be easy to be critical of you," I say, "however; I cannot say what I would have done under the same circumstances. We all make bone head decisions for which we regret later on. What is important now is what can be done to help correct the wrong."

"I told Allen I will cooperate with the authorities in whatever way I can."

"Good. I believe for now we need to wait until tomorrow mornings meeting.

Hopefully Allen will have direction from agent Weber."

We chat for a few more minutes before I excuse myself and head below to my little cubical. I cannot help but notice how quiet it is without either the engine/transmission or auxiliary generator noise. I sit on my bunk where I review the day's activities and attempt to think at what lies ahead. 'How long will we be here' keeps rattling around in my mind.

Finally I shut off my reading light leaving the cabin in semi-darkness. I lie awake listening to the party sounds from outside together with road traffic of the midnight hour. Eventually I drop off to sleep vaguely conscience of hearing Allen come aboard.

CHAPTER TWENTY

Oh my-gosh

Day 19. Saturday.

07:30. I rub the sleepers from my eyes, disbelieving the late hour. I quickly wash and dress before heading to the galley. Here I find Roger sitting in the TV lounge, seemingly in a good frame of mind. I fill my coffee mug and together we head to the cockpit where we slide into the aft settee. Paco and Allen join us before long.

08:00. Allen begins by reporting that he has not heard from his contact in San Diego. He suggests that Paco remove the turbocompressor in order to be certain nothing of the engine is damaged. Later, Paco and I should take the parts in need of repair to the welder.

"I have heard from Special Agent Weber," he continues. "He suggests that we proceed as though normal. He strongly recommends that I place you, Roger under house arrest for your own protection. I convinced him that was not necessary; however he cautioned me that you were my responsibility so do not disappoint me by doing anything foolish.

Weber believes that once we have been detected as stopped for a prolonged time, Roger will be contacted as in Acapulco. This time he may not be so lucky with just a scolding. Therefore I am ordering Roger to remain in the continual company of at least one of the three of us. The exception will be while in his cabin. OK?"

We each shake our heads in the affirmative.

"Depending on how long we are required to remain here will determine the degree of risk. If Weber is correct in his assumption that the package contains a monitoring device, it will not take Mendoza long to see that we are not where we should be. All of us need to establish a heighten degree of awareness of the people around us. It is not unreasonable to believe that they will not think twice about doing bodily harm to any of us in order to get to Roger and the package. We can all be at risk." He pauses. "I don't want to be an alarmist, but it is best that we take precautions." Once again he pauses to allow his words to have effect. "Lastly, Weber wants me to inspect the package, so Roger please go get it."

Without hesitation, he slides out from the settee and disappears below to his cabin. "We need to keep a close eye on him," says Allen. "Weber is not convinced that Roger is as innocent as he claims."

I ask Allen if he mentioned the envelope from Gaston to agent Weber. "Yes, I have," he replies.

Upon his return, Roger places the gaily-wrapped package in the middle of the table. Initially no one says a word as we each stare at it. Finally, Allen reaches to pick it up saying, "It looks innocent enough." He gently shakes it while turning it over. Cautiously he unties the ribbon and slips it off. Next he removes the wrapping paper to reveal a plain white cardboard box sealed top and bottom with scotch tape. Removing his pocketknife, he slices the tape and slowly unfolds the box top. I hold my breath, leaning in for a closer look. The box is further divided into two sections each containing another box. Allen lifts one of them out and places it on the table. He gently opens it and unfolds tissue to reveal a radio transmitter about the size of a nine-volt battery. A tiny blinking red light signifies that it is active. He sits it on the table careful not to disturb it in any way. Next he removes the second box to find that its content is wrapped in bubble wrap. Nestled inside is a velvet pouch with a gold cinch cord. Removing it, he unties the cord allowing the contents to slide out into his left hand. I am thunderstruck. It is a very large violet-blue gem. In a word, it is spectacular.

"Oh my-gosh," I exclaim.

"This is no diamond," exclaims Allen. "This is a blue star sapphire, a big blue sapphire, perhaps as large as the Star of Bombay. It could be worth millions."

He explains that although he has limited knowledge of The Star of Bombay, he knows that "it is housed in the National Museum of Natural History at the Smithsonian Institution in Washington, DC and like The Star of India it is considered extremely rare and quite valuable." Immediately he replaces it in its pouch together with the transmitter and returns them to the box.

"Well, we now know what we have to contend with," he says. "Roger, I believe for all of our safety, the box shall remain from now on in the ships safe."

Roger agrees, outwardly relieved.

"What I guess I don't understand," I say," is who would ever consider sending as valuable an item as this with a young man who knows nothing of what it is he is carrying? No offense to you Roger, but this is bizarre."

There is a protracted silence around the table.

Roger speaks, " I believe it was done because of its simplicity. Who would guess that anyone would be that arrogant and daring to try such a stunt? Also consider Captain Daniel's impeccable record of honesty and care in boat deliveries. Who would guess?"

"Roger is probably right. And if it had not been for an anonymous tip to the FBI, they might have pulled it off," says Allen. "But for now let's go about our business in our normal way," states Allen as he stands to retire to his cabin with the package in hand.

Roger agrees to help Paco in the engine room while Allen walks up to Kitty's to further pursue an update on the turbocompressor search, to also notify the bank of our delay and undoubtedly talk with agent Weber. Left more or less to my own devises I gather dirty clothing for washing, clean the galley and replace the cleaned carpets.

12:00. I make sandwiches together with a vegetable and fruit plate. I find that I very much miss having Emilia on board. We gather at the settee for lunch where Paco expresses his opinion that when the turbocompressor was rebuilt it was incorrectly assembled at the factory before being placed on the engine. The engine appears to be OK.

13:00. Paco and I prepare to leave for the welder by gathering up the articles for repair. We elect to take a taxi because of the distance to the shop, described by Kitty as beyond the center of town. After several minutes of standing by the roadside we are able to stop an empty taxi. Paco provides the driver with the name of the shop as he takes the front seat while I get in the back. The taxi is an older Datsun, in rough shape after years of hard driving and little care. There is no headlining and little in the way of seat cushions. The young driver guns the engine to accelerate with spinning wheels out of the gravel roadside onto the macadam. We rocket down the road into town. I hang on for dear life, being battered about from the rough road and shifting gears. Passing through town he abruptly slams on the breaks while veering onto the right shoulder and comes to a stop amidst a cloud of dust. Before I am able to gather my wits, both rear doors open whereupon two men climb inside pinning me in the middle. Without waiting for the doors to fully close, we are off again with spinning wheels and flying dust. The two speak to the driver in Spanish, obviously thankful for the lift. My new companions at least prevent me from bouncing around as we continue to zip along at a fast pace.

The road we are travelling is the one I could see from Athena upon our arrival. To my left I recognize many of the buildings set on stilts extending out over the tidal waters of the bay. Rows of coconut palms line the road to the right. Through them and across an open field I am able to see what looks like a military two-story housing complex.

Shortly, our driver shifts down to slow before turning right into a side street where he stops to discharge my two bookends. Immediately we blast off, only to quickly decelerate in order to turn right and then right again paralleling the front of the earlier seen housing complex. The buildings are identical; each painted white with beige trim. They appear to be four-plexes, well maintained, nicely landscaped and neat. Not slowing, we pass the last of them before leaving the smooth roadway to encounter a rough dirt road that takes us several hundred feet to a fenced in compound consisting of a large metal building set behind a rundown house. We drive through an open gate and into the compound where we come to another abrupt stop. Paco pays the young man while I thankfully crawl out of the rear seat.

The building, we learn is the machine shop of the welder. It is built of corrugated metal, measuring I guess, at sixteen hundred feet square. Its walls are twenty feet high with a flat roof. The yard is littered with junk cars, wheels and tires, heaps of scrap metal and dozens of fifty-gallon drums. A single story wooden frame house in need of paint and general repair is also part of the compound.

Paco and I step inside the shop through an open rod iron gate to a floor of uneven dirt. Several men are at work in various parts of the cavernous building. A small office is located in one corner that we approach in an attempt to locate the owner. One of the men calls to us in Spanish from where he is working at a metal lathe. Paco explains that we are looking for the mistro, (the owner) Carlos Orosco. He replies that he is Orosco, shutting down the lathe to come to meet us.

I estimate he is in his mid-thirties, husky, over six-foot tall, weighing 250 pounds, all solid muscle. Clean shaven he has a round happy face with a wide smile displaying beautiful even white teeth. He wears a baseball cap worn backwards, a colorful blue and white stripped tank top shirt, kakai shorts and a pair of hiking boots with heavy wool socks.

We introduce ourselves, learning quickly that his English is limited. Paco therefore explains in Spanish what we would like done to each of the items while I can only standby catching a familiar word and phrase now and again. I gather by his gestures that he can repair the water pipe and the turnbuckle and knows an electrician who can repair the alternator. He is not certain what if anything he can do with the engine control cable. He and Paco step into the small office providing me with the opportunity to look around.

The shop consists of several lathes, drill presses, bench grinders, a welding machine, acetylene tanks and a variety of power hand tools. I hear an air compressor running somewhere outside providing power for many of the hand tools. Fluorescent lights suspended from above provide adequate light over workbenches and machines. The men entering and leaving the shop make it difficult to know who may be an employee, who is a friend passing to say hello or a relative from the house. A shaggy dog wanders in to check me out before choosing a shady spot to lie down.

Exiting the office, Paco shakes hands with the mistro and informs me that we can expect the items, excepting the alternator, to be ready later this afternoon.

Leaving the compound, we are faced with the prospect of having to walk back to the marina. We follow a well-worn footpath to the main road where as luck would have it, the same taxi picks us up. I speculate that he knew we would need a return ride, so simply waited.

Following another exhilarating taxi ride, I relax and read in the settee in the comfort of Athena's air conditioning. Exposure to the heat and humidity of the day has me worn out. I had forgotten how uncomfortable this kind of weather can be as experienced by eighteen years of living in Houston.

17:30. Paco and I prepare to return to Orosco's. Again we take a taxi although as it turns out not the same one as before. This fellow proves far tamer than the previous one together with a good command of English. He explains two things about taxi travel. One, that when you hire a taxi, it is not yours exclusively. If there is room for additional passengers, they are picked up and you are expected to make room for them. Two, locals get to ride free. Arriving at the shop, we smartly ask that the taxi to wait. There has been progress with our repairs. The water pipe has been successfully welded. The alternator has been delivered to the electrician and can be expected to be ready Monday afternoon. The steering cable has been declared unfixable as the internal flexible cable is broken and cannot be welded. A new cable can be delivered from San Jose by air on Monday or Tuesday. Lastly, the turnbuckle is not cooperating. The eye stem is cross-threaded inside the barrel. They have tried heating the barrel in order to expand it enough to back the eye stem out, but have been unsuccessful. Carlos (Paco now uses the mistro's first name) is afraid that any further heating will destroy the barrels temper. His solution is to cut the barrel in half, adding a new stainless piece and re-threading. Likewise with the stem, cut off the damaged (cross-threaded) section, weld a new piece in place and re-thread it also.

Rather than risk making a poor decision, Paco and I return with the barrel and eye stem to the boat for Allen's evaluation. Needless to say his initial reaction is disbelief in what was, in his opinion, to have been a relatively simple job has turned into something major. Yet now, there is little choice, the alternatives are poor to none. He gives his approval and has us return via the waiting taxi. Carlos assures Paco that the results will be satisfactory. It will be ready Monday afternoon.

"What is the significance of the buildings to our right?" I ask our driver as we pass the housing complex on our return to the marina.

With help from Paco he explains that they were built as housing units for employees of the now departed United Fruit Company and that most are owned by wealthy Costa Ricans from San Jose and North Americans as vacation homes. He tells us that we are at the extreme south end of what was company land, all of which was left to the state after United gave up its banana business in 1985. I begin to sense there is a good story here.

19:00. Allen has prepared a dinner consisting of hamburger steak smothered in fried onions with mashed potatoes and carrots. Roger makes a dessert of vanilla custard that we eat in the television lounge held captive by an HBO movie. Afterwards, Roger and I wash the dishes and clean the galley.

23:00. I turn in after what has been an interesting and busy day. I crawl into bed, snap off the reading light and quickly drift off into a deep and restful sleep.

Day 20. Sunday.

08:00. Despite some noise earlier outside, I have remained comfortable in my bunk enjoying the first real opportunity of the trip to be truly lazy.

08:30. Washed and dressed I go to look for my companions. Allen is in his cabin stretched out on his bunk. He tells me that he has a slight headache and mild upset stomach.

Roger and Paco are outside at the chain locker inspecting and repainting chain depth marks. There is no activity in or around the two rafted boats. It makes me think they have probably gone into town.

I descend to the galley for juice and coffee where I decide to whip up a batch of pancake mix. I heat-up my favorite flat iron skillet.

I invite Paco and Roger to join me, but they decline, as does Allen.

I put away three hotcakes with a fried egg, washing them down with fresh hot coffee. After cleaning the galley I gather my book from below to settle into the aft settee with its 360-degree view.

There is very little boat traffic; not unusual as it is Sunday morning. The few that are on the water appear to be transporting families, perhaps to church or to visit a relative. One in particular is fully loaded with women and children in their finest clothing, while the men wear their everyday blue jeans and T shirts.

10:30. Paco and Roger come inside, their project outside completed. They are wet with perspiration, dirty and hungry. I send them off to shower while I prepare another batch of mix for pancakes with eggs and bacon. Allen joins them. I find it difficult to keep up with the demand for pancakes, but ultimately manage to satisfy their appetites. Afterwards we sit around the main salon table where Paco entertains us with stories about his family and of the time he spent in the United States. I enjoy his outlook on life and his insight of living in North America.

12:00. Allen declares the rest of the day as a holiday and suggests we take the dinghy to explore the bay. Paco improvises with a broom handle lashed to the outboard engine to substitute for the damaged steering mechanism. I fill a cooler with soft drinks, bottled water and ice. I gather towels for swimming and several tubes of sunscreen.

Our timing is good as the tide is at half full and rising. Departing the marina we motor south paralleling the land towards the end of the bay. We pass many similar structures as seen to the north, built out over the water supported by wooden poles. Now, unlike when we arrived, the poles or stilts are partially exposed above the water line, clearly showing their extreme length. Some buildings have ramps leading to floating docks where boats are kept as I have seen on the coast of Maine.

Just ahead is the fishing fleet anchored and rafted together in two rows of five. As we approach them, they give the appearance of being a large funeral barge because of the many black flags flown from the marker buoys stowed upright atop the cabins. Outside on both sides of the cabins are water jugs strung together like pearls on a string. The black flags, like the lobster buoys of Maine, signify who the owners are of this fleet. These boats are used for the long line form of fishing of which we have seen examples on several occasions over the past few days.

We pass two closed marinas that at one time were part of the popular sport- fishing and yachting scene. One, The Golfito Yacht Club was, together with the Hotel Las Gaviotas, highly recommended by Charlie's Charts (a boater's guide) as recently as 1991. The network of docks and ramps are gone. The only remaining evidence is the concrete pier that protrudes fifty feet from the shore that all else was once attached. Another is The Tres Marlin Marina. Unlike its sister, it is operational as a warehouse/cold storage facility for local catches of shrimp and sardines.

We turn west and cut across the bay to Punta El Cabro where we follow the shoreline. Here the rain forest comes to the water's edge. The high tide line is clearly marked where the salt water stops growth. I have read, and now can visibly see, what is meant when Costa Rica is described as a nation of 'green upon green upon green.' My reading tells me that the tall, shapely trees are called Medina and can grow to heights of twenty to thirty feet. It is a soft wood and is being actively harvested for use as pulp. But, the most abundant flora in the rain forest is the ferns, found from sea level to the highest elevations. Here they are numerous. The big tree ferns rise twenty feet with fiddleheads to catch the sunlight. Lower or smaller species are known as eaphytic, arboreal "nesters" or climbers whose long leaves can grapple upward for one hundred feet or more. Additionally are the bromeliads, brilliantly flowering spiky leafed "air" plants. Costa Rica has more than two thousand species of bromelaids (including the pineapple); the richest deposits are found on this isthmus. Another prominent plant is the poor man's umbrella (sombrilla de pobre), a name you will remember if you get caught in a downpour while in the rainforest as its giant leaves make an excellent shelter.

Before long we come upon a small indentation in the shoreline and a clearing. In the clearings center is a thatched roof palapa that Allen believes was once The Jungle Club. Again as recently as 1991, it is described by Margo Wood, the widow of Charlie of Charlie's Charts as a popular anchorage for cruisers. Owned by a couple, Barb and Whitey, they operated this rustic facility successfully for a number of years gaining wide notoriety within the cruising community. Today it is eerie quiet, abandoned, as the jungle slowly over runs it.

We continue to follow the shoreline before reaching a shoal area where we decide to turn around and head back towards the deeper water of the bay. After rounding Punta El Cabro, we run directly to the north end of the bay, a distance of several miles, ultimately crossing the shipping channel used upon our arrival. We drop anchor and wade ashore on a sandy beach known as Playa Cacao, a popular relaxation spot for locals. Today is no exception. There are a number of buildings including a restaurant, The Seven Seas. It features a nice menu and cold beer. I have a great chicken salad served with Italian dressing and roll. The four of us enjoy a lengthy meal, occasionally going for a swim for relief from the oppressive heat and humidity.

The Seven Seas is a few hundred yards east of another well-known cruisers hangout of the seventies and eighties, Captain Tom's. We motor over, dropping anchor some fifteen feet from shore. The story goes that a Thomas Gilmore arrived here in the early sixties on this badly storm damaged converted World War II gunboat. He came ashore at this spot where the boat has since been encased in concrete that Gilmore turned into a bar and restaurant. Over time he added three small guestrooms with a shared bathroom. He enjoyed life up to his death in 1991. Although his widow and son have taken separate turns at running it since his death, neither had been successful. Today it is a battered, beat-up relic of what was once a lively, in-place to meet and greet the cruising world's notables.

Deciding to have a closer look, I swim to shore joined by Paco and Roger. Much to my surprise I find that Captain Tom is indeed here. He is entombed in an above ground white marble crypt, only a few yards from the restaurant, where a marker shows him as a United States Marine and a member of the American Legion, born 1924 died 1991.

A woman is inside the restaurant. I saw her go in as I was coming out of the water. As I stand at the crypt, she exits after securing a bamboo door with a piece of string. I ask if she speaks English. "Only a little," she answers as she rushes past me. "Are you Captain Tom's wife?" She does not answer, quickly disappearing into a nearby motor home.

The three of us take a closer look inside the boat of what at one time was the eating area. Large pieces of the corrugated roof is gone; blown away I would guess, exposing the ribs of bamboo. The floor or what may have been the deck of the boat is badly rotten particularly where tables and chairs once were. The aft cabin where the kitchen was located is a shamble of rotten wood and rusty metal. I would be afraid to go inside for fear of falling through the floor.

We walk the grounds on a stone footpath that winds throughout the property. Once manicured grass areas and tropical gardens are now over-grown with weeds and tall grasses. In departing I admire the work that went into a retaining wall and steps along the beachfront. The old boat itself remains well situated in its concrete cradle where at high tide it has the appearance of being once again afloat. A lot of Captain Tom remains; his hard work is on display for anyone interested to see.

Once back on board the dinghy we continue our exploration of the northerly end of the bay. It is now full tide so we are able to motor in and out of several estuaries that would be dry at mid to low tide. Much of what we see is part of the Golfito National Wildlife Refuge.

Our trip begins its conclusion by our motoring south along the face of the one thousand-foot long commercial loading dock. There are no ships docked to obstruct our view of the enormous conveyor belts. The facility is in excellent condition showing signs of being well maintained as well as heavily used. There are several people fishing from the dock that wave as we pass.

Continuing south we pass The Samoa Yacht Club. Two sailboats tied to a pier that is partially underwater are the only signs of activity although a palapa at the pier's end has the appearance of being open.

Next we stop at the Texaco fuel dock to determine whether Athena's twenty-five foot beam will allow her to come here for fuel. Determining that she will fit inside the tiny basin, Allen will come tomorrow to make arrangements for fueling here rather than have it brought by truck to the marina.

Next we come abeam of the public swimming facility. Today being Sunday and with a full tide, the area is alive with families enjoying the relative cool water as relief from the ever pressing heat and humidity. The sandy beach provides space for the children to run and play with squeals of delight.

18:00. Returning to Athena, we raise the dinghy onto the fantail unwilling to leave it in the water for fear of it being stolen. We each shower before relaxing for the balance of the evening. Allen's uneasy stomach and headache has returned. He does not look well. I convince him to take a couple of aspirin and go to bed. Paco, Roger and I confine ourselves in the TV lounge where we find a HBO movie.

22:00. I turn in for the night. The day's activities together with too much exposure to the sun have worn me out. I read for nearly an hour however, before snapping off the reading light. Sleep does not come quickly as I am stiff and sore from the sunburn. Eventually, I do drift off with thoughts of needing to call home tomorrow.

CHAPTER TWENTY ONE

Turbo search

Monday. Day 21.

Mendoza, standing at the chart, cannot believe that the instrument continues to place Athena at Golfito. He confirms what he already knows that there has been no movement for this the third day. Angered and frustrated, he returns to his deck. By his earlier calculations, today or certainly no later than tomorrow, the boat should have been in the Bay of Panama. *What is holding them at Golfito, of all places, over two hundred miles behind schedule?* he asks of no one.

He lifts the receiver from his desk telephone and dials a sequence of numbers. Leaning back in his chair he closes his eyes while the instrument dials and a connection is made. "Bueno," a male voice answers.

In Spanish, Mendoza asks to speak to Ernesto who after several minutes, comes on the line. Mendoza asks if he has anyone in Golfito who he can trust to do a favor. Answering yes, he is told to contact him to determine what is delaying Athena. Mendoza instructs Ernesto that his man is not to make any contact with the boat. He ends the call by saying he wants a quick response.

Mendoza, in an uncharacteristic decision, decides to leave his office where he normally would spend the morning. Secretly he admits that he does not want to have to talk with the cartel who will certainly be looking for an update.

The morning hours are quietly spent by Paco, Roger and I performing a variety of maintenance and household tasks while Allen continues to locate a rebuilt or new turbocompressor. Still not feeling well, but working with his contact in San Diego, they do locate a replacement. They decide to first have it shipped to San Diego to verify that it is the correct make and model. It will be tomorrow before we will know the outcome.

14:00. After lunch, Paco and I return to Orosco's where we are told that the alternator will not be ready until tomorrow or perhaps Wednesday, that the steering cable assembly will be arriving on a morning flight tomorrow and the turnbuckle is ready. Carlos hands it to Paco with a smile, obviously quite pleased at the results. I am amazed with the outcome. It looks shiny and new, but more importantly both stem pieces turn freely inside the barrel.

Carlos, learning of our engine problem, tells Paco that he has a good friend who has a Volvo marine dealership in San Jose. A telephone call by the mistro confirms that in all probability he does have what we need but will require specific information on the year of manufacture, the model and part number.

Buoyed by the prospect of a quick solution to our troubles, Paco and I return directly to the boat to obtain the needed information. Allen is skeptical but decides that there is no harm trying. At Orosco's, the mistro telephones his buddy who promises to have word back to us by morning.

Taking our well-traveled route, we walk to town unable to find a taxi. I ask Paco to join me for a beer at the hotel bar. We are hot, sweaty, dry and in my opinion deserving of a cold beer. As I had hoped, Winter is bartending. I introduce her to Paco before sliding onto the same stool from my previous visit. "I figured you had left," she says after taking our orders.

"No not yet. We may be able to leave soon, depending if replacement parts arrive to fix our broken engine."

"Well, I'm glad you're still here," she says with a smile while placing our drinks on a napkin before us.

"Salud," I say to Paco raising our bottles in a good health toast. The beer goes down smooth and easy in a most refreshing way.

"What have you been doing with yourself?" she asks.

I briefly recap yesterday's exploration of the bay and how I came upon the woman at Captain Toms. "That is his wife," Winter confirms. "She still lives out there on the acre of ground he purchased in 1962. She is somewhat of a recluse, only seen rarely, mostly in town when she comes for groceries."

"She did speak to me. I thought she might be of oriental decent."

"No, she's Costa Rican, dumb like a fox."

"There appears to be a ton of history here. How would one go about learning more of it?" I ask her.

"Not to boast, but I'm as knowledgeable of the history of the area as anyone. If you'd like I'll spend time with you."

"Wonderful. When?" I ask, delighted with the offer.

"Wednesday afternoon, meet me here at one o'clock."

"If we are still here," I say thanking her. I pay our bill and return to the boat. Allen I learn has developed a bad case of diarrhea together with stomach cramps and a bad headache. He has confining himself to his cabin.

Roger has prepared a dinner of ham steak, mashed potatoes and a vegetable. He has baked dinner rolls and a white vanilla cake. We eat in the main salon rather than in the cockpit, hoping not to disturb our leader, who we sorely miss.

I do scullery duty after having sent Paco and Roger to the TV lounge where they find a James Bond 007 movie on cable. I am able to listen from the galley before joining them with cake and ice cream.

22:00. I peek in on Allen before retiring. He says he feels somewhat better but continues to have to run to the head.

"I have Imodium AD in my kit. Nurse Pat placed them there for just such an occasion." Without allowing him to decline the offer, I go for them. He takes one tablet without complaining.

I say goodnight before going to my cabin where I prepare for bed. I'm a little worried about Allen so decide to set my alarm for two AM in order to check on him. I read for a few minutes before snapping off the reading light and drifting off into a restless sleep.

Day 22. Tuesday.

02:00. Allen, I find is resting comfortably. Relieved, I return to bed where I sleep soundly until 06:30 when I again check on him. I find him at his desk on his computer. He admits that he continues to have diarrhea and flu like symptoms. I have him take an aspirin and Imodium while I fix a cup of hot tea with honey. He asks me to go up to Kitty's for any information from San Diego.

"Bad news, I'm afraid," Kitty says handing me a fax.

I read that the turbocompressor received is not the correct part for our model engine. The broker advises that a second one is coming from a dealer in Minneapolis.

"Allen is under the weather," I inform her.

"What's wrong?"

I explain his symptoms and what we have done for medications.

"I didn't think he looked well yesterday. Would you like me to look at him?" she asks. "I have a small amount of medical training."

"Yes, please."

She informs her helper Maria, a young Costa Rican girl that she will be back shortly. Taking a small bag, we walk to the boat where we find Allen stretched out on his bunk in a cold sweat. He tries to make light of his condition but Katie knows differently. I watch as she takes his temperature and pulse and listens to his heart and chest. She politely asks that I leave.

I step outside, closing the cabin door. Paco and Roger are at the settee with concerned looks. I tell them what I know while slipping in beside Paco to wait. I show them the fax from San Diego.

After several long minutes, Kitty emerges from below. "Allen has a good case of the flu together with what I suspect is a touch of food poisoning. After learning where you guys ate the other night I am surprised that you are not all sick. He needs rest, plenty of liquids and an aspirin every four to six hours," she states. "I'll come back to check on him at noon." We thank her as I see her to the cockpit door.

I spend the morning polishing bright work while Paco and Roger install the turnbuckle and retune the standing rigging. I also reinstall the window covers to help keep the cockpit cooler.

While eating lunch Allen joins us. Bedraggled and weak, he asks, "What is the status of the turbocompressor?" I show him the fax, explaining that I am hoping to hear more later on today. "What about the one from San Jose?"

I explain that Paco and I plan to go to Orosco's after lunch.

Kitty comes on board where she scolds Allen for being out of his cabin. She takes his temperature and pulse. Her prognosis is that continued rest and fluids are necessary. "I think you'll feel much better tomorrow, if you will stay quiet today."

"Keep me apprised of any developments," Allen says, returning to his cabin.

I walk with Kitty back to her office having asked if she will call Orosco to get any information regarding the turbocharger from San Jose. I learn that her Spanish is excellent. After several minutes she covers the mouthpiece to speak with me. "Orosco's friend confirms that he has the needed part and will sell it for $650.00. He stipulates that the total amount must be placed in his Banco National account, refundable if the part will not fit or is not what we need. Once acknowledgement of deposited funds is received, he will ship via the commuter airline."

"How do we get the money to his bank?" I ask.

"There is a branch office locally that will accept the deposit and notify his branch immediately. It is early enough in the day that there should be sufficient time for the transfer by this evening. You probably can have the part on the first flight in the morning."

"Please tell Orosco that I will need to get approval. I'll get back to him as quickly as possible."

Kitty relays my response and thanks him for his help.

"Is Allen well enough to be going to a bank?" I ask. "He controls all of the Athena's money."

"I wouldn't want him to take the chance," she answers. "There may be an alternative," she continues after a short pause. "If Allen will agree, I'll put up the money."

"Let's go ask," is about all I can say.

Without much discussion or resistance, Allen gives his approval. "Bob, you should accompany Kitty in the event there are complications," he says. She offers to drive her Honda Accord to the branch office that is located approximately one mile beyond Orosco's shop. The bank is little more than a doublewide mobile home with room enough inside for two tellers and a manager. Much as at Coco, you are required to take a seat and advance from chair to chair until reaching the front of the line. Our wait is fifteen minutes. Kitty explains in Spanish to the young man seated stiffly at the desk what our needs are, together with her identification, the two bank account numbers and the dollar amount of the transfer. Gathering the items, he excuses himself to confer with the manager who eventually asks that we come to his desk. Kitty and he know one another and the transaction is completed smoothly and quickly. Outside she says, "I should have anticipated the need to go to him. The first fellow is not trained for this high finance."

We stop at Orosco's to ask that he telephone his friend with the transfer information which he does. He then informs Kitty that the part can be expected on tomorrow mornings flight arriving at ten." Uno momento," he continues while going after a cardboard box containing the repaired alternator. Handing it to me I ask for the factura (receipt) knowing I have no money to pay. He tells Kitty that I should not worry about payment for now.

After thanking him we drive back to the boat where I thank her for her help. "That's what I'm here for," she says with a smile. On board Athena, I find Paco to give him the alternator. Allen is asleep in his cabin while Roger is reading, stretched out on the TV lounge floor. I decide to relax in the settee where I can read and relax.

✍

"Engine trouble. What sort of engine trouble?" bellows Mendoza into the telephone receiver. Impatiently he listens as Ernesto explains what the informant has conveyed to him.

"How long will they be there?"

"It is difficult to know. They are waiting for parts."

"Keep me updated," says Mendoza dropping the receiver into its cradle.

Nervously he plays with a paperweight from his desk while attempting to decide his next move. He fully understands that he can no longer escape not talking with his cartel contact. Resigned to the inevitable, he places the call. Sweat breaks out on his forehead as he places the headset to his ear.

"Bueno," says a voice.

"Bueno, this is Mendoza."

"We have been waiting for your call. Is everything in order?"

"Not exactly," Mendoza responds. He explains the situation attempting to remain calm and in control. "My people tell me that the boat is safe and that once the new part is received they will be back underway," he states in hopes that this will satisfy the needs of the cartel.

"The merchandize must be at its destination at the prearranged time, otherwise there will be grave repercussions. Do you understand?"

"Yes," replies a deflated Mendoza.

"Do whatever is necessary to assure its delivery as specified in our instructions." The line goes dead.

Mendoza sits in shock, unable to concentrate. He reaches in his bottom desk drawer to withdraw a bottle of tequila. Removing the cap he takes several long swallows.

18:00. Roger prepares dinner for three. Allen joins us for a few bites of nourishment before Kitty stops, pronouncing him "on the mend." Following dinner and galley cleanup, I watch TV for a while until deciding to excuse myself to walk to the marina office.

Using the outside pay phone, I place a call to Pat. Initially upon hearing my voice, she is fearful that something is wrong before I can assure her that everything is fine. I explain the unscheduled stop together with our quest for a replacement part. She tells me that she has had no further contact from the FBI and things at home are normal; however, I can sense her loneliness. We chat for over fifteen minutes before signing off with love and kisses.

Reflecting on the early hour, I walk up to the hotel bar where I slide onto my favorite barstool. There are but a few people here tonight and no Winter. The barkeeper, a man whose name I learn is Bill, turns out to be her father who tells me that she has the evening off. I order a beer to relax and watch the view from above.

"I understand my daughter is playing tour guide tomorrow?"

"Yes, I'm interested in the town and it's peoples history."

"Good, then she'll fill you in on what you want to know."

"This seems like a strange place to raise a family," I say after several minutes.

"Not really. When I first came here, this was as good a place to live as any place in the United States. Things have of course changed over the years but still we feel the living is good. By leasing this bar and restaurant it provides us with a decent income. We return home once or twice a year to visit family, see a doctor and have our teeth cleaned."

"What brought you here initially?" I ask.

"The United Fruit Company."

"What did you do for them?" I continue.

"I was hired as a chemist, fresh out of college to work in a laboratory developing insecticides to control banana pests. Another beer?" he asks.

"Ok," I answer as he walks to the cooler at the other end of the bar. The restaurant has had several new arrivals. "Here you go," he says before returning to fill a drink order for the lone waitress.

"Hello stranger," comes the familiar voice of Winter from behind. She slips onto the empty stool beside me. With a wisp of a smile, she asks, "May I join you?"

"Of course," I answer.

"Are we still on for tomorrow afternoon?"

"Yes, I believe so," I answer, feeling a little awkward at having such a pretty gal show me so much attention. "Can I buy you a drink," I'm finally able to ask as Bill comes back towards us.

"Sure. My usual, please," she tells her Dad.

"He has been quite informative, explaining how he happened to come here and his working for United Fruit."

"I tell him that he needs to write a book. He is one of a handful of American workers still living that can tell the story."

"Are you two conspiring against me?" asks Bill delivering Winter's drink.

"Nothing more than what we have talked about before," she answers.

He shrugs his shoulders while departing to the other end of the bar.

"Give him a tape recorder and have him talk to it if he feels uncomfortable with writing things down," I offer.

"He is so impossible. At times, I question whether he would even do that."

"Then you need to be the repository of his stories and recollections," I say gaining some self-composure. "I sense there is a lot of good reading material here that needs to be told."

"I'm sure you're right," she answers before offering a toast.

We sit in silence for several minutes watching the passing foot traffic below as well as Bill's activities behind the bar.

"How are the repairs coming?" she asks breaking the interlude.

I offer a quick update, concluding with our hopes that the part from San Jose will fill our needs. "If the part comes on the morning flight and fits, we may not have time to get together before you depart," she comments.

"I doubt that we can be ready before Thursday," I respond. "We have fueling to take care of and I would discourage us going until Allen is feeling one hundred percent."

"What's wrong with him?"

"He has the flu, complicated with diarrhea from apparent food poisoning."

"How are you and your Mexican friend feeling?" she asks.

"Fine, we seem to have escaped."

"I'm glad."

Glancing at my watch I realize I need to return to the boat.

"I'll walk part way with you, if you don't mind."

I pay the bill and thank Bill for his hospitality. Winter and I descend to the street level before turning right onto the narrow sidewalk to follow the curve of the street leading down the incline to the main road. She slips her left arm through my right pulling me tight to her side as we weave in and out of theoncoming foot and bicycle traffic.

We stop at the intersection where she stops to explain, "This is the physical center of the south part of town known as Pueblo Civil. The northern part, which we will visit tomorrow, was the Zona Americana and where the administrators of United lived. As a kid growing up, we seldom if ever came here. It was considered too dangerous because of the number of bars and brothels that prospered along these two streets. But, I'll explain all of that and much more tomorrow. Good night." With that, she gives me a kiss on the cheek and slips away into the crowd, leaving me alone to walk the short distance to the marina.

On board I find that all is quiet. Both Allen and Paco are asleep while Roger occupies the TV lounge, stretched out on the floor. Upon seeing me he raises up on an elbow. "I was beginning to worry about you."

"I walked up to the hotel for a beer and the time got away." I inquire about Allen and am told that he has been in his cabin the entire evening. We chat for a few minutes before I say good night and retire below. I am in bed and asleep in quick order.

Winter hurriedly walks to a tiny storefront bakery where she steps inside. Although the store is closed and in semi-darkness, she moves with ease to the rear of the shop. A cloth curtain hangs in the doorway that she quickly brushes back to reveal a man and woman seated in their living room. Without pausing she addresses the man, "Ernesto, I have updated information for you." The woman rises to leave.

The man listens as Winter relates her latest findings regarding Athena's mechanical difficulties. "Also the captain is sick and may not be able to leave until Thursday even if the part fits."

"Do you think you can get onboard?"

"I don't know," Winter answers.

"You will need to smuggle the package off. My instructions are that the merchandise must be in Panama no later than this Monday."

"How do I do that, may I ask?"

"That is for you to figure out. You have two days in which to bring this about. If caught, you are alone. Good night."

Careful not to be seen, she steps back outside into the night air deciding to head for home. She feels confident in her ability to succeed in this assignment as she has in the past. But, she needs time to think and plan.

CHAPTER TWENTY TWO

Winter

Day 23. Wednesday.

06:30. Despite the urge to be lazy and remain in bed, I rise and prepare myself for what I anticipate will be a busy and interesting day. I find little activity by my shipmates, although someone had made coffee not long ago.

Allen tells me from his cabin that he feels better, but admits he is weak from the ordeal. He remains below.

08:00. After a light breakfast I walk up to Kitty's where I ask her what time the flight from San Jose can be expected. "Ten fifteen is the first flight, then another at two."

She volunteers to call Orosco to ask that he contact his friend for the arrival information. While waiting for the reply I tell her about Winter and my highly anticipated tour of the town with her.

"I know who she is, but have never met her. She and her family are old timers, so she should know her way around. I understand they own the bar over the hotel."

"I believe so," I comment.

"She is known around town as someone not to cross or disagree with."

"Oh," I say rather surprised at Kitty's frankness. "How come?" I ask.

"People who have been in conflict with her have been mysteriously beaten up and/or slandered. I'm told she is vindictive if she doesn't get her way."

The telephone rings before I am able to pursue my questioning further. It is Orosco saying that the part will be on the early flight. I thank her, deciding to leave the other matter alone for now.

Back at Athena I inform Allen of the part arrival time and suggest to Paco that we leave for the airport within the hour.

09:30. At the road we are able to catch a taxi without much delay. We join two local women who make room for me in the back seat. They smile and giggle as I first peer inside and then somehow shoehorn myself into the small area left of the seat. I find it necessary to ask Paco to close the door, as I am unable to pull it shut.

Thankfully they get out after a short distance, allowing me to once again breathe normally. Paco and the driver are regaled in laughter as we resume our course towards the airport.

Travelling the now familiar road, the only road for that matter, we enter what must have been the American zone as explained by Winter last night. There is design and order to the passing scenery where evenly spaced stately palm trees line the wider paved roadway, together with hedges of bougainvillea, groomed grass and flowering bushes. Individual white stucco houses pass in parade, set well back across wide lawns from the road. A hospital and schoolhouse pass before we turn left to follow a road that crosses an open space preceded by a sign that says, 'beware of golfers.' Shortly we come to the modest single story red roofed terminal building together with an empty hanger building both adjacent to the partial dirt and grassed runway. I fail to see anything resembling a control tower, however I do notice a windsock placed atop the hangar.

We ask the driver to remain while Paco and I go inside the terminal building. Not surprising, it is very small. A ticket counter is set along one wall with the daily arrivals/departures of the single airline, Sansa, serving Golfito listed on a board behind. A check of the arrival board shows that our plane is on time, about ten minutes away.

We return outside to pass the time and explore the grounds. As expected, I find that the airport also serves as part of the golf course. Several yards from the terminal building I find a carved wooden marker signifying the number five tee box. Looking out on what I guess is the number five fairway I see another wooden post in the distance. Walking out to it, it turns out to be a yard marker. In this case it has the number two hundred clearly carved on the side facing the fairway, signifying the distance to the green. Continuing to walk ahead I realize that as I approach the green, I am paralleling the runway. The greens apparently were nothing more than where someone decided on any given day to place the flagstick. There is no difference in type or quality of grass from the fairway. Six-barrel palm trees surround the green, but no sand traps or other hazards.

Searching for the number six tee box I hear the engine sound of the aircraft approaching from the south. I watch as the pilot lines the twin engine turboprop up with the runway together with reducing power and lowering landing gear and flaps. It has always been a tremendous rush of adrenaline for me at this point in landing a plane, whether I'm watching or flying one. Seconds later it gracefully touches down, a puff of dirt from the main landing wheels before rolling past me towards the terminal building.

The part is indeed on the aircraft and by the time I walk back it is off loaded and in the care of Paco. There were several passengers on board, one in particular I recognize as Special Agent Weber. Wishing not to be seen, I hurry with Paco to the waiting taxi.

Anxious to install the part, we drive directly to the marina where Paco takes it onboard and goes below to the engine room. He unwraps the part to learn that it is dirty and well used, not new as we had been told. After cleaning it of grease and dirt, he attempts to install it with Roger's help. I stand off to the side in an effort to watch but not interfere. In attempting to place the part on the mounting plate of the engine, it is quickly obvious that it is too large in diameter. Paco tries several times to make it fit, but to no avail.

"Don't torment yourself," says Allen, having come down from his cabin, "there is no way that will fit. Send it back."

Frustrated and angry, Paco prepares the part for return. I convince him to have lunch before taking it to Orosco's. "It can go nowhere until tomorrow," I explain.

Following Allen to his cabin, I tell him of my sighting of agent Weber. "I do not think he saw me. My guess is that he believes he is here undetected."

12:00. During lunch, Kitty brings a fax with good news from San Diego. The turbocompressor shipped from Minnesota has reached San Diego and has been confirmed that it is what we need. It will be booked on a flight to Los Angeles, connecting to Miami then on to Panama City arriving early Friday morning. "Getting it from Panama City to here will be a problem," Kitty says. "There are no direct flights from Panama into Golfito. I'm surprised your agent didn't realize that."

Without hesitation Allen writes out a reply to San Diego for Kitty to send asking that the part be consigned to Patrick Foley, his agent in Panama. He and Patrick will figure out a way to get the part to Golfito.

With lunch finished and the boat squared away I discuss my plans for the afternoon with Allen. "Have fun," he says still looking tired and weak.

Roger joins Paco to return the part. I share a taxi with them on their way to Orosco's. I disembark at the town center and walk up to the bar where I find Winter waiting. She is dressed in a halter-top, shorts and tennis shoes. Her hair is tied back in a small ponytail, a pair of sunglasses set atop her head.

"Are you ready to go?" she asks.

I answer in the affirmative.

We descend to the street level where she leads me to a parking area next to the hotel for two wheel vehicles. "I hope you don't mind riding double with me," she asks while unlocking a moped. "It's the easiest and cheapest way to get around."

She wheels the machine around to face the street before mounting it with ease and grace. Turning the ignition key, the small engine comes to life with a puff of blue smoke from the exhaust. Lowering her sunglasses, she guns the engine by a twist on the handle bar accelerator with her right hand. "Come on, get aboard," she says looking towards me over her left shoulder.

"I won't bite."

I swing my right leg over and settle onto the narrow black seat behind her.

"Put your feet on the bars below, your arms around my waist and hold me tight."

She engages the clutch, applies power and away we go down the street from the hotel to the main road where we make a right turn. My heart skips several beats as she accelerates the machine to a high speed along the rough road. "Our first stop is at my house. So relax and enjoy yourself," she says sensing my tension as her ponytail twitches my nose.

We travel north passing Orosco's, the bank and many other now familiar sights. I do manage to relax some and before long we enter the wider, smoother streets of the American Zone. "These are known as banana company homes," she says pointing to rows of single-story white houses with their characteristic extended roof overhangs. Several have shutters and window air-conditioners. All are on good-sized plots of grass and landscaped grounds, set well back from the road.

Winter slows as we approach a cross street. She swings right onto it, accelerating again before pulling into a gravel driveway taking us to one of the single story white wood house perched on stilts.

"Hold still," she says as she drives the moped across the lawn to the side of the house where she parks under the house. Dismounting I am surprised at how much cooler it is here than out in the open. "This space is where cars and boats were kept by the previous owners," Winter explains. "This was, over the years, the typical home for many white collar workers of United Fruit and their families. It is quite unique. Follow me."

She leads to the front where a wide set of stairs rise up to the main level and to a magnificent set of carved, polished mahogany doors. Unlocking the right hand door, she invites me inside. My eyes take a few minutes to adjust from the bright sunlight to the semi-darkness. Winter closes the door before sweeping past me. "Come along," she says leading me towards the back of the house. Following her, as my eyes adjust, I see that we are in a wide wood paneled hallway from where the other parts of the house can be entered, both left and right. Colorful throw rugs are randomly scattered on the hard wood floor accentuating the handsome paintings on the walls.

At the hallway end, she opens the door to a 1950's era kitchen. For me it is like stepping back in time. "Wow," is all I am able to say repeatedly as I walk about. All the appliances are matching white enamel, together with a soapstone sink, black and white square floor linoleum and a tin ceiling. Four ceiling fans, each with white paddles driven by a wide leather belt from a concealed electric motor, whirl from above.

"Can I offer you an ice tea?"

"Please," I answer. "I'm amazed that anything like this would be found here."

"There were many of these homes built, part of the incentive package to find and keep managers," she says handing me my tea. "Come let me show you the rest."

There are two bedrooms, one bathroom, a living room and the kitchen. She concludes the tour back in the kitchen where we sit at a chrome leg table. "I thought you might enjoy seeing this."

"Tell me, how did you come to acquire this house and do you live here by yourself?"

She explains that it was her parent's residence for many years and it is here that she grew up. She bought it from the Cost Rican government after United deeded it to them in 1985 and "yes, I do live here alone."

My history lesson of the area begins with an explanation of United's move to the Golfito region in 1938 after banana diseases, depletion of good soil and massive labor strikes led it to abandon its plantations in Limon. She explains how Golfito became a major part of the company empire and a main shipping port to the world, building the huge loading dock that could handle 4000 bunches of bananas per hour and a 246-km railway from the plantations in the surrounding valleys. "The company constructed houses and barracks for its employees, schools, a hospital, stores, a dairy farm, even an airport and a golf course. About 15,000 people migrated here from throughout the region to work for United. By 1955, over ninety percent of the nation's banana exports were shipped from here. In its heyday, Golfito was a crowded, steamy banana port."

"Your Dad said he was a chemist?"

"Yes. He joined a team of research chemists embarked on vigorous projects to conquer tropical diseases such as malaria and dengue fever. His laboratory also worked very hard to conquer the specialized diseases of the banana plant."

"Were they successful?"

"Yes, to a degree. Where once whole areas of bananas were wiped out by diseases these labs developed specialized insecticides and fungicides to halt the problem. Some of these laboratories are still at work today."

"So tell me, what happened to end all of this prosperity?"

"In a word, profits. Production costs increased over the years coupled with violent labor conflicts. The Costa Rican government raised its export tax on bananas and the Pacific markets of California and Japan were considered too small. The company changed its name to United Brands before running into financial difficulties during the 1970's. United Brands stopped production and moved out in 1985 leaving most of the facilities they had constructed to the state. UFCO's lands were bought by the Del Monte Corporation, which now operates the former holdings, converting to African Palm Plantations. The clustered palm fruits are pressed to produce oil used in lards and margarine, unfortunately palm cultivation doesn't require much human labor, so it has not relieved the unemployment caused by United's departure. In an effort to revive Golfito's economy, the government in 1990 opened a duty free zone located not far from here."

Glancing at the large clock on the wall, she announces that we need to go if we hope to see everything. Stepping outside, the heat and humidity of the afternoon takes my breath away. Only the breeze produced by the moving moped offers any relief as we zip along to our next destination. I find I am now more relaxed and able to anticipate Winters next twist or turn.

Before long she reduces speed to enter a gravel parking lot and comes to a stop. Leaving the moped we walk across an open grassy area to where she points towards a large black net suspended high above a grove of towering palm trees held in place by a labyrinth of metal pipes. Moving closer, Winter explains that this is a wild bird sanctuary constructed by United Fruit and now part of the wild life preserve. "If fact," she continues, "all of what you see here belongs to the National Wildlife Refuge."

The sanctuary is alive with a wide variety of brightly colored birds. They swoop and dive in a kaleidoscope of color, remaining in constant motion. We watch intrigued for several minutes before returning to the moped to resume our journey. She points out the Olympic size swimming pool and the tennis courts as she guides the moped through the center of the neighborhood. "These were popular recreation attractions as well as the eighteen hole, par three golf course that surrounds the airstrip," she explains. "I spent many a happy hour as a kid at these facilities."

Next she swings into the grounds of a hotel. "This is one of three hotels for tourists coming to the refuge and to the tax-free zone," she says as we park the moped to walk along a stone pathway towards the front entrance. We step inside to the front desk, a cocktail bar and restaurant to the rear. She explains that this was the social center of the American Zone before becoming a hotel. "The restaurant and bar were well used by the employees, families and visiting guests of the company. It was subsidized and cost very little to eat and drink here."

Our next stop is briefly at the former headquarter offices and warehouses of United Fruit now used primarily by the vendors of the tax-free zone for storage. "Dad's laboratory and office was in there," she says pointing to a two story metal building that is now the home of an electronics vendor. Circling the complex, I am surprised at its small size. Winter explains that because the bananas never stopped here from the fields as they went directly to the loading docks for immediate shipment, these were administrative offices for the several dozen managers required.

Within a short distance, we arrive at the tax-free zone, where we again park the moped and walk. The complex, an outdoor mall ringed by a circular concrete wall, is several acres in size comprising of eight to ten metal buildings each measuring, I estimate at two hundred feet in length and twenty to twenty-five feet in width. The buildings are arranged in groups of two, each facing into a common courtyard or plaza. Stores and shops are subdivided within the buildings with as many as fifteen spaces under one roof. A majority of the spaces offer high-end or high-ticketed home appliances of televisions, VCR's, video equipment, furniture, refrigerators, stoves and microwaves. Others have jewelry, watches, cameras, perfumes and toiletries while others focus on hard liquors, wine, mixes, etc. A few are set up to sell groceries of canned goods, sweets, cake and pie mixes.

The competition among the vendors is fierce. The salespeople stand outside their doors like barkers at the circus, stressing how good the values are inside. Without going inside, all the stores appear to be offering the same merchandise.

Winter explains that a permit is required by the tourist/shopper in order to buy merchandise. The permit, although not expensive, requires a twenty-four hour waiting period before it may be used.

"Why is that?" I ask.

"Its intent is to keep you in town where you will spend money on food and lodging while waiting."

"What I don't understand from walking and looking around is where are the people coming from that theoretically can afford these items? Certainly not from the town of Golfito or from the North Americans who are not here. What I have seen today are mostly locals."

"Ticos," she answers. "From San Jose who come to buy manufactured goods imported from Panama without the one-hundred percent tax normally levied."

Walking to the moped, I ask, "I notice how when people see you, they shy away. Why is that?"

"I'm an American, considered by many as a throwback to 'La Yunai' as United was called. There is a resentment and nostalgia against those who ran the company, including my father. I've lived with this for years."

Our next stop is at the huge loading dock with its four mammoth loading conveyors standing silently at attention. Supported by an elaborate rail system, they are able to travel the length of the dock in tandem or individually, servicing several cargo ships simultaneously.

"Rows of track ran parallel to the dock allowing several trains to offload together. At one time the train ran parallel with the main road through the center of town and along the water's edge," explains Winter. "An old steam engine is on display in a park close to the hotel. Have you noticed it?"

"Yes, I have seen it on several of my walking trips."

We leave the moped to walk along the deserted dock. The low shadow of the Osa Peninsula shimmers in the distance as the sun sparkles off the waters of the bay, Golfo Dulce. Winter takes my left hand and pulls me towards the loading dock edge where we sit with our legs dangling out over the side. The temperature is quite pleasant as we are shaded by one of the giant cranes together with a cooling breeze off of the bay.

"How do you get to Captain Tom's from here?" I ask.

"From back at the duty free complex where there is a road. Would you like to go out there? I should have asked earlier."

"No. I believe I saw enough on Sunday."

"Perhaps another time."

"This has been a very pleasant afternoon," I say after a long interlude of silence. "I cannot thank you enough."

"I do have a favor to ask."

"What is that?" I ask.

"I'd like to see your boat before you leave."

"I will have to ask Captain Daniels. I don't see any problem, but may I ask why?"

"I've never been on a boat of that size. I'm curious I guess. Nothing more. If it is a problem I will understand."

"Tomorrow, say about noon?" I ask.

"That will be fine. Now it's time for me to go to work."

Heading southwest towards town we pass the multi-level hospital, also built by the company. It too has the original style of the local construction. "A new emergency ward and operating room were recently completed, as well as waiting rooms and doctor's offices," I'm told.

The road gets rough as we enter Pueblo Civil. We pass the Catholic Church; a two-story white stucco building featuring Moorish shaped windows and a multicolored steeple where a traditional gold cross stands aloft. A cemetery is located behind where the round gold domed structure seen from Athena upon our arrival sits. She explains that this area of town is known as Barrio Bella Vista, (beautiful view.)

16:30. She drops me off at the marina with a quick kiss on the cheek. I promise to let her know about tomorrow. I watch as she maneuvers the moped out onto the busy street and disappears into the crowded afternoon traffic.

The boat is wonderfully cool after so many hours out in the hot sun.

"How did it go?" asks Allen as I peek into his cabin.

"Very well." I tell him of her house, the tax-free zone and some of the other things I had seen. "She would like to see the boat tomorrow."

"What did you tell her," says the familiar voice of agent Weber from the darkness of Allen's cabin.

Startled by his unexpected presence, I need a minute to answer; "I told her I didn't think it would be a problem."

"This may work to our advantage," says Weber coming forward to shake my hand. "Good to see you again."

"I was sure it was you getting off the airplane earlier."

"Have you told anyone else?"

"Only Allen."

"Good. Let me bring you up to date," says Weber. "First; however, do you have anything cold to drink?"

I scramble above to return with a bottle of cold water.

"Should we bring in the others?" asks Allen.

"Good idea," says Weber while wiping his brow.

I go above to where I find Paco and Roger watching TV in the lounge.

The five of us convene in the settee where Allen introduces agent Weber to Paco and Roger. Weber starts by cautioning us that his being in town needs to be kept quiet. He continues, "I believe that the heat is about to be turned up by the cartel. We have intercepted two telephone calls; one between Mendoza and a male contact here in Golfito named Ernesto and another between Mendoza and an unidentified cartel member. In them we learned that an effort to remove the package from the boat will be attempted soon." Weber pauses for a swallow of water and to allow his words to sink in. "Before coming here, I stopped at the Golfito Police station where I made inquiry of all males known as Ernesto. Luckily, there is only one, a baker who owns a shop in town and is considered by the police as 'suspect' with ties to the local Mafia. Nothing serious, mostly petty stuff like roughing up folks who he says had not paid him for purchases on credit. They feel confident that he has someone else do the dirty work for him."

"Were they able to give you a name?" asks Allen.

"Several actually, but one in particular sticks out, a woman named Winter."

My mind goes numb for several seconds unable to comprehend the implications.

"She like Ernesto has been a suspect in a number of beatings and strong-arm tactics. It is known that she frequents his shop often, where his house is located in the rear, usually late in the evening after dark. Another thing is that she seems to have more money than what a bar-maid might earn, even though her family owns the bar."

Katie's words resonate around in my head.

"Bob, did she display unusual curiosity about the boat and/ or you guys?" asks Weber.

"Not really. Her only interest came when asking to see it tomorrow."

"She will need to be watched very closely. Captain, do you carry weapons onboard?"

"No, I don't. We do carry a flare gun which at close range can be deadly."

"Ok. Make sure it's handy and loaded. Better that you be prepared than caught off guard."

"Where will you be?" asks Allen.

"I will be right up there," he says pointing towards the marina office. "I have a room overlooking the water where I can watch your every movement." He pauses before continuing, "Allen, I suggest you resume your watch schedule so that there is someone awake around the clock. This may be over kill, but something tells me that this gal is our main threat."

"What can we expect she'll do?" I ask.

"Good question. I think she's too smart to try to lift the package in broad day light, rather I see her role tomorrow as familiarizing herself with the boats layout in order to return under cover of darkness."

"How will she know where to look?"

"By deduction. She knows who has the package, now she needs to find out where he lives."

"Should you take the package for safe keeping?" asks Allen.

"I don't think that would be smart. If in the event she gets the upper hand forcing you to relinquish the package, I'd rather lose it than lose you."

"Have you seen the contents?" I ask Weber.

"Yes, it was what we were doing upon your arrival."

"Can you place a value?"

"Admittedly, I am no expert; however, what I do know about gems would lead me to believe that this stones value is in the millions."

"Why do you think the cartel chose this method of moving the gem?" asks Allen.

"It was not the cartel's decision as much as it was Mendoza's. He, I believe, stumbled on the idea of using Athena when he learned of your intended trip to Panama. He was betting that no one would bother a private boat in transit with an American Captain. Once Roger agreed, he inserted the radio tracking device in the package and rewrapped it. It was a clever plan and might have worked if it were not for the anonymous tip we received."

The four of us look at one another, each with a grin. It would seem that Roger's summation earlier had nailed it.

"When should we start the watch schedule?" asks Allen.

"Right away. When is your watch, Bob? "

"I have the nine to twelve," I answer.

"Good. I would suggest you go for a beer about eight o'clock and attempt to determine if she has an ulterior motive in wanting to come aboard. Find out her work schedule for tomorrow. She just may give you some indication of her plans."

I ask Allen if he has told Weber about the Gaston envelope.

"Yes, Allen passed it over to me earlier," Weber responds. "I plan to alert the Bureau in my next communiqué and ask for directions."

Paco excuses himself saying he needs to check on dinner he is preparing below.

"Would you care to stay?" asks Allen. "Paco makes an awesome fish dish from Dorado he caught last week."

Weber happily accepts the invitation. He and Allen remain at the settee while Roger and I set the table in the main salon. Paco serves baked

Dorado together with potatoes, onions and carrots acclaimed by all as "outstanding." Dessert with coffee is served in the cockpit settee for the start of the first watch; Allen's six to nine.

After galley cleanup, I go below to my cabin to shower, change clothes and stretch out on my bunk for a brief interlude of silence. I nod off for five minutes; waking refreshed and rejuvenated something I've been able to do for years in order to recharge my battery.

19:30. In the cockpit above I find Allen alone, reading at the settee. He indicates that Weber has left and everything appears quiet.

"I'll be back to relieve you as close to nine as possible," I say.

"Not to worry. Do what is necessary, I'll be here."

The evening air remains hot and humid. The quarter mile walk to the bar brings a slight bead of perspiration to my forehead where I find my favorite stool empty. No one is at the bar including Winter and only a few folks are in the restaurant. After several minutes she emerges from the kitchen with a tray of food. "I'll be right there," she says looking over towards me.

"What's up?" she asks from behind the bar. "I didn't expect you tonight."

"I needed to stretch my legs after dinner, so came this way."

"I'm glad. Can I get you a beer?"

"Please. I enjoyed myself this afternoon."

"Me too," she says, bringing a cold Bud.

"Are you a sailor?" I ask.

"What do you mean?"

"I figure you must have an interest in boating to ask to see ours."

"Oh, I see. Well, I'm really no sailor. My interest is simply to see the inside of a boat and where you live and work while on the water for long stretches of time. If there is a problem, I'll understand and not come."

"No, there is no problem. We are looking forward to having you."

"I admit that given the opportunity, I would like to sail away, especially under the right circumstances."

"Like what?"

"Maybe with the right guy."

"Have you been married?" I ask.

"Yes, just briefly. It was a huge mistake that neither of us will forget."

"That's too bad. What happened?"

"He was twenty years older than I, a womanizer and a gambler. Need I say more? However, he did teach me a few lessons about life and I got a nice alimony settlement."

The conversation turns to her life in Costa Rica where she admits to living a carefree, bohemian life style of nonconformity.

"I've always been independent and outspoken where people avoid and shun me, but I don't care. It's the way I am."

She excuses herself to check on the patrons in the dining room.

"You certainly don't exhibit any outward signs of being inhospitable as a waitress," I tell her upon her return.

"I keep it under control, for my father's sake."

"Not with me."

"Thanks, I like some people better than others." She leans over the bar to pull me towards her and kisses my check. "I do like you," she says.

She leaves as two men come to the other end of the bar. I gather they are here to sport fish from what I can hear of their conversation. Their exchange with Winter is lively with a splash of sassiness, all seemingly in good fun. I watch her while turning the information over in my mind, trying to make sense of what to believe.

With my beer finished, I pay the bill and say good night. It would be easy to remain, but that would lead to another drink and further delay in relieving Allen.

The town is quiet, the street nearly empty as I make my way home. There are a few shops open, but not like on the weekends. The marina too, is virtually deserted, only a few boat show interior lights.

Rounding the marina office, I am startled by movement from a dark corner. It takes the shape of an individual who steps forward into the eerie yellow illumination of the dock light. My heart skips several beats before I recognize the facial features of special agent Weber. "Sorry if I scared you. I saw you coming and wanted to ask what you may have learned."

I explain that her interest in the boat is to see where the living spaces are located on the premise that she might one day take a boat trip. As for money, she says she received a "nice alimony settlement" from a busted marriage.

"What do you think about her? Is she our villain?"

"I'll be very disappointed if she is."

"Did she mention that she is wanted for questioning in the States?"

"No."

"I thought not. Goodnight. See you in the morning," he says returning to the shadows.

"I just now spoke with Weber on the dock," I tell Allen, repeating what I told him.

"What are his feelings?"

"I think she is his main suspect."

I relieve Allen. "Call me with anything," he says, going below to his cabin.

21:30. I note the time in the logbook. Both Roger and Paco are below watching a movie as I start the watch that goes without incident.

At midnight Roger relieves me. We spend several minutes discussing my visit with Winter. He questions me about her physical appearance, having not met her. I give a brief description before saying, "You'll meet her tomorrow. I don't believe she will bother us tonight."

Tired, I say goodnight and go below to my cabin where I quickly prepare for bed. No reading tonight; I snap off the light but lie awake turning the events of the day over in my mind. I eventually do fall asleep.

CHAPTER TWENTY THREE

The Sting

Day 24. Thursday.

07:00. I roll out of bed after a night of unrest. I wash, dress and head for the galley where I make coffee before joining Allen in the cockpit. He is looking more like his old self. He confirms that he is feeling much better.

"Was there any activity during the night?" I ask.

"No, very quiet."

09:00. After taking over the watch from Allen, he informs me that he is going to walk up to Kitty's office. "I want to telephone Patrick and discuss how he thinks it's best to get us the part," he says stepping out through the cockpit door. I watch him make his way along the dock and up the ramp, relieved to see the familiar bounce back in his step.

The watch proves uneventful; my time spent reading and watching Paco and Roger wash the boats exterior.

10:30. Allen returns, looking none too happy. Settling into the settee, he says, "Good news, bad news. The good news is that Pattrick will ship the part after its arrival tomorrow to the airport at David, Panama. David is located just over the Costa Rica border, about thirty-miles from here. The bad news is that we will have to go for it ourselves."

"Sounds simple enough," I say.

"Yes except that you are forgetting customs and the import duties required."

"No, I had not considered them."

"Kitty is checking with a friend who is an import/export specialist for advice and directions."

Changing the subject I ask, "Do you have any thoughts for when our lady arrives?"

"You need to be the tour guide. You call the shots. Show her what you think may be of interest to her. She is after all, your guest."

"Have you seen or heard from Weber?" I ask.

"No. He is keeping a low profile."

Roger relieves me a few minutes before noon enabling me to ready myself for Winter's arrival. At 12:15 I begin to worry that perhaps she is not coming. 'Had I misunderstood the time?' I ask myself.

Minutes later I see her coming down the ramp from the street above. She hurries along, dressed in white shorts, a yellow short sleeve blouse and white deck shoes. Her auburn hair held in place with an elastic headband.

"Welcome aboard," I say extending my hand to help bring her through the lifeline opening and onto the boat deck.

"Thanks," she says giving me a polite kiss on the check. "I'm sorry for being late."

"Not a problem. I have all afternoon. Where would you like to start?"

We elect to remain outside where I describe Athena's characteristics as to length, beam, draft, height and sail design. "She is one of a kind, built in Great Britain for the charter business," I explain as we walk the deck perimeter ultimately stopping aft under the sun awning. Here I show the inflatable and how it is raised and stowed on deck.

"What are these?" she asks pointing to the deck hatches.

"They lead down to the swim platforms where guests can swim, snorkel, scuba or water ski."

"Nice, I would enjoy a vacation with activities like that. Can you enter the main part of the boat from down there?"

"No," I respond, knowing full well that access is possible. She does not press the issue, seemingly satisfied with my answer.

We enter the cockpit where I introduce her to Roger, now on watch.

"I'm glad to finally meet you," she says in shaking his hand. "You're the only one I've not met."

"Hello Mamm. It's a pleasure meeting you."

Remaining on the bridge, I point out the navigation aids, engine instruments and controls before taking her to the chart table and logbook. Her interest seems genuine as I describe their various functions.

Next, we go below into the main salon. "It's beautiful. I had no idea," she comments as she stands beside the highly polished dining table. "And look over here," she exclaims, walking towards and stepping up into the TV lounge. "This is gorgeous, the fabric colors are wonderful."

Following my lead we move into the galley.

"Have you had lunch?" I ask.

"No, but I thought we might go somewhere later."

"Let's see," I say unsure if I want to accept the invitation.

"Where do you all sleep?" she asks.

I explain that there are three staterooms and three crew compartments that provide sufficient space for a charter of six passengers.

"Where is your cabin?"

"Follow me." We exit the main cabin to follow the passageway beside the port engine room, stepping into Paco's and my shared head and then into my cabin. "Here it is, small but ample," I offer as she looks around.

"I'd call it cozy."

"How do you get in and out of bed without banging your head?"

"You crawl on your hands and knees or slide on your behind," I say as I demonstrate by wiggling onto the bunk, butt first. Not totally surprising she does likewise causing us to fall backwards, collapsing as one in a tangle of body parts. Turning towards me her mouth smothers mine, her tongue extending inside. She shifts her weight to roll on top, her hands probing at my crouch. I feel myself grow in desire as she unzips my shorts. Unable to free herself of her tight shorts, she pulls away to roll off of me and on to her back where she easily slips off both shorts and panties, revealing her auburn pubic hairs. Reaching up she pulls the blouse off over her head to expose her well-formed firm breasts and pink nipples. She turns on her side towards me, her hazel eyes flashing with excitement and expectation. For a moment the temptation to take her is over-powering. She is unquestionably a very desirable woman, but we both recognize in the next instance, it is not to be.

"I'm sorry if I suggested in any way I, ..." She places her right index finger over my lips to silence me.

We linger for a few minutes in a silent embrace.

"Let's get back before we are missed," she says sliding off the bed to dress.

"If you need to use the restroom, I'll wait outside."

"Thanks. I'll only be a minute."

She joins me to return to the main salon where Paco has prepared a light lunch. "Will you join us?" he asks. "We are all at the settee."

"Thank you. It all looks so good," says Winter apparently now opting to eat on board.

With plates full we go above, sliding in to where Allen was seated before excusing himself to return to the galley.

"Welcome to our house," says Paco raising his soda can.

"Cheers," she replies. "It appears you fellows eat quite well."

"I believe that's a fair statement," I respond with a nod of agreement from the others.

Allen returns with a generous supply of food. "I believe I'm regaining my appetite," he says with a wink.

The conversation centers on our trying to learn as much about her as possible without being obvious that we think she is a suspect. In most part she answers our questions willingly and with an easiness that has me partially convinced that she is innocent of our suspicion. Slowly however, she turns to become the inquirer, asking questions of the boat that would suggest she has some knowledge of boating. I'm surprised by Allen's willingness to tell her where his cabin is located as well as invite her in to see it. Paco, Roger and I, while clearing the settee and cleaning the galley, comment that perhaps she has won him over or is he the fox luring his prey to the den.

"Thanks fellows, I enjoyed your hospitality," she says upon returning to the cockpit with Allen. "I want to invite you tonight to the monthly gathering of expatriates at the restaurant. It is very informal, cocktails and snacks. The group is quite small at this time of the year. Come about seven o'clock."

I walk with her to the moped in near silence. Without fanfare she says that she hopes to see me this evening and is gone. I watch her disappear into the rush of afternoon traffic as a feeling of emptiness surrounds me. I stand at the roadway for several minutes before starting my return to the boat.

"Wait up, Bob. I'll walk with you," says Kitty coming from her office. "Was that who I think it was?"

"Yes. She wanted to see the boat, so I gave her a tour. Are you and Tim going to the expatriate get-together this evening?"

"I doubt it. We don't fit the mold. Did you get an invitation?"

"Yes. I'm not certain that any of us will go however."

Reaching the boat, we enter the cockpit to find a full house. A stranger has come aboard joining Allen, Roger and Paco on the settee. "Come in and join the discussion," says Allen. To my complete astonishment, the stranger is none other than agent Weber in a very clever disguise. He has changed his appearance with a bushy mustache and a long hair wig under a cap. Wearing a ragged pair of shorts and a faded T-shirt, he has taken on the look of a boater.

"What do you think, Bob?" Weber asks. "Can I pass for a yachtie?"

"You certainly fooled me until I got up close."

"It provides me with the ability to move around without raising suspicions."

Allen speaks, "I didn't expect to have a meeting, but here we are. Let's have Kitty's report on import duties."

"Simply put, my man tells me that the procedure for legally bringing the part into Costa Rica can be time consuming, several days minimum and quite expensive." She pauses before continuing, "Now, as I understand it, the part you have coming is of a medium size and weight," she states.

"That's correct," Paco replies.

"Can it be disassembled in some way and brought back in pieces?"

Paco and Allen look at each other, the wheels turning inside their individual heads. Their joint opinion is that it can.

"Then his recommendation is that you simply go get it, take it apart, conceal it in your luggage and bring it back with the hopes no one gets wise."

"You mean smuggle it back?" asks Allen.

"Call it that if you wish."

For a minute there is silence around the table as all eyes turn towards Allen.

"I'll need to give it some thought," he says, "especially with a US federal agent in our presence."

"I'm here on a different matter," says agent Weber. "I haven't heard a word."

Kitty, feeling her duty done, excuses herself to return above. "Thanks, I'll let you know what my decision is," Allen says walking her to the door.

After a pause to allow Allen to reseat himself, Weber asks, "How did it go with the visitor?"

I provide a recount of what I showed her and what we talked about omitting the interlude in my cabin.

"What is your impression? Is she our threat to steal the package?"

"I wish I knew for certain. She may be using me to get information and to win our confidence. For someone without an ulterior motive, she has spent a lot of time wooing an old married guy that cannot possibly be of any interest to her except as a means to a higher goal."

"Our intelligence suggests that she is a player in a local Mafia group with ties to the underworld, most notably a cartel from Columbia."

"You mentioned that she is wanted for questioning back home. What for?" I ask.

"Interstate trafficking of illegal goods."

"Why haven't the authorities done anything about it?"

"She is only a small player. With patience, we believe, she will lead us to the bigger players."

"Do you believe she will make her move tonight?" asks Allen.

"Yes. Time is running out for her. I believe she will come aboard when she feels everyone is asleep. She knows the boat layout and by now has decided where and how to enter."

"How so?" I ask.

"I'm not certain. It is unimportant, what is important is that we make it as easy as possible without raising her suspicion. Do you normally lock the cockpit door at night?"

"Yes," answers Allen.

"Leave it unlocked tonight. Leave whatever night-lights are normally left on. Whoever has the watch should be well concealed"

"What happens after she is aboard?"

"I will be responsible for apprehending her once on board," answers Weber. "My goal will be to sequester her for questioning before turning her over to the local authorities for trespassing. Understood?"

Each of us answers in the affirmative.

"For now, it is business as usual. Any questions?"

"What about this evening?" I ask.

"If you wish to go, I have no problem."

"Do you have any information you can share with us about the envelope given to me by Gaston?" I ask.

"I can say nothing more than that he is dead."

"Dead, what happened?" I ask.

"He took his own life. The Coast Guard report states that he swallowed a cyanide pill while being raised up to the helicopter. He was dead before they could strap him in."

"And the others?"

"They are fine."

The meeting concludes.

Allen and Weber depart the boat to go to the marina office. They look like two old fishing buddies as they meander up the ramp with stops to look and point at items of interest. I would like to hear their conversations.

Paco has the watch as I curl up in the settee with a book while Roger goes below.

Winter parks the moped in the hotel parking lot and walks down to the bakery now closed for siesta. She steps inside and proceeds to the rear door where she peeks inside to the sparsely furnished room. "You are taking a chance coming here in daylight," says Ernesto from a corner.

"I'm here to buy bread, if asked. Why did you send for me?"

"We have a visitor in town, a US federal agent. He's been snooping around, asking questions about you and me. I thought you should know."

"I know. He came in yesterday and is staying at the marina."

"Do you know his mission?"

"To safe guard the delivery of the package to Panama."

"Why?"

"He is in hopes that the package will lead to the cartel's big wigs."

"What are your plans?"

"I don't feel the risk of going for the package is worthwhile. We are playing hardball with the United States Government and that puts a new light on the situation. The package can stay on the boat until Panama as far as I'm concerned."

"Mendoza will not like this decision."

"He can go to hell, or come down and do it himself."

"I'll let him know."

"Not for the moment. I could change my mind. See you later." She departs the store but not before taking two loaves of bread.

My arrival at the bar is met with rounds of welcome handshakes and hellos from the ten or so couples in attendance. Winter acts as my escort and hostess making me feel comfortable and welcome. I learn that all are North Americans, either from the U.S. or Canada and all live in banana company houses that they purchased from the Costa Rican government. All are my about my age, retired and living here year round with occasional visits home to children and grandchildren. They tell me that living expenses are less here than "up north" with little or no loss of comfort or services.

The social hour passes quickly with most attendees leaving to return home or have dinner elsewhere. Being in no rush to leave I sit at the bar on my favorite stool to watch the traffic below while Winter helps clean up from the gathering.

"Are you in a rush to leave?" she asks.

Indicating that I am not, she suggests we go sit in the restaurant. We find a table to the back where we can enjoy privacy but she can see up front. Her body language tells me that she has something on her mind as she fusses with rearranging the salt and pepper shakers while having difficulty getting comfortable in her chair.

"I need to talk to someone I feel comfortable with and I can trust. I trust you," she finally says.

I thank her for her confidence and ask what is on her mind.

Very much to my complete surprise she confesses that she has been planning on breaking into the boat to steal a package. She explains that this is not unlike other services she has performed over a period of years for a variety of individuals, none of whom she has met. The money paid her has been very good, enabling her to enjoy many comforts she otherwise could never have been able to afford. It started as petty thievery, but of late has escalated to far more serious crimes of violence and theft. "I know that the guy who flew in yesterday is an FBI agent which tells me that whatever is in that package is hot. I don't want to go to jail for the rest of my life over something like this. What should I do?"

Studying her face and eyes, I ask if she is willing to speak to the authorities about who is paying her?

"As much as I know, which isn't much."

"Are you sure? This is a big step. Should you at least speak with your Dad?"

"My Dad knows nothing of this. This is my own decision."

"I suggest we go to agent Weber and see if he will make a deal."

"Where and when?" she asks.

"I'll go get him and bring him here if you wish or we can go to him at the marina."

"Not here. Is he there now?"

"I'm sure he is."

Starting to cry she puts her face in her hands. "I'm scared, really scared for the first time in my life."

Reaching across the table I hold her hands in mine.

"What will happen to me?" she asks.

"It is impossible to say. I believe that you coming forward will help agent Weber in his recommendations to the authorities back home."

We remain at the table several minutes while she composes herself. "Ok, I'm ready, let's go," she says regaining her old confidence. We walk rather than ride to the marina, her arm through mine as if we were out for a casual stroll. A delightful breeze coming off the bay makes it a comfortable time to be out doors. Neither of us speaks, as we both are absorbed with our individual thoughts.

Arriving at the marina, we stop at the office where I step inside. I learn that Weber is not in his room, leaving me to believe that he is already on board. We make our way down to Athena where I suggest she remain in the shadows on the aft deck.

The cockpit is empty. The boat is as quiet as a church mouse. I call for

Allen as I approach his cabin. Startled, he bounces out of his bunk asking what is going on. "I need to find Weber, quickly," I respond.

"I'm not sure where he is."

Without explaining, I leave him to duck down into the main salon that I find empty. Panic-stricken I bound back up into the cockpit and quickly exit to the aft deck to discover that Winter is not where I had left her. I repeatedly call her name in hopes of finding her nearby. My stomach turns over as I frantically search the entire fantail.

"Bob, we are over here." It is the voice of Weber from the direction of mid-ship.

Going forward I find him and Paco standing at the lifeline with a handcuffed Winter. "What is going on?" I ask.

Weber explains that although he saw us come on board, he wasn't certain what was happening and so when I went inside he approached her but because she resisted, he handcuffed her.

"Is that so?" I ask.

"He came upon me so fast from the dark that I panicked."

"Have you told him why we are here?"

"I haven't had the chance."

I suggest that we go inside where I will explain. I convince Weber to remove the handcuffs before entering the cockpit. Allen greets us with an inquisitive expression. Paco excuses himself to retire below. The four of us slide into the settee. I bring Winter a bottle of water and damp towel to help settle her nerves. Weber starts a tape recorder he places in the center of the table. I provide a recap of our earlier talk at the bar together with her willingness to confess her intention to steal. I don't attempt to embellish her statements; however, I do try to put as positive a spin on them as possible.

Weber sits and listens, stone faced. He offers little in the way of a sign of his feelings. Finally I run out of gas and stop talking. Winter has remained in silence, as has Allen. For several minutes there is total quiet except for the evening breeze buffeting against the cockpit windows.

Weber breaks the silence by asking if she is doing this of her own free will, which she answers in the affirmative. "Ok, here's the deal. If you'll provide the names of those you know within the cartel and cooperate with the investigation, my report will recommend you receive the maximum possible leniency."

She looks towards me, her eyes asking for my advice. I assure her that Weber can be trusted. "All you need to do is tell the truth."

"Alright," she responds, knowing her fate is sealed.

Weber asks Allen and I to leave them alone, explaining that it is for our own protection.

"Call me when you're done?" I ask. "I'll be outside on deck."

Allen joins me to sit on the large storage locker under the sun awning on the fantail. "This has turned out to be a quite an interesting evening," he says.

"I'll say. Not what I had expected."

"You have developed a strong relationship with her. You are to be congratulated."

We remain silent both in our own thoughts.

"I've been thinking," he says. "I believe it may be best that you and Paco go for the part tomorrow. Do you have a problem with that?"

"No," I respond.

He explains that if Paco and I run into trouble, his remaining behind will provide a better chance of bailing us out. "Once I get the particulars from Peter in the morning, I'll decide who goes and when." Glancing at his watch, he stands to excuse himself for bed. After several steps he turns back towards me. "Did I mention that Athena may have been sold?" he asks.

"No. When and where?"

"Not totally sure, but possibly in Panama as soon as we get her there."

"When did you learn of this?"

"Earlier this afternoon from the bank. It was your fellow, Matt that brought the deal to the table. Small world, huh?"

I'm overwhelmed and speechless. So many questions flood my mind that before I can sort them out, Allen is gone. I conclude that he probably doesn't know any more either. My questions will be answered in due time. More importantly for now it is a matter of waiting for the meeting inside to conclude.

Time drags as I remain seated with my arms folded and my head bobbing about as I slip in and out of sleep. Now well past midnight, I long for the comfort of my bunk below. Occasionally I sneak a peek inside to assure myself that they are still talking.

"We are done," says Weber, waking me with a hand on my shoulder. I snap into consciences, startled and embarrassed, realizing that I had fallen hard asleep. He invites me inside where Winter looks relieved and smiling. She motions for me to sit beside her where she slides her arm around mine to take my hand. Allen emerges from his cabin to join us.

"We believe we have struck a good accord," says Weber. He explains that in exchange for her testimony, he is releasing her on her own recognizance. I squeeze her hand in celebration. "It is to be business as usual however. She does what she normally does as if this meeting never occurred. Additionally, she has agreed to stonewall any and all informa-tion about her plans to take the package until after the boat departs, then she will admit that she was unsuccessful in removing it."

"What if they seek retaliation against her?" I ask.

"It is our feelings that she won't be bothered in a harmful way until you leave. Afterwards she is entering protective custody as soon as I can arrange it and returning to the United States for arraignment."

Although there are several additional minor items discussed, the meeting concludes shortly thereafter. Weber excuses himself saying that he has considerable paperwork to do in his room. Allen says his good night and retires to his cabin. We sit alone for several minutes before I escort her back to the bar, now long closed, to her waiting moped. She wraps her arms around my neck to pull me close. "Thank you for every-thing," she says. "You are a good friend. Now get on the back."

"Why? What for?" I ask.

"You don't think I fell for all that bullshit back there do you? You and I are going back to the boat and you are going to get the package and bring it to me."

"And just how do you expect me to do that?" I ask.

"No one will expect you. You will simply get it from where ever it is and bring it to me."

"I don't know where it is," I respond.

"I believe you do. Now let's go or else."

"Or else what?"

"You will not see your family again."

Unlike the Winter I thought I knew just minutes before, this is a very different, determined woman.

"Just what does that mean?"

"You really do not want to know, but suffice to say, I have the ability to see you and your family hurt."

So the rumors about you are true?"

"Then more so for you to cooperate with me. Get on the back or I'll make you wish you had."

Feeling I have little choice I mount the moped and settle in behind her. She turns the ignition key. The little engine cranks and cranks, but will not start. Again she tries, but the result is the same.

"It is of no use, it will not start, comes the familiar voice of agent Weber from behind us. "I have disabled the machine."

Like a cat, Winter leaps off of the machine and runs. Another fig-ure, equally as fast appears from the shadows to join Weber in the chase. Together they head her off before she reaches the sidewalk where she is quickly subdued, handcuffed and led to a parked automobile where she is placed in the back seat.

"Are you OK?" asks Weber of myself.

"Yes," I respond. "You had her figured out all along, didn't you? You never believed her. Right?"

"Let's just say that there were several gray areas about her story that didn't add up."

Weber's accomplice joins us from the car.

"Bob, meet police Chief Arturo Romano."

"My pleasure," I say with a handshake.

"I have been watching her for months," says the chief, "suspecting she was working for the cartel but was never able to prove it."

"I'll call you in a few days to finalize extradition papers for her return to the United States," says Weber. "Thanks for your help."

"My pleasure," says Romano as he walks towards the waiting car. I catch a glimpse of Winter as the overhead light illuminates the car's interior. She is not a happy camper.

Back on board, I find the boat quiet. I leave the door unlocked and leave the cockpit light on. I peek in to check on Allen who I find is awake and invites me to join him. Knowing nothing of the bazaar events of the past hour, I fill him in.

"It doesn't surprise me," he says after my discourse. "I had a feeling that Weber wasn't buying her story."

"Well, I'm glad it is over," I say. "Perhaps we can all get some rest."

"Don't forget, we have a turbo-compressor pickup to contend with yet."

"I nearly forgot. I am off to bed," I say excusing myself.

I go directly below to my cabin and quickly prepare for bed. I wonder how all of these evening's events will play out. I am in no mood to read so snap off the overhead reading light. Exhausted, I listen to the sounds of the night and Athena before sleep overtakes me.

CHAPTER TWENTY FOUR

Stinky

Day 25. Friday.

07:30 Although tired from the late evening, I am up and about in anticipation of yet another busy day. Washed and dressed I stop at the cockpit en route to the galley. Allen, seated alone in the settee, offers his morning greetings. I ask if I can bring him anything from the galley. "No, I'm good," he replies, "However, I'd like for us to get together after you get your coffee."

Paco and Roger are assembled upon my return. Allen gets right to the point. He has decided that Paco and I will go for the turbocompressor.

"You'll leave at noon, crossing the border before one o'clock where they should be a bus departing for the airport at one o'clock. I estimate the travel time as an hour and fifteen minutes to the airport where you'll be met by Patrick Foley's agent. Paco thinks it should not take more than one and one-half hours to disassemble the unit, pack it and be ready to return. Do not come back across before five o'clock, well after the border crossing guards shift change at four. This should reduce the chances of your being recognized by the same guards who were on duty when you entered. I suggest that your excuse for entering Panama is for sightseeing. Each of you will take a duffel bag in which to carry the parts back in, filled with the stinkiest clothes in your possession that hopefully will deter customs from conducting too thorough a search if you are stopped." He provides us with the name and description of the man we will meet at the airport together with sufficient money. He elects to omit the issue of what we are to do if caught and apprehended.

I pack my stinky bag, borrowing several of Paco's dirty clothes for the right aroma. I make sure I have my passport and dress comfortably for

218

what I anticipate will be a hot and sticky drive. I eat a light brunch, drink lots of water and generally try to relax.

At noon Allen and Kitty walk us to the street to wish us well. "We'll expect you back between seven and eight," says Allen as we load into the waiting taxi that will take us to the Costa Rica/Panama border.

Our driver is Orlando Espinoza, who together with his brother Cirilo, own the taxi and have been selected by Kitty to provide transportation. "Good luck," she says as they wave goodbye.

Travelling on the two-lane road from town, we parallel the bay to its end before turning east for several miles to join up with the Pan American highway that takes us south. The roadway is in surprisingly good condition allowing Orlando to travel at a good rate of speed taking us through a mixture of villages and towns not unlike those I've seen in Mexico. The topography of the land changes from the hills and lush flora of Golfito to flat, treeless rolling plains. Moving away from the water has increased the outside temperature by several degrees. The cab, unfortunately, has no air-conditioning. Now it is really hot.

Before long we enter the dusty border town of Paso Canoas, a sleepy village whose principal existence would seem to depend on the border station located on the south of town. Once through the town, Orlando pulls over to the roadside and stops several hundred feet from the border crossing.

"I will be over there for you tonight after six o'clock," he says, pointing across the street.

With my duffel bag slung over my shoulder, I follow Paco to the gray single story corrugated metal building where the flag of Panama flies in the afternoon breeze on a handsome aluminum pole at the entrance door. Inside, we find our way to the immigration section where I fill out the necessary form and present it to a uniformed gentleman seated behind a glass enclosure. Apparently satisfied after only a cursory look at my passport and then at me and that I pose no threat to his country, he stamps the form and my passport allowing me to enter the country. At the window beside me, Paco is also admitted without question.

Outside we walk to a kiosk to buy tickets for our desired bus departing within ten minutes to San Jose de David. I learn from a brochure that David is the official name of Panama's third largest city.

Before boarding, I purchase a cold Fresca. There are but a few passengers, allowing us to occupy seats across the aisle from one another. The bus is air-conditioned, providing a welcome relief from the outside heat. On schedule the driver closes the door and pulls away from the loading area to enter the busy highway that remains the Pan-American. *So far, so good*, I say to myself.

The brochure describes David as the hub for the province's commercial activities, mainly agriculture and cattle raising with an estimated population of 124,500. It is the capital of the province of Chiriqui known for its flower and coffee highlands of Boquete and Cerro Punta. It serves as the port of exports and imports with neighboring Costa Rica and is connected to the rest of the country by the Enrique Malek airport.

Paco and I for the most part, remain silent, each in our own thoughts. From my window I watch as the countryside rolls past. The flat land creates vitas of open space to the horizon. The brochure calls this the coastal plains or low lands of western Panama, hot and humid most of the year.

The city of David appears slowly at first but before long we are in the outskirts and then the suburbs. Leaving the Pan American highway we swing onto a wide tree lined paved road leading, according to the many road signs, to the airport. Passing through an industrial area of manufacturing and light industry, the bus arrives at the airport entrance and proceeds to the passenger departure area where we get out.

Inside the modern steel and glass structure, we follow the signs to the baggage claim area located on the floor below. At the foot of the escalator, a man carrying a placard with "Daniels" displayed catches my eye.

Indeed he is our man who motions that we accompany him to a small room reserved for our needs and where the turbocompressor waits.

Paco wastes no time in unpacking the unit and verifying that it is what we need. The deliveryman, John and I stand aside as Paco, with tools brought from Athena, disassembles the unit. He carefully places the seals and O rings into plastic bags before removing and wrapping other component parts, leaving the single largest item, the compressor casing, as the heaviest and bulkiest. He first wraps it in paper before placing it inside his duffel bag secure amongst his clothes. The other parts are intermingled in the clothing and place in my bag along with his tools in preparation for leaving. The process has taken just over one hour and a half. We thank John who then dissolves into the crowd of people.

Returning to the main floor, we find the bus kiosk and purchase our return tickets. Unfortunately, we find we have an hours' wait having just missed the four o'clock bus that would have taken us directly to the border. The next bus makes a stop at the central station in downtown David. We consider taking a taxi, but decide against it. Finding comfortable seats we relax with soft drinks and candy bars to help pass the time.

The bus departs on time taking us into the city with a stop at the downtown bus terminal. I note that David is not a particularly pretty city. There are but a very few pleasant parks or green spaces or buildings with any pleasing design features. It is a faceless city I conclude, with little to compel me to return.

There are a considerable number of riders returning to the border requiring Paco and I to place our bags overhead. Mine is comparably light and I have little trouble, but Paco's is heavy and requires extra effort by him.

Once settled in, we relax for the one-hour plus ride back over the same terrain as we had traveled earlier. Again, I note the barren landscape, devoid of trees and houses or anything else for that matter. On the distant western horizon under a lowering sun is the spine of the Sierra Madre Mountains covered now in a purple haze. I actually relax enough to doze off for a few minutes.

Arriving at the border, we wait to be last off. We are in no rush, noting the time as 5:45. Wrestling with the heavy bag we manage to load it on Paco's shoulder in as unassuming manner as possible. Entering the single story customs office, the procedure to leave the country is simply a matter of relinquishing our immigration papers to a smiling official.

Next, we proceed to a similar style structure that houses the Costa Rica customs and immigration officials, a distance of several hundred feet. A welcome to the country sign stands beside a flagpole where the Costa Rica flag flies in the strong afternoon breeze. We find and complete the proper forms before queuing up for the next available agent.

"How long do you stay in Panama?" asks the uniformed man seated behind the glass enclosure after a careful scrutiny of my papers and passport.

"Only a few hours," I respond spontaneously. I know better than to lie because he has my stamped passport showing my arrival time into the country.

"What is purpose of your visit?" he probes.

"Pleasure."

"Why were you in Panama for so little time?"

"My friend and I were sightseeing."

"Where you stay in Costa Rica?"

"Golfito."

Apparently satisfied or totally confused, he stamps my passport and form allowing me to re-enter his country. Paco is processed without question.

Bags are being randomly checked by two disinterested uniformed customs agents from among the steady stream of pedestrians filing through the two isles towards the exit doors. Paco and I put on our most innocent of faces and join the procession of folks who appear to be transients, each carrying little in the way of luggage or packages. We decide to split up. I go first as Paco follows, intermingled with ten people behind me. Our timing seems good as one of the agents is involved with a bag, leaving the other one as our only obstacle. Without wishing to make any eye contact, I look straight ahead and stride confidently towards the exit doors.

"One momento, Señor," calls the officer in my direction. I pretend not to hear him; but his second command, clearly meant for me, gets my attention.

"What is in the bag?" he asks after I place it on the examining table that separates us.

"Dirty clothes," I answer.

"Open, please."

I unzip the duffel bag, revealing the jumble of dirty clothes. He steps forward and asks that I spread it open so that he can look inside. The odor from within is overwhelmingly bad causing him to step back from the table. For an instant I fear he is going to have me empty the contents, but alas he does not.

"Go, go," he says while directing me towards the exit. Casually I zip closed the bag, walk to the exit and to a waiting Paco outside.

"That was close," he says as we move towards the taxi.

"I'm glad he picked me."

"Why, don't I have an honest face?" Paco asks with a boyish grin.

"It would not take him long inside your bag to find the casing, that's all."

"But my bag is stinkier."

We both laugh: much relieved.

Orlando is waiting as expected and ready to depart. Once inside the taxi and underway I begin to relax, confident that we have been successful. It has been my first and hopefully last smuggling venture.

The return trip to Golfito is uneventful with us arriving at the marina at seven-fifteen. Orlando, I learn has been previously paid for by Kitty. We thank him for his service. "Anytime I can be of assistance, just call," he says as I exit from the back door.

The boat is quiet as we come aboard.

"Hola, you're back," says Allen coming from his cabin to the settee where we have placed the two bags. "How did it go?"

"No problems," answers Paco while unpacking the parts. Together we give him a brief description of the afternoon events expounding on the wisdom of taking the stinky clothes that saved the bacon with customs. Once our debriefing is completed, Paco and I take the parts below to the machine shop for reassembly. Like at the airport, I remain mostly out of Paco's way but am able to hold the flashlight and help in small ways. Allen joins us in the small non air-conditioned room that provides me with the needed excuse to leave. "Oh, I almost forgot," Allen says. "Winter's dad was by and expressed an interest in seeing you before we leave."

"Any idea where I might find him?"

"Undoubtedly at the bar."

"Am I needed here for an hour or so?" I ask.

"No; however I want an early start tomorrow."

20:00. I shower and change clothes before walking into town. The streets and sidewalks are busy with the evening rush of shoppers. Reaching the hotel, I climb the stairs to the bar where I find the bar is full of young men that appear to be on a sport fishing party. The restaurant is busy as well. I see Bill behind the bar who asks me to be seated.

"You'll be leaving in the morning?" he asks after several minutes of delay in waiting on customers.

"I believe so."

"I wanted to tell you that there are no hard feelings towards you for what has happened to my daughter. It was going to happen sooner or later."

"Did you have any inkling of her activities?"

"Yes and no. But I felt that as she was an adult, I should not interfere with her private life."

"Are you alright with her leaving?" I ask after several minutes.

"Yes, although I will miss her."

"I just hope it all works out for you and her."

"I should go," I say. "I have lots to do."

"You are welcome. Have a safe trip home."

I find my three buddies on the settee upon my arrival back onboard. I learn that the turbo-compressor has been successfully installed and tested. The water pipe however, repaired by the mistro, continued to leak at the weld but was repaired by creatively replacing it using a length of high-pressure hose.

Secondly, I am told that Weber and Winter have flown out to San Jose. Thirdly, we must vacate the dock by early morning as the marina had earlier booked reservations for an incoming boat, requiring this space. Fourthly, the port captain cannot be found to sign us out of the country. Best guess by Kitty is that he is drunk somewhere and probably will remain so for the weekend. Lastly, we still need fuel.

Allen determines that come morning we will anchor off the marina and use the dinghy to shuttle back and forth to shore. It is clear that we will not be leaving early in the morning as once had been expected.

Realizing I am hungry from no dinner and little for lunch I go below to heat a can of soup together with several hunks of bread with butter. It is filling and satisfying.

23:00. As the watch schedule has been cancelled; I say goodnight to Allen and turn in. Despite my best efforts to read, I am unsuccessful, as I am unable to keep my eyes open. Giving up, I snap off the reading light and fall quickly to sleep. A content and satisfied feeling engulfs me.

Day 26. Saturday.

06:00. First light. The port engine turns over and starts. I ready myself for the day. I peek into the engine compartment to learn that there is no leak and that the turbo compressor appears to be functioning. After several additional minutes to allow the engine to reach normal operating temperature, the hose continues to hold. Allen declares the repairs successful until we reach Panama. The starboard engine is started so Paco can do a leak check. We make final preparations to leave for the fuel dock.

07:00. Paco, Roger and I release Athena's tie downs as Allen maneuvers us away from the marina and towards the Texaco fuel basin. As early as it is, we are confronted with several boats already in line for fuel. Paco raises the dock master on VHF who explains that it will be an hour or more before he can accommodate us, suggesting we return later. Feeling there is little in the way of an alternative, Allen takes us to a position off of the marina at mid channel and has Paco drop the anchor.

07:30. With the anchor down; Allen has the dinghy launched in preparation to going ashore. Taking the ships papers, he and Paco depart, leaving Roger and I to make Athena ready for departure. There is little to be done, as the boat has been ready for several days. We double check the safety equipment and make certain that there are no loose items. Window covers are removed and stored as before.

10:30. Allen and Paco return with the news that we have a twelve-noon appointment for fuel. "Not at the fuel basin," informs Allen, "they want us at the cargo dock where they will have a fuel truck." He further explains that the harbormaster is still missing.

"What happens if he doesn't surface?" I ask.

"I'm not totally sure, but somehow we are going to leave this place today."

11:45. We stand off the giant cargo dock to wait. A rising tide has us ten or so feet below the top.

12:30. No fuel truck. Paco uses the VHF to call the fuel basin. He is told that the truck has a mechanical problem and they are unsure when it can be fixed. They will call when they know more. We return back on the hook off of the marina; we can do little more than wait. We eat lunch and try to relax.

14:30. Kitty calls and asks that Allen come to her office. I accompany him as Paco is asleep and Roger is involved in a movie.

Kitty explains that the port captain remains nowhere to be found. The best guess is that he is gone for the weekend.

"I have an idea," she says with a whimsical smile.

"What is it?" asks Allen. "I'm desperate."

"I can forge a document by whiting out the name on a Xerox copy of another boat and type in Athena and change the date."

"I need to call Patrick to determine whether it will be accepted in Panama."

Katie places the call and fortunately locates Patrick in his office. She puts him on the speakerphone. "What the hell have you gotten yourself into this time Daniels," he asks. Allen and Kitty explain.

"It's a Xerox copy because you lost the original. Right? Hell yes, I can deal with it."

"See you in a few days," Allen signs off. "Go for it," he instructs Kitty. "I'll have it for you in an hour."

We decide to walk to the Texaco station rather than return to the boat. The dock master explains that the truck is expected to be ready sometime soon. He will call.

"Can I buy you a beer?" asks Allen. "We may as well wait here rather than return to the boat."

"Sure," I respond, somewhat surprised that he would have a beer knowing how much he wants to get underway.

We walk up to the virtually empty hotel bar and order a beer served by a middle-aged woman who we learn is Bill's wife. She turns out to be a very likeable gal with a bubbly personality. She tells us that she has been married to Bill for only a few years and hails from California. Her name is Peggy. There is no mention of Winter.

Allen's handheld VHF crackles to life with the voice of Kitty indicating that our paperwork is ready. "Now all we need is fuel," says Allen before calling the fuel dock for a delivery update only to learn that there is no new news.

Paying the bill we walk to Kitty's office where Allen obtains the clearance papers and settles our account. We say our good byes with hugs while wishing she and her husband continued success.

18:00. On board, Allen makes one last attempt via VHF for a fuel delivery time. "In the morning, Senor. 06:00 at the cargo pier."

19:00. Dinner is prepared by Paco with dessert by Roger. I clean the galley and prepare it for an early morning departure.

21:00. I watch TV but before long say goodnight and go below to prepare for bed. I slip in under the covers with a feeling that the next few days will be busy. I drift off to sleep with very little effort being thankful that we are about to leave.

CHAPTER TWENTY FIVE

Golfito to Balboa

Day 27 Sunday

05:30. The mornings wakeup call comes from the rumble and vibration of the port engine cranking over and starting.

Quickly I roll out of bed, dress and dash above to join the guys in the cockpit. Following a quick safety check, we raise anchor and proceed to the cargo dock.

06:00. As we approach it in the mornings first light; the fuel truck is visible as a faint outline. I feel like cheering in near disbelief.

Once secured, two attendants pass down the fuel hose to Paco and Roger while Allen and I plot waypoints on the navigation chart for the journey south.

07:00. Fueling completed. Allen pays and thanks the men who without fanfare release Athena from the final bonds of Golfito.

07:10 Underway at long last. 'Seven days and seven nights in Golfito,' sounds like the title to a book. This steamy former banana port with its many characters will stay in my memory for years to come. I remain outside on the deck as we motor north. The bay is quiet on this partly sunny Sunday morning, too early for pleasure boat traffic.

We turn to port at the southern white buoy to align ourselves with the markers to the open water. Seeing no traffic to interfere with our passage, Allen is given the ok to proceed.

07:35. We pass through the narrow channel and out into the Gulf of Dolce where we take up a course of 230 degrees to our first waypoint, 8.5 miles away.

Boat speed is 7.0 knots with engine rpms at 2600. The starboard engine voltage meter is showing only 11.5 volts output, indicating that the rebuilt alternator and/or the voltage regulator needs adjusting. I inform Paco who is in constant motion, continually checking the condition of the engines. He reports that the hose repair on the port engine is holding up well.

I make fresh coffee and relax in the settee.

09:00. My watch. We are proceeding in a southerly direction and are nearly to the entrance of the Gulf of Dolce. Sea conditions are good with one-foot swells and little wind. Speed remains at 6.5 knots. There is rain in the area but nothing noteworthy. GPS indicates that the distance to Balboa is 245 miles. With an average speed of 6.5 knots, it should take us 53 hours. Our ETA on Tuesday should be at 12:00 hours.

11:00. We round Punta Banco, the landmass that forms the southern boundary of Dolce, Cabo Matapalo is the northern boundary. In entering the Pacific Ocean, we once again encounter a wide area of floating debris. I hand steer to avoid many of the larger pieces.

At noon I hand the watch to Roger. I make my logbook entries, noting that our heading is 150 degrees, with our next waypoint at 25 miles.

My engine room inspections reveal that all is well.

I have lunch before going below for the afternoon to read and relax in my cabin.

16:00. Paco's watch. We have changed course to 100 degrees. He is flying the genoa to take advantage of a steady wind on our starboard beam. Our boat speed is exceeding seven knots. I sit out on the fantail alone. There is some sunshine peeking in and out of a mostly overcast sky.

18:00. Allen takes the watch while Paco starts dinner. Fish again tonight. Oops, we are out of onions. Apparently missed by Allen and Roger when they went shopping in Golfito. I start a provisioning list for Panama.

18:30. Dinner turns out to be not bad in-spite of no onions. Roger and I do the galley clean up.

19:00. We furl the genoa and prepare the deck areas for running at night. Allen has us strike the Costa Rica flag and replace it with the flag of Panama.

21:00. My watch. Our course remains at 100 degrees, boat speed at 6.5 knots. We have twenty-five miles to our next waypoint. I note that there are numerous fishing boats to avoid and that radar is essential.

23:00. Radar is showing an object ahead at one o'clock on the five-mile range. It has the appearance of being a fishing boat, but I see no lights. At eleven o'clock, on the same range, is another object. However, it is showing a port red light and occasionally a glimpse of a white stern light.

23:15. Rapidly approaching the object that has now moved dead ahead, I reduce power and call for Allen. He uses a spotlight to determine that our mystery object is a barge in tow. We allow it to pass.

24:00. I turn the watch to Robin. Allen remains above to help him guide the boat through a narrow, rock infested channel created between Isla de Coiba and Isla Canal de Afuera. Although reportedly three miles wide, our chart shows rock and shoal out reaches.

00:30. I turn in. I'm told that if needed, I'll be called.

I read for a while. I have found a Captain Hornblower epic adventure by C.S. Forrester, The Atropos published in 1953. It is one of many books on board.

Day 28. Monday.

06:30. Bright sunshine in my cabin wakes me but I decide it is too early to get up so remain comfortably in bed. The sea is flat making for a nice ride. I listen for anything unusual from the boat, but hear none.

07:30. Shower and shave. My beard is looking good, I think. I shave only around my neck so that I don't feel scruffy.

08:00. With newly made coffee I join Allen on the bridge. It is a beautiful morning, only a few scattered clouds with lots of sunshine and a deep blue sea. The genoa is flying to take advantage of a five to seven knot offshore breeze. Our boat speed remains at 6.5 knots.

Alone with Allen I ask if he has received any new information regarding the sale of Athena.

"Only that we probably will be met by a sales agent at the Balboa Yacht Club," he answers.

"Is there anything new to report on the package?"

"No. I expect we'll know more upon our arrival."

Because of Allen's seemingly unwillingness to elaborate, I go below for breakfast of cereal and fruit. Returning to the settee I reread parts of Trish Lambert's book, Panama by Water. It has a lot of good information about transiting the Canal. Information I'll find helpful, I'm certain.

09:00. My watch. Course is 125 degrees with next waypoint at eight miles.

10:30. We are off of Punta Mariato where a course change to 91 degrees will take us to our next waypoint at Morro de Puercos at 25 miles distance. We furl the genoa because the wind is now on our nose. Radar shows us as two miles offshore.

Looking towards the land, the dense forest is a dark sap green. It blankets the cordillera or mountain range of the Sierras that forms the spine of Costa Rica, Panama and extends to Columbia. Towering clouds conceal the mountaintops, casting their long shadows on the rolling terrain below. It creates a mood of intrigue and mystery. There are areas of open fields where coffee and sugar plantations exist together with rice fields and a variety of fruit trees.

The surf line tells me that there are but a few places where you can go ashore because of the rugged, rocky terrain. The scene reminds me of the song Bali Ha'i from Rogers and Hammerstein's musical South Pacific.

11:00. A freighter is on the horizon.

11:30. We pass one mile apart. Her name is Poolcraft; her homeport is Amsterdam, The Netherlands. She rides high out of the water, suggesting that she is empty. I calculate her speed at ten knots. She throws out a rolling wake of several feet in height. She does not answer my calls on VHF.

12:00. I turn the watch to Robin. I note our position, speed and that there are no engine room problems. He seems relaxed and in good spirits. After a sandwich, I go below to my cabin where I stretch out on my bunk and read. There is little of anything else to do except relax.

15:00. I go above at the watch change between Robin and Paco. I sit out on the aft deck under the awning. There is a high overcast that breaks the sun intensity. I'm certain it is ninety degrees with corresponding humidity.

16:00. My solitude is abruptly broken by one of Paco's fishing reels that start to sing. Because he is on watch I decide to bring the catch on board. It is something small I soon discover, as it skips across the water as the boat drags it along. It turns out to be a five-pound Spanish mackerel. Paco says it is a keeper. I therefore place it in an igloo chest of ice until Paco is free to filet it. I reset the spinner (lure) with one hundred feet of line.

Once again comfortably seated, I realize that the land height is progressively lowering. The towering mountain range seen earlier has given way to rolling hills. There is still the rich vegetation, a combination of trees and cultivated fields.

Two more fish strikes capture my attention. They are both Bonita. Paco has me throw them back.

I watch with interest as a large thunderstorm has developed over the land behind us. Inside it are several rainsqualls that have lowered visibility to zero with a driving, swirling wind. These are common I have read, especially now during the wet season (invierno or winter) from May through November.

Panama's weather, I have learned, is influenced greatly by the position of the Intertropical Convergence Zone or ITCZ. This is the almost continuous planetary belt of low pressure where the northeast trade winds of the northern hemisphere converge with the southeast trade winds of the southern hemisphere. It is characterized by a great deal of cloudiness, frequent squalls and thunderstorms. The ITCZ moves from the winter hemisphere to the summer hemisphere, reaching its northern most latitude in August and southernmost in February. One of Allen's weather faxes, Tropical Surface Analysis, clearly shows the ITCZ running on a line through Costa Rica at about nine degrees latitude. It is at least part of the reason for the unsettled clouds and rain we have run in and out of since Golfito.

18:00. We have six miles to go before our next turning waypoint off of Punta Mala. From our position, two miles off shore, it is seen as a flat protruding mesa. The chart shows it to be part of a large landmass that creates the northern boundary to the one hundred mile wide entrance to the Bay of Panama.

19:00. Dinner. Allen prepares steak and potatoes with a green salad, a welcome change from our fish diet. Roger and I do galley chores.

20:30. Reaching the waypoint, our new course is twenty-one degrees with our next waypoint as Isla Tobago, sixty-eight miles away.

21:00. My watch. The sea has settled down to flat with one-foot swells and little wind. Our boat speed fluctuates between six and one half to seven knots.

22:00. Although there has been heat lightning all around us, we have remained clear of any storm activity. Now however, radar is showing a group of activity at two miles, directly ahead.

22:20. The activity has blossomed into a full-scale squall, filling the radar screen on the three-mile range.

22:30. Heavy rain, gusting winds and lumpy seas greet us upon our entry into the storm cell. "Nasty thing that we are in," I think. We are being jostled about in a very unfriendly manner. Wave heights are three to four feet coming at us from the port quarter driven by wind gusts of thirty miles per hour. I reduce power allowing the boat speed to drop to three knots. Great fountains of seawater burst up through the metal grating between the two pontoons forward as Athena plunges into the oncoming sea. Torrents of rain and seawater fly up and over the bridge, reflected in the green and red running lights. I haven't bothered to operate the windshield wipers knowing they would be of little value to improving visibility.

Inside the cockpit, all manner of items are being tossed about. The chart table, once well organized, is now scattered with the navigation instruments. One good result of the violent bashing is that the port engine tachometer is working.

23:00. Finally I have limited visibility. Rain has slacked but the wind has not. Wave heights remain at three feet. Athena is pitching and rolling so violently that it is impossible to move about. I need both hands on the wheel to stabilize myself and to make matters worse radar shows a large vessel five miles dead ahead moving towards us.

23:15. By now I have been joined in the cockpit by my three mates. We can see the oncoming boats red port running light together with her two white mast lights, indicating she is over 300 feet in length. Allen has me turn sharply to starboard and apply power but Athena has a hard time making any progress in the storm tossed water. We shine our high power spotlight at the approaching dark hulk in hopes of attracting attention by the watch officer. The spotlight reflects off her large bow wave, telling us that she is traveling fast and low in the water. Allen repeatedly calls the vessel on VHF, but with no response while Robin continually flashes the light.

"Bob set the auto pilot. Get your life jackets and prepare the life raft for abandon ship," says Allen as he unsnaps the EPIRB from its holder.

We take little time before gathering on the fore deck, each in our life vests. Seconds before Paco and Roger are set to release the life raft, Allen calls, "Wait. Let's give it a minute."

Miraculously, the wind and rain diminish allowing Athena to pull away on a thirty degree diagonal, out from the direct line of travel of the oncoming boat. I stand mesmerized, attempting to fathom our distance and whether we can outrun her. I think that this is surreal and cannot be happening.

"Secure your safety harnesses to the nearest deck plate," Allen says in a calm voice. "She I believe is going to miss us, but we are going to get a big swell of water from her passing wake. So hang on."

The bow of the giant hulk passes off our quarter stern at a distance of one hundred fifty feet but that distance closes quickly due to her massive width. Her hull pushes out a massive wall of white water that now rolls towards us. The first of the series picks Athena's port hull up from behind causing her to heal down sharply to starboard, burying the starboard rail underwater. As the swell passes under her, Athena rights herself momentarily before violently pitching to port as the wall of water rolls under the starboard hull. A second and third wave does likewise causing a violent whipping action. I am slammed about, my right shoulder smashed against the cabin on one occasion; while on another I bump my head on a stanchion.

As the ship passes, there is a frightening roar from the powerful engines and driving propellers. Her wake is a churning, furry of wild water for many, many yards behind her. Fortunately we are now far enough away to avoid being sucked into the cavity of space she leaves behind. In a matter of minutes she is gone; a silhouette against the far horizon, leaving us alone under a carpet of stars.

I remain seated on the deck, too stunned to attempt to move. I say a silent prayer of thanks for our good fortune. If we had come upon each other while inside the storm, I'm certain the results would have been far different.

"Is everyone OK?" asks Allen.

Thankfully we all are.

"Let's get inside then."

I unsnap my safety harness and get to my feet, shaky at first. We gather in the cockpit where Allen reduces engine power and brings Athena back on course. I note in the log that the time is 24:00.

"Let's do a safety check to determine what damage we may have," says Allen. "Report back here when done."

I go below to the galley and main saloon, where I find a number of items thrown out of their cupboards, but nothing broken or damaged. The coffee pot and toaster even made it through without landing on the floor.

A check of my cabin shows only a few items disturbed, but overall considering the battering we took, I am pleasantly surprised.

The report from the others is also of only minor damage. The largest single item is the tool chest in the starboard engine room that tipped over and spilled its contents.

"We shall consider ourselves very lucky," states Allen, to which we all concur. "Let's get back to business. Roger, I believe it's your watch."

I make my logbook entries and retire below to my cabin. I lie awake on my bunk where the full impact of the experience sweeps over me, sending chills up and down my spine. An image of the giant hulk bearing down on us sticks in my mind. I think just how lucky we are to have survived such a close call.

Day 29. Tuesday.

06:00. I awake to realize that I am still dressed from last night. Apparently I fell asleep without undressing. My reading light is still on as well. Deciding that there is no need to get up, I remain on top of the covers.

07:30. Showered and dressed, I find Allen at the helm. He declines anything from the galley. I note that our progress has remained good despite poor sea and wind conditions, an overcast sky with rain showers in the area. We are passing the Los Farollones Islands Now eight miles until we reach our next mark.

09:00. My watch. We are coming under the lee of Isla Tabago. The sea seems to be settling down.

09:10. Reaching our mark, the new course is due north, zero degrees. Our next waypoint is the 'whistle" or outer buoy, a distance of six and one-half miles, marking the Canal's entrance. It seems unreal to be on a northerly bearing. Allen tries to contact Patrick on the VHF, but receives no response.

10:10. At the whistle buoy, I note our position as eight degrees, fifty-one minutes, fifty seconds by seventy-nine degrees, twenty-nine minutes, seventy-nine seconds. This is as close to the equator as we will get. In fact this is our southernmost position. Our new course is 320 degrees. We are now travelling west of north. Unreal, I think.

Much like the flight approach to an airport, we contact Flamingo Radio on channel twelve and receive permission to proceed to the Balboa Yacht Club. Flamingo is responsible for the movement of all shipping.

10:15. To starboard through the morning haze, at a distance of ten miles, I can see the outline of the many high-rise buildings of downtown Panama City. It could easily be that of New York Cities lower Manhattan.

Around us I count over twenty vessels at anchor, all waiting to transit. "The ships to our left have dangerous cargo, those to our right are standard merchant ships," advises Allen.

10:25. Patrick comes up on the VHF. We give him our location. He tells us that he'll see us at the yacht club.

10:30. Passing between the number one and two buoys there is no other traffic. The Island of Flamingo is now visible at two o'clock on the starboard bow. Allen explains that it is connected to the mainland by the Amador Causeway to Naos and Perico Islands that together form a chain of anchorages for small vessels. All were created with the spoils from the Canal excavation. The islands are a favorite place for families to picnic, take walks and ride bikes.

10:40. Passing between the number five and six buoys I can begin to feel the influence of the oncoming current of water flowing towards the sea from the locks above.

11:00. At buoy number sixteen, Allen takes the helm. We turn out of the channel and into the outer anchorage of the Balboa Yacht Club. Reducing power we follow the yacht club tender to an open mooring where the young man preceding us, retrieves the hawser from the buoy and hands it up to the waiting Paco.

Allen shuts down the engines while I make the appropriate logbook notation of our arrival time as 11:10.

Patrick hails us on channel sixteen to advise that we should remain on board, as he will bring the necessary paperwork and the Canal representative out to us. He advises that we will be required to hire a fourth line handler because Allen as captain doesn't count. He, Allen, must remain on the bridge during transit. We need to have our four, one hundred fifty-foot lines out and ready for inspection when the fourth handler comes on board.

We collectively busy ourselves with making the boat shipshape for our visitors.

CHAPTER TWENTY SIX

Balboa

11:30. Patrick Foley arrives by the club's launch. He comes aboard through the starboard lifeline opening with a helping hand from Paco who greets him with a manly bear hug, as does Allen. The three stand talking on the aft-deck where I have an opportunity to observe Patrick. He is a piece of work at five foot ten, two hundred-twenty plus pounds, a ruddy complexion and a full head of white hair. I guess his age at 55. He is our agent and the owner of Foley Yacht Services. They come inside after several minutes where Roger and I are introduced.

"Care for a beer?" asks Allen.

"Of course, I thought you'd never ask," responds Patrick as he slides into the aft section of the settee. I break out and open three cold bottles of Pacifico, Paco and Roger both declining the offer to go below to change engine oil and filters. Additionally they are removing both alternators to give to Patrick for proper bench testing and adjusting. Allen requests that Patrick buy a new eighty amp starting battery.

I soon learn that he is a Brit by birth coming to Panama from Kent, England in 1960. Now a United States citizen he is married with a four-teen-year old daughter. He retains much of his English accent, embellishes the kings English punctuated with profanities.

Allen describes our harrowing experience of last evening. "The sad part of it all is that they probably never knew we were even there," he concludes.

"Even if they did see you, there is little they could do to avoid you at that speed. It takes one of those monsters miles to come to a stop."

13:00. Leo, the ad-measurer comes aboard to verify Athena's physical dimensions for use in the formula to determine the fee payment for transit. He is an American, an employee of the Canal Company, about forty-five, lean and tan. It is clear that he and Patrick have worked with one another over an extended period of time.

Patrick is the source of our entertainment, imparting stories of his early life and of many of the characters he has encountered in his lifetime. He has a quick wit and must know hundreds of jokes with an instant recall. Three bottles of beer help loosen him up.

14:00. Somehow the paperwork, started earlier by Patrick, manages to get completed. He informs us that we are free to leave the boat and that we will transit on Thursday (day after tomorrow) starting promptly at 06:00. Additionally, our fourth line handler can be expected on board tomorrow mid-morning to go over line handling duties.

"What do you know of a sales offer for Athena?" asks Allen of Patrick.

"Very little, I must say. I was knocked-up (Brit for telephoned) by a chap who wanted to know when I expected you because he had a client interested in seeing her. That's about it."

"I guess we'll hear soon enough from someone."

14:30. Patrick and Leo depart. "I'll be in contact between 17:00 and 18:00," Patrick calls to Allen from the launch. Paco and Roger ride in with them to help transport the two alternators. Upon their return Allen asks for a brief meeting. We assemble at the settee.

Allen starts by reminding us that we should not let our guard down with regard to the package. "There is still the real chance that we may be boarded at any time. For that reason as well as for the general security of Athena, I want at least one of us on board at all times. I also remind us that Roger is still under house arrest and must remain in the company of one other individual." He continues with our transit date and time and that our fourth line handler will be here in the morning. "I also expect to be contacted by the party interested in buying the boat. Now I need to make a telephone call to the bank for an update." We conclude with a short discussion of maintenance chores to be done before transit time.

15:00. Allen calls for the shore launch, asking that I go with him.

15:10. The launch pulls aside Athena's starboard side where we are careful to time our step to its pitch and roll. We head towards the yacht club under the skillful control of Andres, a young Panamanian at the helm. I sit mid-ship next to the engine compartment with its rattling diesel engine underneath. The launch is a wooden double-ender, steered by a tiller. It has seen years of service with little maintenance yet she remains sturdy with no signs of age.

Athena's mooring is a considerable distance from the club. Out here there is an easy one-half knot of current coming down the channel, together with a ten-knot breeze from the same direction. Both of these factors are perpendicular to our desired course requiring Andre to steer a course thirty degrees high, putting the launch in a sever crab.

As we approach the mid-point of the yacht basin the effects of wind and tide begin to diminish, particularly as we come under the lee of a fuel dock that extends from the shore. We could have landed there but had asked to be taken to the yacht club's office, located in the main building. Directly ahead, the club's three-story building is in full view. It is in desperate need of paint and largely falling down. The initials BYC are brightly painted red against the scaling white concrete wall of the first floor.

As we close in on the building, the tide and current diminish to where Andre is able to steer without hindrance towards a set of concrete steps located at the base of the first floor. Looking above, I am able to see that the second floor is an open restaurant. The third floor is enclosed and it is probably where offices and meeting rooms are located.

Skillfully, Andre brings the launch alongside the steps to where Allen and I are easily able to step ashore. I turn to watch him swing about and head out to the fuel dock before I follow Allen up the eight or so steps to a landing that leads into the spacious dining room. Set for the evening meal, I count twenty tables each with white tablecloths, red napkins and place settings for eight. Continuing to follow Allen we make our way to the opposite end of the room to a magnificent mahogany bar measuring I estimate at thirty-five to forty feet long. A distinguished black man in a tuxedo approaches us. "Captain Allen, may I help you?" he asks.

"Martin, it is good to see you," Allen exclaims accompanied by a handshake. "I would like the use of a telephone."

"Of course, please come this way."

We are taken to a private room located behind the bar with a desk and several chairs together with a telephone and fax machine. Before leaving he asks if there is anything else he may do for us.

Allen tells him no, but thanks him. Allen then contacts an international operator to establish his account and that he may be making multiple calls. Next he dials the offices of the bank where, after some difficulty he is put through to his contact. After the normal formalities, Allen informs him that Athena is at the Balboa Yacht Club and of our transit time. "I am in need of additional cash and can you tell me anything about the boats possible sale?" he asks. I can only watch as he listens. After several I understands, Allen completes the conversation by saying Good-bye.

"Well, here's the deal", he says leaning back in the chair. "Weber wants the bank to hold off on any negotiations until after the package delivery. He does not want anything to interfere with his ability to apprehend the cartels pickup person."

"So, is it business as usual for us?" I ask.

"Yes, with one small twist. There is some thought now of removing the gem from our custody."

"You're kidding. It was Weber who felt it better for us to keep it rather than try to convince someone we didn't have it."

"I know, but something has changed his mind. We need to hope he knows what he is doing."

Next Allen calls Kate to inform her of our safe arrival in Panama and to ask if she would call my wife.

Leaving the room, we walk out to the bar. "I'll buy us a drink," says Allen.

We sit at a small table overlooking the yacht basin where Athena is moored in the far distance.

"Is everything satisfactory?" asks Martin.

"Yes, very nice," answers Allen. "Now we need something cool and refreshing to drink."

"What is your pleasure?"

Allen orders a rum and coke while I ask for a beer. Martin, I learn has been an employee here for thirty years.

A sea breeze off of the water together with several ceiling fans overhead, make this a comfortable spot to relax despite the near one hundred degree heat. There is an Old World atmosphere here, reflecting a by-gone era of wealth and supremacy, from the days of the Canal's development. Although now passed, the physical signs remain in the beautiful wood of the bar, the cut glass of the mirrors and glassware behind it and the brass foot rail in front. The high back barstools, also made of mahogany to match the bar can probably tell many a story. Above the bar are burgees of dozens of yacht clubs from around the world, reminiscent of the San Diego Yacht Club.

"Many folks now consider the yacht club as a relic," says Allen as he watches me look around. "With the transfer of the Canal Zone to the Panamanian's in 2000 this facility, I'm afraid together with many others like it will disappear."

"That will be too bad," I exclaim.

Martin delivers our drinks. Allen and I offer one another a toast of good health. I take a good size pull from the bottle, enjoying the refreshing taste. We sit without speaking for several minutes before Allen breaks the solitude. He feels it best not to say anything to Roger regarding the potential gem transfer. "I think for the time being, there is no need for him to know. I will inform Paco when time allows."

"You don't trust Roger?"

"I have mixed emotions. I think he's too smart a man to have been drawn into a scheme of this magnitude without knowing the consequences."

I simply shake my head. All of this is becoming a little more than I am able to comprehend.

16:30. Our drinks finished and the bill settled we decide to walk out to the launch via the fuel dock. A door to the side of the bar leads us out and down a set of stairs to a small boat repair yard. The yard, quiet in the afternoon heat, has a single railway where a fair size powerboat occupies it for bottom maintenance. The EPA would not be pleased with the conditions here I muse. Oil spills have largely gone unattended together with open drums of paint, lacquers and thinners.

The fuel dock, much like the clubhouse, is in poor condition after years of heavy use and neglect. It is a wooden structure set on posts running out into the boat basin over three hundred feet. Its peaked roof, designed for protection from the sun and rain, has numerous openings where boards are missing. I notice many of the floorboards are splintered and loose as we carefully watch where we step.

The fueling operation consists of two fuel pumps set on a similar type wooden pier but placed perpendicular to the long pier to form a T. There is a small shack set off to one side that is used for an office and also where Andre hangs out. He provides us a lift out to Athena.

It is a short ride to where we join Paco and Roger in the cockpit. They indicate that they have completed all maintenance items until the new battery and alternators are returned. They report no unusual or suspicious activity around the boat. Allen provides a recap of his telephone call with the bank, not mentioning that the package may be removed.

17:30. Patrick comes up on the VHF indicating that he is on his way out. We watch as Andre guides the motor launch through the moderate chop towards us. I am surprised to see two passengers in the boat, expecting only Patrick as they come along side.

Patrick is the first to disembark, nimble despite his weight. The second individual is timid and has difficulty in timing his exit from the launch. Paco finally steps forward to help him make the transition.

"Hello guys. Sorry to be such a klutz," he says approaching Allen with an extended hand. I now recognize him as agent Weber still in disguise.

We move inside to the settee where Patrick asks for a beer and Weber asks for a bottle of water. I slide into the settee across from Patrick.

"The Bureau has ordered the gem be removed," begins Weber.

"Before you ask why, I'll try to explain. The gem has been tentatively identified as one missing for over fifty years. The Bureau is unwilling to risk its disappearance again and is requiring that it be couriered out tomorrow. In its place a fake stone identical in size, color and weight will be substituted. We believe that you are under no more risk with a fake than the real one. Allen, please go get the package."

"What about the monitoring devise?" I ask.

"It will remain with you in the original package undisturbed."

Upon Allen's return, Weber continues speaking while carefully removing the gem from the box in its pouch and places it in a pocket. "The Bureau is asking Mr. Foley to accompany me in transporting it to a reputable jeweler in Panama City that will substitute it with a fake. Mr. Foley will then pick up and bring the fake gem here by early tomorrow morning. The jeweler will in turn make arrangements for the true gem to be sent to FBI headquarters."

"Is there any update on cartel intelligence?" Allen asks.

"Actually there is very little to report. There has been one telephone communication intercepted between Golfito and Mendoza in which the informant Ernesto notified Mendoza of the mysterious disappearance of his accomplice. Otherwise there has been little movement among the participants. Has there been any contact here?"

"No, none," answers Allen.

"We believe Roger will be notified where to deliver the package and to whom possibly during transit."

"Wait," exclaims Roger. "I forgot, there is a card accompanying the package. I was told not to open it until we reached the canal. It will contain delivery directions for the package."

"Where is it?" asks Weber.

"In my cabin."

"Then please go get it."

Without pause Roger slides out of the settee and disappears below to his cabin. We four remain silent, each in our own thoughts.

"Here," says Roger upon his return.

Weber accepts the bright yellow and pink envelope and with Allen's pocket knife, slices it open. Inside is indeed a birthday card intended for a wife. Opening it to the inside right page, in place of a romantic message, Weber finds a simple handwritten note stating that final instructions will come during transit.

"Ok, at least we know when you will be contacted. The question now is how?"

"Do you find the lack of more specifics strange?" I ask Weber.

"Somewhat I suppose. My guess is that Mendoza wrote the note before he had been told who would be the pickup person and where. He therefore decided that 'In transit' was his best way of buying himself time to finalize his plan. Regardless, I would suggest that there be a heightened awareness by all on board for anything unusual occurring."

"What about the sale of Athena?"

"I have asked the potential buyers to hold off with any contact until after the transit. They will wait for my OK before coming forward."

Satisfied that he has explained everything, Weber turns the meeting over to Allen who asks Patrick for his update. He imparts that the alternators will be delivered in the morning together with the new starting battery. He explains that the line handler can be expected about midday. "His name is Jose, a most likeable local chap. I believe that is all I have."

"I would recommend that all of you leave the boat this evening to go ashore for dinner," informs Weber. "Lock her up and go eat as normally would be the case. Athena is under close surveillance by me together with several military police."

"That's good, because I need to get to a bank," says Allen.

"Then you better get going."

Allen informs Paco and Roger while I run below for a clean shirt. Returning to the cockpit, I find Patrick thumbing through Trish Lambert's book left on the table.

"Who is reading this?" he asks.

"I am." I answer. I explain my interest in the Canal and that it has been my hopes for years to one day transit it in our thirty-seven foot sailboat.

"I hope that happens one day."

19:00. The launch picks the six of us up and takes us to the yacht club where the four of us find a taxi at the back of the club for the ride into Panama City. Weber and Foley depart separately in Foley's automobile.

The route to the city takes us through a small part of the Canal Zone still under control of the United States. I am reminded that at noon on December 31, 1999, total responsibility for administration and operations will pass to the Republic of Panama.

We wind our way on a wide two-lane macadam road lined by palms with thick Bermuda grass, running along the roadway in all directions. Neat white stucco homes with bright red tile roofs are set well back from the road, suggesting that we are in a residential neighborhood, perhaps "officers' country."

We pass through an intersection with a fire station on one corner, a one-story office building on another, a convenience store on the third and a strip shopping center on the fourth. We could be in nearly any small town back home.

Further on to our right we pass an open area of lawn where a war memorial sits predominantly. Four flagpoles guard the tribute to a long ago event, their flags waving in the brisk afternoon wind.

Soon we are upon a sentry building signaling the end of the zone and the entrance to the outskirts of Panama City. Although there is a guard in the enclosure, he pays little attention to our leaving. Within minutes it becomes obvious that we are in very different surroundings. The road is pockmarked with holes, narrow and winding with the ever present "silent policeman" to slow speeders. Not so for us, as our taxi flies over the bumps causing us to fly about the inside. There is no grass to be seen anywhere. Buildings are mostly wooden, two to three story, ramshackle frames. The sidewalks, what few there are, are littered with paper, bottles, weeds and a continual sea of humanity.

Approaching the city, Paco asks the driver to stop at an open-air market where he buys onions and a few other fruits and vegetables. I exit the taxi to stand and watch with curiosity the activity associated with this large and very busy market.

Our next stop is downtown in the city center to a bank that Allen goes inside. I recall having been in this area while with McDonalds (1975) because our licensee's office was located somewhere here. Allen quickly returns explaining that he will need to return tomorrow as it is closed except for simple transactions.

Paco provides the driver with the name of a restaurant recommended by Patrick, located in the old section of the city. We depart from the sleek city of finance and trade to enter the charming old district of narrow cobble stone streets overlooked by the flower bedecked balconies of two and three story houses. It is a snap shot of the past.

History says that the original city was founded in 1519, six years after Balboa had discovered the Pacific Ocean. It was located several miles down the bay, but was abandoned after it was sacked and burned by the pirate Morgan in 1671. This present city, a walled city, was begun three years later, at the head of the bay on a narrow tongue of volcanic rock with water on three sides. Fire has ravaged the city time after time. As recently as 1878, nearly a third of it burned to the ground. Rebuilt, the city remains vibrant and alive with theater, restaurants and art galleries. The streets remain narrow where there is little enough room for our vehicle to travel.

Our restaurant is located in a stone building dating back to the early eighteen hundreds. It is set back in a courtyard which in turn faces the west where the sun is now low on the horizon, about to drop into the Pacific Ocean, creating a blaze of streaking color under a row of clouds.

If there is an outside sign advertising the location, I miss it. Through an arched opening protected by a heavy oak door, we pass into a reception area where an impressive host greets us. Allen handles the formalities before we are led down a short flight of stairs and seated in the center of the dining room.

It is a magnificent room with a high vaulted ceiling from which three large lighted chandeliers are suspended. Construction of the building is entirely of volcanic gray brick, set in an interlocking pattern from floor to ceiling. Allen, an architect by training, suggests that no mortar was used in its construction. Large tapestries depicting Panama's history from pre-Hispanic to present hang elegantly around the room's perimeter providing a warm and comfortable atmosphere.

Much like the Spanish, evening meals in Panama are taken rather late which allows us the place nearly to ourselves. Our meal is taken leisurely, without concern for boat operations, high jacking or any of the many other concerns we have encountered. The food proves to be quite good, the drinks generous and the service attentive. I leave with a feeling of warmth and wellbeing.

Finding no taxi, we walk a short distance along the seawall to a park where we find a monument to the French builders who began the Panama Canal together with the lovely French Embassy. On the walkway around the monument we encounter a fine view of the Amador Causeway, the Bridge of the Americas and of Panama City's sweeping skyscraper skyline to the east. The quarter moon hangs over the bay making for a lovely view. A plaque on the walkway commemorates the firing of canon shots from here to drive away a Colombian warship and consolidate Panama's independence from Columbia in 1903.

Eventually an empty taxi comes to our rescue that takes us to the yacht club. There is little activity at the club except in the bar and a few couples in the dining room. There are no signs of Weber or his military contingent as we walk out to the pier's end where we board the launch for the short trip to Athena. She is wet from the evening's dampness making footing tenuous. Inside she is dry and comfortable.

We say goodnight to one another and head to our respective quarters. I am in bed having barely undressed. Sleep is upon me fast, in spite of it being only ten-thirty.

Day 30. Wednesday.

07:00. The sunlight streams into the cabin through the porthole at the foot of my bunk. It dances about, reflecting off the bulkhead and overhead saying, "get up, get up, you sleepy head."

07:30. I find Allen busy at his desk. He has been up for quite a while by the looks of the paperwork and empty coffee cup. Sitting back in his chair to stretch he tells me that we can expect Patrick soon with news of our alternators and battery. "He may have our line handler with him as well. Paco is working on the windlass and I haven't seen Roger."

I go below to start a fresh pot of coffee when I hear the motor launch come aside with Patrick. He is alone. I put the teapot on for hot water.

"Hi, Bob," comes Patrick's booming voice from above.

"Good morning Patrick, I'll be up with tea in a minute."

"Lovely," he responds. I think, a Brit he is.

Patrick is comfortably seated in the settee as I hand him his tea. He hands me a soft cover book. "What is this?" I ask.

"A little gift from me to you," he replies.

The little gift proves to be David McCullough's book, The Path Between The Seas, a chronicle of the creation of the Panama Canal-1870 to 1914. He has signed the inside cover page, To Bob, Best Wishes-Patrick, Balboa 1977.

I am deeply touched. It is a gift I shall cherish and know I'll use as reference material for many years.

Patrick's attention quickly switches to a smallish size paper bag that he hands to Allen. "This is a little gift for you," he says with a wink.

Knowing the bags contents he asks, "Can we take a peek?"

"I'm only the courier, you do as you please."

Allen removes the fake gem from its box. "It looks exactly as I remember the genuine one," he exclaims holding it in the palm of his right hand for all to see.

"As it should," says Patrick.

Allen places it in the box next to the transmitter before carefully rewrapping them using the original paper tissue and ribbon. He excuses himself to take them to the ships safe.

"I still need to get to the bank," says Allen upon his return. "They were closed last night."

"No problem. I can arrange for a representative to come here if you wish."

"Great. Here is the voucher for the amount to be drawn."

Patrick, using his VHF radio, contacts his office with instructions.

"Que Pasa," says Paco coming into the cockpit from on deck.

"Buenos días," says Patrick before informing him that the parts will come this afternoon and the line handler, Jose.

"Gracias," replies Paco with a broad smile.

"Can we get fuel now?" asks Allen of Patrick.

Patrick radios the fuel dock. "Right away," comes the response in Spanish.

By now we know the routine for getting underway. Although the fuel dock is only a few hundred meters away, taking Athena any distance requires the same amount of preparation.

Allen cranks the engines while Roger, now up and about, handles the aft fenders and mooring line while I tend to the forward fenders and line. At Allen's command, Paco releases the hawser allowing us to drift away from the mooring buoy. We rig for a starboard side tie at the fuel dock.

Allen applies power to ease us through the three rows of boats and buoys which separates us from the dock. Alongside, we throw our lines to the waiting attendants who quickly tie us off. Paco and Roger handle the fueling operation.

Patrick departs. He assures us that all is in order. "Not to worry," he says as he strides confidently down the long pier to the clubhouse.

With Roger standing by helping Paco and Allen inside at his computer, I relax in my deck chair under the sun awning on the aft deck with Path between the Seas. I read that before all that is before me today, this was nothing but mud flats reaching out several miles at low tide. This low tide effect was in some part the reasoning that led to the long held theory that there was a water height difference between the two oceans.

Balboa, in the early years was known as LaBoca. It became the dumping grounds for dirt excavated from Culebra Cut that I guess I'll learn more about later in the book. Twenty-two million cubic yards were deposited here with the results that six hundred seventy-six acres were reclaimed from the Pacific as a site for the town. Noas Island breakwater was also built from some of the same spoils.

"Mr. Daniels, I presume?" asks the voice of a slender gentleman dressed in a black business suit, a black bowler hat set squarely upon his head and carrying a slim expensive leather briefcase. He has come aboard without my realizing his presence.

"No, no, I'm not," I say rather sheepishly.

"I am Ralph Abernathy of the Royal Bank of England to see a Mr. Allen Daniels at the personal request of Mr. Patrick Foley. Is Mr. Daniels here?" he asks with a clipped English accent.

"Yes, of course. Will you follow me, please?"

I rise and take him into the cockpit where he removes his hat, placing it under his left arm and stands at rigid attention. I cross to Allen's cabin and peering inside I announce that the banker is here.

Emerging from below, Allen's facial expression upon seeing Mr. Abernathy standing at attention is priceless.

"Mr. Daniels?" asks Abernathy.

"Yes," answers Allen moving forward to shake hands. "Welcome aboard."

Ignoring Allen's out stretched hand, he gives a slight bow of recognition before indicating that he has come at the request of Mr. Patrick Foley to transact business. "If we may be seated, I'll take only a moment of your time, Mr. Daniels."

"Will this be sufficient?" asks Allen of the settee.

"Yes, quite nice."

I leave the two of them alone to return to my chair and book. Paco and Roger are filling the port fuel tank apparently finished with the starboard tank.

I am no sooner settled in my chair before Abernathy and Allen step out from the cockpit. "Thank you for coming," offers Allen.

"It is the banks pleasure, Mr. Daniels." Without fanfare Abernathy strides smartly to the lifeline opening where before stepping off onto the fuel dock he turns to doff his hat and says, "Good day." He departs with short quick measured steps across the fuel dock and onto the covered pier leading to the yacht club.

"Who was that?" asks Paco as he and Roger stand and stare.

"That was our banker delivering money," answers Allen.

"He is as good an example of a proper Englishman as I believe I have seen," I offer as commentary to my three companions.

10:00. Paco announces that fueling is complete. Allen pays the cashier and with help from the two attendants, we cast off. The reverse procedure of before sees us back on our mooring at 10:30.

12:00. The motor launch pulls alongside bringing what would appear to be our fifth crewmember. He easily swings himself up onto Athena's deck from the launch bulwarks. He is a muscular, middle aged man obviously accustomed to being on the water from his timing the pitch and roll of a boat. "My name is Jose," he says in broken English once onboard.

"Hola and welcome aboard," says Allen with a firm handshake.

We learn that he understands English but has some trouble speaking it. After a cool drink in the cockpit, we show him the four one hundred fifty-foot lines required for the transit, which are laid neatly coiled on deck. Inspecting them, he seems pleased with their condition. "Good, good," he says. "I will be a forward handler in order to be able to assist with any trouble that may occur," he then announces. Paco agrees to be the other handler forward, leaving Roger and I to take the aft lines. He advises that gloves are helpful in preventing rope burns together with several other tips and advice.

We learn that he makes a transit four to five times a month, that his pay is one hundred dollars a trip plus the expense of being picked up and delivered to his home. He is licensed by the Canal authorities and has been doing this for ten years.

13:00. Satisfied that all is in order he asks that the launch be called. "I'll see you in the morning," he says departing over the rail into the moving launch.

Allen sums up what each of us has been thinking. "He knows his business and we will do as he says."

Until the battery and alternators arrive, there is little for any of us to do. Allen and I discuss doing further provisioning but decide it is unnecessary until we know more of the sale of the boat.

I go below to the relative coolness of my cabin where I stretch out on my bunk and quickly fall asleep. It is a deep and refreshing interlude but too soon interrupted by the bumping of the shore launch outside my porthole. Going above I find Paco and Roger off-loading the alternators and battery with help from Andre. I help by taking the battery below where I leave the two guys to do their thing.

It is far too hot to be outdoors so I curl up with Path in the aft settee. Allen is stretched out asleep in his cabin.

The more I read from Path the more fascinated I become with the history and development of this waterway as brilliantly told by David McCullough. If ever I had read that a French company, (Campagnie Universelle Du Canal Interoceanique de Panama), started the Canal in 1880 by a Mr. Ferninand de Lesseps, I do not recall. What I do remember is that President Teddy Roosevelt was commonly credited with having built the Canal; however, in reality it was built under three Presidents, Roosevelt, Taft and Wilson. And in fact of the three, it was Taft who gave the project the most time and personal attention. When Taft replaced Roosevelt in the White House, the Canal was only half finished.

16:00. I go below to check with Paco to ask if he or Roger need anything.

"Aqua, por favor," Paco responds.

I bring them both large bottles of cold water that they gulp down almost without interruption. It is hot and humid in the engine rooms without air-conditioning or outside ventilation.

"Gracias," says Paco.

"De nada."

Returning to the cockpit, I find Allen busy at his desk on his laptop. I don't disturb him but go back to my book.

McCullough devotes the first two hundred forty-one pages of Path to the unsuccessful efforts of the French in building the Canal. The extraordinary venture lasted more than a decade. It had cost two hundred eighty million dollars, far more than had ever been spent on any one peaceful undertaking of any kind. The number of lives lost has never accurately been determined; however, from analysis of the French records, it would conclude that at least twenty thousand died.

It all came to an end for the French with the death of de Lesseps late on the afternoon of December 7, 1894 three weeks after his eighty-ninth birthday.

His death, together with fraud and political corruption, led to the decision by the French government to place the assets of the company up for sale. Their asking price was one hundred nine million dollars.

Theodore Roosevelt made it clear that he felt a passage across the isthmus at some location (Nicaragua was his first choice) was essential to America's control of the Pacific. As President he formed an eight-member commission to study the French proposal that concluded that what the French company had to sell was worth much less than their asking price. The commission established a total value at forty million dollars, which, interestingly was the precise figure the French were now offering to sell it for.

Roosevelt, in a reversal of his support of a Nicaragua route, threw his full support to Panama after seeing the commission report. Panama was declared the unanimous choice for the canal.

A bill was introduced in Congress to authorize the President to acquire the French company's Panama property and concessions at a cost not to exceed forty million dollars; to acquire from Columbia perpetual control of a canal zone at least six miles wide across the Isthmus of Panama; and to build a Panama Canal.

After considerable debate and heated argument from the pro Nicaragua element, the test came in the U.S. Senate on the afternoon of June nineteenth. The vote was forty-two to thirty-four; Panama had won by eight votes. On June twenty-six, the House passed the bill by an overwhelming vote of two hundred fifty-nine to eight. The President signed the bill two days later, June 28, 1902, and so it became the law.

18:00. "Dinner is ready" announces Allen. Paco and Roger make their appearance, both looking tired and hungry. Allen has prepared the last of the Dorado. He has breaded and baked it serving it together with Mexican rice, refried beans and flour tortillas.

Following dinner Allen reminds us of the early start and long day ahead tomorrow. He suggests we all get to bed early.

I wash dishes and clean the galley, as everyone else seems to have retired. Although a good cook, Allen is messy. It takes nearly an hour to get the galley squared away.

21:00. I go above and step out onto the deck. The evening's air is heavy with humidity although a nice breeze off the water makes it comfortable. I stroll forward to where I am clearly able to see the outline of the majestic Bridge of the Americas spanning the canal. Its coat hanger design with its numerous white lights is reminiscent of the Sydney Harbor Bridge in Australia.

Boat traffic this evening is plentiful in both directions reminding me that the canal operates twenty-four hours, seven days a week, three hundred sixty-five days a year. A large container ship slips quietly outward bound, loaded high with containers, riding low in the water. Numerous smaller boats dart up and down the channel, including tugs and some I assume are pilot boats.

I watch as the yacht club's power launch makes several trips to and from the club transporting personnel and goods to boats moored like us within the club's inner basin. Nothing comes our way, which makes me feel easy. Yet I wonder who or what may be watching over us on the eve of our transit.

21:30. With one final look, I retire to my cabin with Path. As tired as I am I cannot seem to put it down. Finally, at eleven o'clock I extinguish the reading light to slowly drift off to sleep, David McCullough swirling around in my head.

CHAPTER TWENTY SEVEN

The Transit

Day 31. Thursday.

05:00. Although there has been faint sunlight in my cabin for several minutes I have laid in my bunk in quiet anticipation of the day's activities. I'm excited and eager to fulfill my dream of transiting this man made wonder known as The Panama Canal. My reading from the wonderful book given to me by Patrick Foley has further heightened the desire.

05:30. Washed and dressed I find Allen is in his cabin where I know this is a busy time for him so do not linger. Paco and Roger are at the settee engaged in quiet conversation. I go below to the galley where I pour a cup of coffee and settle into the settee next to the guys to wait. They, like me, are anxious for the day's activities to begin.

05:55. The boat delivering our pilot approaches. "Hola" calls Paco, signaling that they can discharge their passenger on the port side. The pilot comes aboard at the lifeline opening while almost simultaneously Jose comes aboard on the starboard side via the yacht club's motor launch. Both boats depart without fanfare. Allen joins us from below where introductions are made between one another before the pilot enters the cockpit and Jose goes forward.

The pilot's name is Luis. He is about 35 years old, very professional in appearance with an air of authority. He brings a laptop computer together with a black soft cover briefcase. He is shown into the cockpit where he sits at the settee, looking forward. "You may start your engines," he says. "As soon as you are ready you may proceed into the channel."

"Yes, sir." replies Allen.

"No need for formalities, please call me Luis."

"OK, thanks, Luis."

Allen brings the two engines to life, allowing them to come up to their respective operating temperatures.

Through the foredeck external speakers Allen tells Paco that he may cast off when he is ready.

Paco answers with his usual thumbs up gesture. Once free, Allen applies starboard engine power with the wheel hard to port. Athena answers smoothly. We clear the anchorage, entering the channel. I note in the ship's log the time of 06:30.

"We are going to be transiting with three other vessels," informs Luis. "One is a 650 foot cargo ship, one is a United States Navy drug intervention

boat and the third is a sixteen-foot ski boat. The ski boat will raft up with us,

but will only be with us to Miraflores Lake."

Jose calls us together on the foredeck for a final briefing. Each of our respective one hundred-fifty foot lines is coiled neatly at our stations. I am positioned aft and port, Roger aft and starboard, Paco is forward and starboard and Jose is forward and port. He explains, "Once we are inside a chamber, we will each be thrown small hand lines (sometimes referred to as 'painters') from handlers on the wall. Attach it to the bitter end of your line and slowly play it back out to them. They will secure your line to mooring cleats on the top of the wall. Thereafter, it will be up to the four of us to keep our boat in the center of the chamber. We will adjust as need be as we rise up. Watch for my hand signals. Any questions?"

Each of nods, no. It seems simple enough.

The ski boat joins us. They seemed to have materialized from nowhere. It is heavily loaded with a variety of items. Numerous boxes both large and small, several pieces of household furniture, a 8x10 sheet of Plexiglas, a undeterminable item strapped on top of the Plexiglas and six good size men. They wave and then maneuver in behind us.

They are slightly overloaded. I think to myself.

"They will follow us to the lock, before rafting up", informs Luis.

As I now look up, we are directly under the Bridge of the America's. I again admire its graceful coat hanger design. I know that it stretches across the channel at a soaring 384 feet above mean average high tide. It was inaugurated on October 12, 1962 and it is part of the Pan American Highway that carries motor traffic between North and South America.

"What is the speed capability of your boat, Captain?" asks Luis.

"Comfortably, seven knots in smooth water," replies Allen.

"You are required to do eight knots in crossing Gatun Lake in order to be in position to descend with the others," Luis explains.

"We will do our best."

To our port, at a starting point just to the right of the America's bridge and running north, is a United States Naval Base. The docks, piers and buildings look to be in use; however, there are no ships or signs of human activity.

"Your navy occasionally brings boats here now," tells Luis, "only for short stays. It is one of the many signs of the American departure."

"What are your feelings with regard to the canal transfer?" I ask.

"I am both sad and glad. Sad to see so many of my American friends leaving, many of whom I have known for my entire life. Glad because it gives Panama independence. We can now show the world of our ability to manage our own affairs. To control our own destiny."

Are not seventy-five percent of the jobs presently held by Panamanians?" asks Allen.

"Yes, perhaps as much as ninety percent." replies Luis.

"So the American influence is quite small?"

"Yes and no. The canal is still considered to be in the possession of the United States and until the final day of jurisdiction arrives, we are under the influence of domination. Until we reach independence, we are subordinates."

Quite interesting and opinionated, I say to myself.

We are now in sight of the first locks at Miraflores. It is a two-lock system, four chambers total. As we draw closer, I can begin to make out the two side-by-side locks rising out of the channel while directly in their center is a pier stretching out towards us. At the end of the pier is a white building with a metal tower positioned on top. On the tower are signal lights together with a large red arrow, which rotates left to right designating which chamber to be used. To the left and right of the white building are tracks laid at the concrete pier edge for the electric engines, or "mules" to run upon.

"We will be using the starboard or right chamber according to the arrow," states Luis.

"Roger," answers Allen.

"Can you see the cargo ship nearly inside the chamber being helped by the tugboats on the outside and the mules on the inside?" asks Luis.

"Yes," we all answer in unison.

The naval boat is just ahead of us. It is being prepared to be moved forward by tugs and electric mules.

"We have been given the green light to proceed. Remember, we will be under our own power until well into the chamber."

"Yes, I remember," says Allen, recalling previous transits.

"Captain, we need to raft up with our little friends before going any further."

"OK. Paco have them come forward on our starboard side where you can receive their lines for attachment."

Paco motions for them to join up with us.

"Do you have fenders?' he shouts.

"Yes," is their response.

"Please place them so that we can tie you off."

Two of the men place four dirty, beat-up, deformed fenders along their port side.

"Ai ya ya," mutters Paco," this is no good. Go get our fenders."

Roger and I scurry for four of ours. We secure them at what we consider the correct heights and separation before signaling them to come alongside.

Their lines are not in much better condition than their fenders, but will do. We secure them fore and aft together with two spring lines after which Paco signals to Allen that we are ready.

As we proceed forward we pass a forty-five degree incline, which the mules must climb to get to the top of the chamber wall. The cargo ship and naval ship, I can see, are securely in position.

Allen skillfully guides us past the massive gates or leaves of the chamber.

The two forward line handlers, one each on the top of the left and right walls, yell down to Paco and Jose, "Ready Amigos?'

"Si, ready."

With little delay, two painter lines with baseball size knots on their bitter ends come spiraling down from twenty feet above with a singing, whistling sound. Each of the knots is capable of knocking one out cold if struck on the head. Both lines land on the foredeck with a resounding thud, where the guys retrieve them. Next they tie each line to our one-inch lines and play them back up to the handlers above. Once the length of our lines are fully extended and cleated to the wall, Paco and Jose take up the slack and secure them .

Instinctively I look up to see my handler looking down.

"Ready?" He shouts.

"Yes."

The whipping ball and line come whistling at me like a lariat. Automatically I cover my head with my hands and arms for protection. There is a thud as the rawhide ball lands on the canvas sun cover behind me while the remaining line rains down on top of me. I thrash about finally finding the line leading to the knot.

"Take your time, we are in no rush," comes the reassuring voice of Jose, "let me help you."

"Yes, thank you." I am more than relieved for his help.

"It is not an easy thing to do, especially the first time."

Jose skillfully attaches the painter to my line with a rolling hitch knot and signals above to begin pulling up my one inch line.

"I must go forward to care for my line."

"Thank you, again."

As my line nears tautness, I cleat it off. As I look up I think I see a big grin on the face of my partner, the grin of "I gotch ya."

With all four lines attached, it is now up to the four of us to keep Athena centered in the chamber.

For the first time in several minutes, I have the opportunity to survey my surroundings. Initially I realize that the two sets of gates are closing behind us, shutting us in. Each gate consists of two leaves. Each is sixty-five feet wide and seven foot wide. Here at Miraflores they are eighty-two feet tall. These are the tallest and heaviest (745 tons) of all of the locks because of the extreme variation in the Pacific Ocean tides.

For safety reasons, there are two duplicate sets of gates throughout all of the chambers. One set of double doors is backed by another, in the event that the first fails to function properly or is rammed by a ship.

With the gates now completely closed, there is the sensation of being on a five-block long city street with four story tall buildings on either side; however, there are no doors or windows, nothing to give it scale. And to realize also, because the chamber is never less than one half empty, I am looking at one half of its total size and volume. Statistically, if placed on end, this single lock would be among the tallest structures on the present day Manhattan skyline, surpassed only by the World Trade Center, the Empire State and Chrysler building.

Slowly at first, but increasing steadily, I can see the swirling currents of water entering the chamber from deep below. The water is being admitted through giant tunnels, or culverts, running lengthwise and crosswise within the center and sidewalls. There are seventy well holes in the floor to evenly distribute the turbulence of the incoming water over the full area, thereby subjecting minimum disturbance to ships.

No force is required to raise us, other than gravity. Water simply flows from Miraflores Lake above us into the chamber and we like a giant cork float to the top. It will require 26,000,000 gallons of water and approximately fifteen minutes for us to reach the top. The sensation is as if we are on a slow moving elevator.

As Athena rises, we as line handlers keep her centered. I find that I can easily keep my line taut by running it through the eye of the cleat where I can then pull in or release line as need be. As a team we are working well together.

Fifteen minutes after our start, we are at eye level with the top of the chamber. I try to comprehend all that there is to see, as well as pay attention to my job.

To my right and aft over the starboard rail is a swing bridge, set in an open position parallel with the lock. A duplicate one is to my left and aft, also in an open position. Both, when closed, provide railroad tracks for crossing the two chambers. Open fields of green grass continue from the bridge on my right to the end of the lock.

Reaching our maximum height, Athena's deck is now equal to the top of the wall. Our mooring lines are stretched parallel to the water's surface. Our line handlers are no were to be seen.

"We will remain tethered here until the two larger boats have moved well forward," says Jose.

Directly behind me I sense a flurry of activity. Workers with their various equipment crossing back and forth from one side of the chamber to the other by means of a metal ramp or bridge atop the leaf gate. Men and women in their bright yellow hard hats rush about their business, oblivious to our presence. A quick look at my watch tells me it is just 08:00.

Beyond the gates, I look down over the landscape below. The view is afforded me by the elevation just achieved. The bright morning sun, still relatively low in the southeast sky, provides a backlighted image of Balboa, Panama City and the waterway leading to the Pacific Ocean.

Click, click goes my camera.

Again I have read that the original plans called for the construction of one set of Pacific locks at La Boca (Balboa), much nearer the Pacific entrance than this current one. However, geological conditions were found to be unsuitable for construction without incurring excessive expenses. Accordingly, this and Pedro Miguel, were built three miles inland at their current, more geologically sound and more economical locations.

At the extreme other end of the chamber, the gates are opening. Although we are still secure in our position, the cargo ship is being moved forward. The naval vessel is about to follow.

"Captain Daniels, we will proceed under our own power, passing from this chamber to the next well behind the navy."

"Understand," answers Allen.

The handlers release us from the wall; however, they retain possession of the lines as they walk forward staying with Athena's boat speed. We pass out of the first chamber and into the second. The handlers climb the forty-five degree ramp taking them up to the new wall height as we remain at water level. We play out our lines to them. Once inside, they secure us as before to the chamber walls. The gates close behind us and once again we are elevated by the incoming water.

The walls of the chamber seem in excellent condition, considering their age, the amount of traffic they have handled and what was known over eighty years ago of concrete construction. By latter day standards the engineers were novices in the use of concrete. Many discoveries had yet to be made about the critical water-cement ratios and the susceptibility of the material to environmental attack. To build anything this large was an unprecedented challenge, but what was built has held up even in a climate where almost everything, concrete included, can go to pieces rapidly.

As we reach the top of the chamber, I find that I am just forward of the control house tower. It is a three-story stucco building with a bright red tile pagoda roof. It sits in the middle of this uppermost lock center wall in order to provide an unobstructed view of the entire flight. A series of windows, set at an angle to the ground, similar to an airport control tower run around the entire building just below the roof eves. Two large banners, side by side, stretch across the building just under the windows; one in Spanish, one in English. They read: Providing passage into the 21st century.

Each of our four lines is now stretched parallel to the water indicating that we have reached the top.

Looking aft provides an even more panoramic view of the Pacific, more so with the lower lock as the fore ground. There are a few white puffy clouds now, signifying the heating of the earth by the sun. A light breeze stirs from the west.

Without first realizing it, to our right, I recognize the viewing stands where I, on a previous visit to Panama, had come to watch ships in transit. I remember it was then that I promised myself that I would someday return to do a transit; however, never thinking it would be on as small a boat as this. Today, unlike then, the stand is empty of spectators.

My attention is drawn to Roger who is engaged in conversation with one of the men in the small ski boat. The man is saying something that is holding Rogers attention. He also hands Roger a folded sheet of paper. They are too distant for me to hear or see more.

"Prepare to move forward," calls Luis.

Allen has restarted the engines. He moves us forward as the line handlers walk us to the end of the chamber. They toss us our lines as we clear the final few feet and prepare to enter Miraflores Lake.

To our immediate right is the spillway that helps to control the level of Miraflores Lake and serves as a flood control measure. Several administration buildings can be seen through the trees further along the lake. Their white stucco walls and red tile roofs are strikingly colorful nestled in among the green foliage of the rolling countryside.

"Once we are beyond the end of the staging pier," Luis tells Allen," we can drop off the ski boat. They can be on their own from this point."

"I understand," replies Allen.

Clearing the pier, he stops Athena to allow Paco, Roger and I to untie the smaller boat and toss them their lines.

"Thank you for the ride and good luck," comes from one of the men.

"You are welcome," replies Paco. We wave as they slide away under their own power to take up a 90 degree heading away from us.

"I thought you looked upset while talking to one of them," I say to Roger.

"Not really, they live here on the lake," he says attempting to make light of his conversation. "That is a new boat they have just purchased in Panama City together with other items for the house. The sheet of Plexiglas is to be used for a roof repair."

I decide to leave it at that although I sense there is much more.

Allen proceeds slowly at first before accelerating in order to stay reasonably close to our fellow chamber dwellers.

"Bob, look to the right of the Pedro Miguel Locks," calls out Allen, "do you see the marina?"

"Yes, now I do," I reply after a few moments of searching.

"That is where many pleasure boaters lay over when transiting, wishing to spend time resting, exploring and sightseeing."

Actually, I had read about the number of cruisers who remain here resting and provisioning. Many leave their boats in the care of the marina while they return home to handle affairs, after which they return to continue their adventure. The marina has been extensively written up in cruising magazines as safe and well operated. From this distance, it looks to be very crowded. There are many telephone poles, as my one grandson would say.

The lake is, of course, manmade, created by the building of Miraflores locks and the damming of the Rio Grande River. By my estimate it is two miles long and at its widest point two miles wide. The shoreline is dotted with trees and open fields. Buoys mark the channel to Pedro Miguel.

At mid lake on our port side, we pass a large floating structure. Moorings and steel cables hold it in position. It rises to a height of thirty-five to forty feet and is easily sixty feet long. As we pass one end, I can see it is narrow, maybe six foot thick. Two cranes, a white construction shack and numerous other pieces of equipment are perched on top.

"That is the leaf of a gate under repair," informs Luis. "We are only seeing about one half of its total. As you can tell it floats, like a ship. It is watertight.

"Was it damaged?' I ask.

"No. It is here as part of the ongoing preventative maintenance program of the canal. This is one of eighty gates that are systematically refurbished."

From this position I can see that a large sheet metal plate of skin has been removed. It is like looking inside the hull of a ship with the exposed ribs showing. Several workers can be seen inside.

"Because of the buoyancy, the leaf offers very little weight upon the hinge pins and bearings," continues Luis. "The opening and closing of the gates swing as easily and steadily as one would open an ordinary door."

" How are the gates operated?" my inquisitive mind asks.

" The gates are connected by steel arms, or struts, to large horizontal wheels concealed inside the lock walls. These wheels are nearly twenty feet in diameter and are geared to a large electric motor. To open or close, the wheel revolves about two hundred degrees delivering power to the gate through the strut."

"Stand by for chamber approach," warns Allen.

Our position is at the outer end of the staging pier. The red arrow points to the starboard chamber. We have a green light.

"All of the locks have the same dimensions, 110 by 1,000 feet and are built in pairs, two chambers running side by side in order to accommodate two lanes of traffic," continues the very informative Luis. "The single flight at Gatun consists of three pairs. Miraflores as you know has two sets and here at Pedro Miguel there is one set, making six pairs or twelve chambers in all."

The cargo ship has advanced to its forward position in the chamber as the naval boat starts to take up its place just aft. We, like the tardy child, hurry to catch up, finally gliding into the vast chamber under the skillful hand of Captain Allen.

The line handlers above signal if we are ready? Unlike earlier, I time the advancing rope ball making a nice Willie Mays basket catch. I secure the painter to my line with a half hitch. The handler above takes up the slack as I feed him my one-inch line. The entire procedure takes less than two minutes. I thread my bitter end through the cleat eye and stand ready for further instructions from Jose.

"Nice job," yells Allen.

Jose and Paco each give me a thumb up.

I think to myself, "What a difference one hour can make. At Miraflores I looked like a bumbling landlubber. Well, I better not strut too much I have this lock to exit and Gatun to go down."

With Athena securely tethered, the gates start to close. They appear to swing effortlessly and with no perceptible sound. I now have a much better understanding and appreciation of the scope of their operation, thanks to Luis.

There is comparatively little noise as water begins to fill the great chamber. Something this large and so vital to world commerce, ought somehow to make a good deal of noise. But there is very little. In the distance I hear thebells clang on the towing locomotives now and again together with the low whine of their engines, but little more than that.

"Keep a steady pressure on your lines," encourages Jose from his forward position, "we are approaching the top of the chamber and need to remain centered."

Our ascent has taken us just under fifteen minutes. The gates forward swing open to the waters of Gatun Lake.

With the few minutes available before moving, I go forward in order to get a closer look at the naval vessel.

Although it is over one hundred feet in length, she appears much smaller, perhaps in part by a narrow beam. There is little question that she is built for speed and maneuverability. She sports a camouflage paint color combination of olive green and earth brown. There is light armament; however, I do not recognize any of the weapons.

At the stern or fantail is a small open area accessible by a large sliding glass door into the ship while protected from the outside by stantions and chain. It may be a staging area for deploying or retrieving small boats or personnel. It is only a few feet above water level, much like the swim platform on a water ski boat. Above this is a deck with an electric hoist and numerous other non-descript articles of military value. United States Marines, in combat fatigues man the vessel.

Allen has started our engines. I return to take up my station. Our line handlers walk us forward to the front of the chamber before heaving us our lines. My handler waves and yells "Good trip".

The sun is now hot, as it has climbed high above.

"It is a good thing I have my hat," I holler over to Roger, "otherwise the top of my head would be fried." He smiles back. He has a very full head of hair. No problem for him at his young age.

It is now a few minutes after eleven as we gather in and secure our lines.

"We are on our own to make it across Gatun Lake," says Luis, "we have approximately four hours to make the thirty-five mile trip."

"OK, let's do it," responds Allen. "Everything secure?"

"Everything is secure, Captain," answers Paco.

Allen brings the engines to 2750 rpms. Athena moves out to a speed of 7.8 knots.

"I think you will find the channel well marked," comments Luis, "each of the buoys are in sight of one another generally."

"Thanks," replies Allen.

"Technically we are not yet in Gatun Lake," continues Luis with his narrative; "we are at the beginning of the nine-mile transit of Gaillard Cut that in earlier years was known as Culebra Cut. This was the focus of attention, regardless of whatever else was happening along the canal route, for seven years, from 1907 to 1913."

"Why so much attention?" I ask.

"The major problem was in the excavation of the unstable soil which led to countless landslides. Originally, the cut was to be 670 feet wide; however, with each slide as further depth was attempted, the width increased proportionately. Further ahead as you will see, the distance from side to side approaches 1,800 feet."

As we proceed into the Cut, the surface of the water is smooth allowing forward movement to be without resistance. Our boat speed at times exceeds eight knots.

With line handling duties terminated for now, I am free to move about. I join Roger seated on the foredeck where the breeze created by our forward speed is enjoyable, taking away some of the heat and humidity of the early afternoon.

The Cut seems narrow here. It is if we are in a river. The channel buoys set as they are add further to the feeling of narrowness. Natural jungle growth starts at the water's edge and marches up the hilly terrain on both sides to heights of several hundred feet. Like Costa Rica, there are dozens of shades of green. Over the years since excavation, the jungle has reclaimed the land with a wide variation of ferns, plants and trees.

"Wow, look what is coming!" I blurt out, pointing forward.

From around the bend, now in full view, is an American warship, the guided missile cruiser, USS Ticonderoga. She makes an impressive sight as she steams towards us filling the channel with her size and presence.

Click, click goes my camera as we quickly meet and pass. Many of her officers and crew are out on deck; some on duty, many not, all hopefully enjoying this memorable experience. In passing there is little wake. Athena is little bothered as we continue to make good time towards our rendezvous at Gatun Locks.

"What happened with the ski boat people, Roger?" I ask. "You're bothered by something. Can I help?"

He slowly looks towards me. "I knew you saw too much this morning. They delivered a message from the cartel," he blurts out.

"And?" I ask after several moments of silence.

"The package is to be turned over to a man tonight."

"Where and when?"

"All I was told is that I should have the package ready for pickup at the Panama Canal Yacht Club."

"Had you planned to tell Allen?"

"No. I was told that serious harm would come to anyone who tried to interfere. I don't want to put you guys in any more of harm's way."

"Don't you think it's a little late for that now?"

"I don't know. I'm so confused I don't know what to do."

"I think you need to inform Allen so he in turn can get to Weber. If you'll stay I'll get him out here to talk." Without waiting for any rebuttal, I rise and make my way aft to the cockpit where Luis remains seated at the salon with Allen at the wheel. I stand at the chart table pretending to be interested in the log while in fact I write a note. ROGER NEEDS TO SPEAK TO YOU. I fold it and hand it to Allen.

"Allen, can you use a break?" I ask, "you have been at that wheel for hours."

"Yes, I could as a matter of fact."

"Is there anything special to be aware of?"

"No, stay to the right of center and maintain present speed."

With that, I take over while he disappears below into his cabin.

"I understand you will be leaving us up ahead at Matachin?" I ask of Luis.

"Yes, that is so. I must attend to some personal matters. A friend and fellow pilot has agreed to relieve me."

"I see."

"My wife and I are expecting our first child. She wants me home."

"I understand," I say, thinking back to my own times.

"Do you have children?' asks Luis.

"Yes, my wife and I have five."

"You have been very busy." Luis says with a broad grin.

"They are all grown and on their own now, the youngest will be thirty years old in two weeks."

"We think we only want two. One boy and one girl. That would be ideal."

"I think that's smart," I reply.

Allen emerges from his cabin and without comment steps outside. I watch as he walks forward to where Roger is seated and sits down beside him. On any ordinary day it would be a friendly chat between two friends, only today it is much different, I suspect.

We are in sight of an approaching super cargo ship.

"I would give her added room to pass," suggests Luis, "that type of ship is hard to control at slow speed and has limited visibility."

I ease more to the right of the channel.

"It is called a PANAMAX," offers Luis. "It is the largest size vessel in terms of width and length to fit into a chamber. From container ships to car carriers to dry bulk carriers to tankers, they squeeze through the locks with only inches to spare. They comprise more than a quarter of the 12,500 annual Canal transits."

To describe the leviathan, I would think in terms of a cardboard box set atop a boat hull. The bridge is set high atop of the box. The sides rise from the water line vertically to a height of fifty feet where there are no windows, only companionways. She is painted black above the waterline to midpoint on the hull, then white above including the superstructure. Eurasian Dream is painted boldly at her bow. She flies the flag of Japan. We pass one another without incident.

13:30. I estimate we are at the five-mile point into the Cut. Here the channel begins to widen. No longer does it feel that we are in a river, more like a small lake. The sides of the Cut slope back at more like forty-five degrees rather than the near vertical drop we had seen earlier. They are pock marked by bare earth with only occasional foliage.

"What is happening here?" I ask.

"This is part of the ongoing Cut widening program which is currently the Canal's largest improvement project. PANAMEX vessels, and certain other ships, are, for safety reasons, restricted from passing in this narrow, 500-foot-wide section. Widening and straightening the Cut to a minimum of 630 feet in straight sections and a minimum of 730 feet at curves will allow for virtually unrestricted two-way traffic for all vessels throughout the length of the waterway. Incidentally, we are at the continental divide. Here rain waters flow either north to the Caribbean or south to the Pacific."

In rounding the next curve, we come upon the mainstays of the canal's excavation program, the dipper dredge "Christensen" and the drill boat "Thor" as explained to me by Luis. "The dredge is used for the removal of spoils from underwater while the drill boat is used for blasting."

"What happens with the spoils?" I ask.

"They are taken to various locations, depending on what might be needed.

"You realize that it was the spoils of this nine-mile section of excavation, which created Gatun and Miraflores Dams, and the land area for the city of La Boca, the largest, which was renamed Balboa. At Balboa, 22,000,000 cubic yards were deposited, with the result that 676 acres were reclaimed from the Pacific. Have you been to the Zone?"

"Yes, although for a short time. I was impressed by the wide streets, neat houses and green grass."

"The United States takes very good care of it."

A conventional cargo ship passes. She is low in the water, heavily laden although without signs of her cargo above decks. She is the type of ship, a tramp steamer, that I have always felt would be great to book aboard as a passenger. She displays a Panamanian flag from her transom as she moves smartly on her way.

"Here is where I shall depart," warns Luis pointing to a pilot boat making its way towards us. I bring us to an idle while the pilot boat comes along side. Paco and Allen rig fenders on the port side where Luis with his belongings waits at the gate opening.

"Good luck and thanks for the information," I say.

"Thanks to everyone," waves Luis as he nimbly jumps off to the waiting tender.

Our new pilot comes quickly aboard. Allen extends a handshake while showing him onto the bridge. The pilot boat moves away, accelerating to high speed back in the direction it had come.

I move Athena into the channel and back to speed.

The terrain is changing once again. It is flattening out and widening as we enter Gatun Lake. GPS calculates that we have approximately twenty-three miles to go.

Allen relieves me at the wheel. I introduce myself to the pilot, Felix.

"Glad to have you aboard."

"Thanks, I look forward to working with all of you."

Felix, I learn is Panamanian. He appears to be in his mid- thirties, married with one child, a boy. Like Luis he comes with a laptop computer and black briefcase. He settles in at the settee.

"What is your ETA at Gatun, Captain?"

"16:00 hours at our present speed of seven and one-half knots," explains Allen.

With only light chop, Athena is making good time. There is none of the cavitation of water being trapped under the superstructure as we had previously experienced in heavier seas. Undoubtedly, this is the type of sea condition for which the boat was principally designed. Unfortunately, there are few places where you are apt to find water this smooth for a boat with this configuration.

I elect to remain in the cockpit area, at least for now.

"I understand you and Luis are good friends," I say to make small talk.

"Yes, he and I attended ship pilot training school together and have remained close friends since. In fact we were each other's best men at our weddings. We work closely with one another on many activities, both on and off work. He is more like a bother."

"I was impressed by Luis's history and general knowledge of the Canal," I say.

"Yes, we both have taken special interest in becoming familiar with the Canal's past and present. After all, it is our heritage and our future."

"I find both subjects fascinating. I never realized the scope and magnitude of this engineering marvel."

"Most first time visitors do not. It is only after they have done a transit do they realize the significance of what man created here over eighty years ago."

I nod in understanding.

"Luis and I like to watch people's expressions as we tell them some of the little known facts about the Canal. Generally we do not have a large audience; mostly ship's captains, first and second mates, the helmsman and a few others involved in the management of the vessel. Much like we have here today. Some are interested, others could care less."

"Speaking at least for myself," I say, "I am very interested. I hope you will not mind continuing."

"No, not at all. Captain, may I use your restroom?"

"Of course, use mine," offers Allen pointing towards his cabin.

Once Felix goes below I ask what he and Roger may have decided about this evenings package transfer.

"Very little. My suggestion is that we proceed normally and hope for the best."

"Do you intend to contact Weber?"

"No. I feel it would be difficult at best to reach him and I don't want to cause alarm with our pilot"

"Perhaps he should be brought into the loop?"

"That only implicates additional innocent folks. We need to stay calm and let this play out as it wants." Recognizing that Allen has made his decision, I turn my attention back to the view before me.

Gatun Lake now spreads out before us under a broken sky. There is little definition at the horizon so I am unable to see a shoreline ahead or on either side. The only points of reference are the navigation buoys that march across the open water, red to starboard, green to port and an occasional passing vessel.

"This is one of the largest manmade lakes in the world," Felix says on his return. "It covers approximately one hundred sixty four square miles." He goes on to tell how much land area vanished under water in the lakes creation.

"Every village between Gatun and Manachinis covered, a prospect that the native populace found impossible to believe. Mile after mile of the ill-tempered Chagres River disappeared, as did the Panama Railroad, which would have to be rebuilt on higher ground to skirt the Eastern Shore. Residence of the old village of Gatun, hearing that a dam was to be built where the village stood, refused to leave. Later as the actual construction began and several houses were crushed from dumping rock, did they agree to move out to the new village.

Water spills from Madden Lake, located a short distance to starboard of our present position, together with Gatun Dam controls the level of the lake. Supplied from rainwater that falls on the Canal watershed, the lake furnishes the millions of gallons of fresh water necessary to operate the waterways as well as generate electric power."

"I understand the Canal supplies its own electric power," states Allen.

"Our electric generating facilities at Gatun provide sufficient power to operate all of the approximately 1,500 electric motors and their controls, the towing locomotives or mules, all Canal lighting. We added night lighting in 1967. We supply power to all of the villages and towns within the Zone, including Colon and Balboa. Yes, the Canal is self-sufficient as to energy needs."

Felix I learn is a third generation Zonie. He is able to trace his family history to a grandfather who came from Spain in the early part of the 20th century as an engineer to work for John Foley, then chief engineer for the Panama Canal Company. His grandmother was a native Panamanian of Indian and Spanish blood. Both of his parents are of mixed native blood, giving him his dark olive skin, deep brown eyes and high cheek bones. He was educated within the Canal's school system, where his father like his grandfather worked for the Canal Company. After high school he attended the University of Panama where he earned a degree in math and science.

"The general details of the Canal I learned from my grandfather. He arrived here in early 1906 and was involved in many aspects of the design and planning of the locks and chambers. Although too young to either understand or remember much of the detailed work in which he was involved, before his death he made sure I knew that all of the Canal's detailed plans, drawings, maps, surveys, contracts, meteorological records, had been saved and where they can be found. Someday I am in hopes

of being able to visit Washington, DC, where the major portion of the surviving records of both the French and American efforts are on file at the Library of Congress and the National Archives. Fortunately, there is an abundance of material closer here at the Canal Administration Building."

As we draw nearer to Gatun, Felix continues, "Gatun dam and locks extend a mile and one half across the river valley, a ridge of earth that is fifteen times as wide at its base as it is high. The building of the great dam, for so long the most worrisome part of the plan, turned out to one of the least difficult tasks of all. A tremendous man-made embankment simply grew year by year."

15:00 The locks and dam at Gatun are now visible on the far horizon.

"I see the navy boat to our starboard. Is that the cargo ship further down the line?" asks Allen.

"Yes," answers Felix, "They are waiting for us. This time we will enter first. When given the green light move forward into whichever chamber they designate."

15:50 Allen has throttled us down to minimum speed for steerage. To port, well- guarded by safety buoys, is the giant spillway of Gatun Dam. From beyond it come a thunderous roar and a giant cloud of mist from the falling water.

The red arrow at the end of the staging pier moves to designate the starboard chamber. We are given a green signal light to advance.

"Paco, make ready for the transit down."

"Yes, captain."

Each of us takes our positions as Allen moves us forward past the staging area and into the chamber. It seems strange to be entering a full chamber of water and to be the first to enter.

The line handlers easily toss their painters, which in turn we secure to our lines and pass back for attachment to the wall.

The view towards Colon and the Caribbean is as spectacular this late afternoon as was the view this morning of the Pacific. The sun over my right shoulder gives full illumination to the lower chambers and the waterway leading towards the broad expanse of the ocean beyond. This elevation gives the impression of "standing on top of the world."

"Hey Bob" yells Allen, "we are about ready to start down."

I scurry back to my position, a little embarrassed at not having been more aware of our situation. Looking aft I can see that our partners are in place and the gates are fully closed.

Slowly at first, the waters start to drain. Now in reverse, we play our lines out as we slowly begin the decent, as gently as if a giant hand was lowering us. The decent takes about the same amount of time as the ascent, twelve to fifteen minutes.

"Tie it off," informs Jose, "we are at the bottom."

Almost immediately the gates open to expose the second chamber, its waters shimmering in the late afternoon sun, waiting for our arrival.

As Allen powers us forward, the four line handlers move with us to our new position and secure us once again to the wall.

"What can you tell me about the towing locomotives?" I ask Felix while we wait for our partners to load in.

"Well, certainly they have become one of the most familiar features of the canal. Each is just over thirty-feet long, weighs forty-three tons and has identical cabs at either-end with duplicate controls and driving engines so that they can run in either direction without turning around. Each has an independently powered, center-mounted windlass that can handle over eight hundred feet of steel cable. Line can be played out or reeled in at rapid speed and with loads on the line of as much as twenty-five thousand pounds. With the windlass, the locomotive can control a ship without it moving."

"Where are they manufactured?"

"In Schenectady, New York by the General Electric Company. G. E. has supplied, over the years, virtually all of the motors, relays, switches, wiring and generating equipment."

Again in this chamber as before the draining waters lower us effortless. The gates open to the third and last chamber. Allen moves us forward where we are tethered for the final decent. All too soon we reach the bottom.

Now, in the shadows of the chambers above us, it is much cooler than when we were high above in the bright sunlight.

"It will be dark very quickly, in less than an hour," warns Jose as we gather in and coil our lines for the final time.

Allen moves us out from within the chamber and into the channel.

We pass several large ships to our port being readied to go up the ladder. Tugboats, pushing their burdens into position, churning up the waters with their mighty engines and propellers assist them. Their wake, together with the remaining water emptying out of the chamber, gives us a bumpy but speedy ride down the path to Colon.

I glance at my watch, six o'clock straight up. It has taken us twelve hours to this point to make the transit, much as had been expected.

"Careful, behind you, Allen" yells Paco.

The naval boat moves pass us to port at a high rate of speed. In the fading light of day, despite her running lights, it is difficult to identify her features with the camouflaged paint.

"They are in a big rush, wherever they are going," says Allen.

"They are afraid to be late for chow," says Roger.

"Captain, here comes my ride," points Felix to an approaching boat. "My duties are completed."

"Paco, prepare for personnel transfer."

The pilot boat comes along our port side where Roger and I have set fenders.

Allen reduces speed to steerage as the two vessels come together.

"Good meeting you and good luck," Allen says on behalf of all of us. I wave from my position as Felix steps aboard. "Thanks for all of the information," I yell. He acknowledges with a wave in return. He disappears into the cabin as they pull away into the evening's twilight.

Continuing down the channel, Allen guides us to the entrance buoy of the Panama Canal Yacht Club where under the cover of near darkness we make a right turn into the mooring area. "We'll take the empty mooring at ten o'clock," he informs Paco over the foredeck speaker.

As in so many times before, Paco with hand signals to Allen guides us up to position where Roger retrieves the painter on the buoy, bringing it and the hawser onboard where it is secured.

With engines shut down and the boat secure, Allen calls for a meeting in the cockpit, careful not to include Jose. "We should all go ashore," he says. "I don't believe I have to remind you that we may be in for a rough time. We need to act as if everything is routine and normal. If we do our part, I believe Weber's team will keep us safe."

"Shall I bring the package?" asks Roger.

"Yes," replies Allen.

CHAPTER TWENTY EIGHT

The Transfer

We immediately go about the business of preparing to go ashore. Paco runs the electric winch while Roger and I guide the tender off of its cradle and away from the boat. We secure it on the port side at the boarding gate.

After a final security check and locking the cabin door, Allen joins us in the waiting tender. We power away from Athena under the steady hand of Paco. The southerly wind on our nose creates waves at close intervals that make for a bumpy ride. Although still hot and humid the sea breeze has a cooling effect on the exposed skin.

The anchorage is very large containing many boats of varying sizes and shapes. A few of them display lights but most are simply silhouettes against the far distant shore lights.

"Do you remember the way in?" asks Allen.

"I believe so," answers Paco.

"Head straight ahead to the low building with lights," offers Jose.

After several minutes of threading through the maze of anchored boats, Paco brings us to the crowded dinghy dock of the yacht club where he is able to maneuver us up to the dock. Allen and Roger tie us off. We each in turn scramble out of the dinghy onto the slippery deck, wet from the evening's humidity. Gathered together we walk towards the clubs entrance. Although the area is well lighted, it is difficult to see beyond a short distance of the light's penetration into the night darkness. At the clubs entrance, Jose stops to offer his well wishes, "It has been a pleasure serving with you," he says while offering his hand to each of us. "I hope I have the opportunity to do it again."

"How will you get home?" we ask.

"My daughter is here waiting in the parking lot," he responds with the wave of a hand as he turns away and is absorbed by the darkness.

"Ok, are we ready? Let's see what happens," says Allen as he pushes open the double glass doors. "To the right are the clubs offices, straight-ahead is the bar and to the left is the dining room. Bathrooms are at the other end of the bar. I need to check in with the manager. I will be right back," continues Allen. "I'll meet you in the bar." With that, he strides down the hallway before disappearing into the manager's office.

The three of us make our way into the bar. There are but a few patrons at the far end so we have little trouble finding three bar stools. I make myself comfortable, glad to be out of the heat and humidity.

"What can I get for you gentlemen?" asks a young man.

"A cold Pacifico," I respond. My two companions each order a soda.

"Be right back," he says.

I am surprised at the perfect English. I was fully prepared to try my Spanish.

For reasons that I am unable to explain, I am very relaxed and at ease in light of what may be expected. I sense that this is not so with Roger who looks tired and worried. I try to make conversation, but he has pulled back into his shell. Paco also remains silent.

My observations tell me that The Balboa Yacht Club pales compared to this facility. It is clear that this is newer and much better maintained. It is fully enclosed against the outside elements with air conditioning to provide comfort from the heat and humidity. The bar is well stocked, clean and properly manned. The dining room over my left shoulder is equally as nice with tables set with white table clothes, napkins, stem-ware and center pieces. It would appear that the club caters to an affluent membership.

Our drinks arrive followed shortly by Allen who informs us that we have permission to spend the night on the buoy where Athena is presently moored. Rather surprisingly, he orders a rum and coke.

"I was able to speak with agent Weber," he says in a low voice so as not to be heard beyond our group. "He assures me that the club is under full surveillance as is the boat. He says we need to stay calm. He suggests we remain here for dinner."

"You guys need to split from me," Roger announces very emphatically after sliding off his stool to stand in front of us. "This is my mess and I don't want you hurt or killed because of me."

"Don't be foolish," says Allen. "We are all in this together."

"No you are not. You are innocent bystanders. I am the guilty one for allowing myself to get involved in a foolish scheme. You three need to go back to the boat and leave me here to face the consequences. I can handle myself alone, as I have for years."

Allen's silent look at Roger reveals his mind at work. Before he can respond a lively group of four couples burst through the front doors. They are dressed in evening attire, suggesting they may be headed for the theater. I estimate that they are all in their late twenties or early thirties, each sporting an air of affluence and opulence. In approaching the bar it becomes clear that they are out on the town for the night and this is not their first stop. It is difficult to determine who belongs to whom, as they seem to be quite familiar with one another.

"Drinks for everyone," says one of the men. "Especially for the four visiting yachtsmen," he says looking in our direction. His offer comes at an inopportune time; however, to decline would be considered inappropriate.

The revelers introduce themselves with polite handshakes as they mingle with us as long lost friends. They have many questions about where we are from and where are we going. I am struck by how friendly they are particularly the young ladies.

"Who has the package?" asks one of the young men rather abruptly and without candor. I am caught completely off guard. My heart races in the gravity of the moment, I go stone silent.

"I do," answers Roger without hesitation stepping forward.

"May I have it please? It is my wife's birthday present."

"How do I know that you are its rightful owner?" asks Roger with an air of authority I had not seen before.

"I have the balance of your money. Perhaps that will convince you," answers the young man as he reaches inside his jacket to withdraw a white envelope.

Roger reveals the package keeping it close to his chest with both hands.

"Darling, it's wrapped so pretty, what is it?" asks one of the women.

"You will see it if the young man will turn it over to me."

Realizing he has little alternative, Roger hands over the package in exchange for the envelope. The package immediately goes into the man's jacket pocket.

"May I see it, please?" asks his anxious female companion.

"In due time my love," he answers. "But now it is time for us to say goodbye to these nice people," he says moving away from the bar.

Abruptly, four men burst through the front door with FBI prominently displayed on their hats and jackets. "Drop to your knees with hands on your head," orders one of them as each has a handgun prominently displayed. The young man grabs his female companion, pulling her to him as a human shield. He brandishes a handgun from his jacket.

"No one needs to get hurt," say the same FBI men whose voice I recognize as that of agent Weber. "Let's all stay calm."

"Get out of my way, "yells the young man forcing his lady to stand in front of him. The other party members scatter to take cover leaving him and his hostage alone in the center of the room. The four agents quickly fan out making it nearly impossible for the lone gunman to cover them all.

"I'll kill her," he shouts, now cocking his gun and aiming it at the woman's head. "I'll do it if you don't let me out of here without interference."

For several seconds it is a Mexican standoff as each faction sizes one another up. The gunman now starts to half drag; half push the woman towards the door.

"Wait, let talk," says Weber attempting to distract him.

"There is nothing to talk about," replies the gunman as he continues to force his way out.

Without warning Roger sprints from his bar stool towards the young man, tackling him from behind in a bone crushing crash that causes the gun to discharge. Roger, the woman and the gunman fall into a pile of human entanglement before Roger is upon the man pinning his hands behind his back. The FBI agents rush forward to further restrain him. The woman does not move. She lies in an increasing size pool of blood. Allen and I hurry to her aid where we find her unconscious with a gunshot wound to her scalp. She is bleeding profusely. I hold her head while Allen applies his handkerchief to the wound while Paco goes for a wet towel from the rest room. The bartender is asked to call for medical help.

Meanwhile, the gunman is lifted to his feet, handcuffed and relieved of the package.

"What is your name?" asks Weber.

"I think you know the answer to that," he says sarcastically.

"Who do you work for?"

"No comment."

"Where were you taking the package?"

"No comment."

"Do you understand the seriousness of withholding information to a United States Federal Agent?"

"Go to hell."

Following several more outbursts of defiance, Weber has the shackled young man led away.

The woman begins to stir from the wet compress applied to the wound. "She is coming to," says Allen. "I don't believe it is serious but she should be taken to a hospital for observation."

20:00 "Your duties with me are completed," says Weber having joined us in the clubs restaurant. Matt and Patrick accompany him. It is good to see them; especially Mathew whom I certainly didn't expect would be here.

"I hope we have performed to your expectations," says Allen after a few minutes of introductions.

"But in fact you have led us to one of the top men within the cartels Panama operation. For that we are grateful."

"Can you divulge more about him?"

"He is from a prominent and well to do Panama family. His family and their connections will undoubtedly see his release without reprimand. Local authorities have known that he and his family is and has been connected to the Columbian cartel for many years. What is different here is that smuggling is not typical of their mode of operations. It leads the Bureau to believe that this may have been a one-time endeavor. It is again believed that their intention would have been to have the stone cut up and sold off in small units."

Patrick joins in. "The gemologist in Panama City, after examining the stone, confirmed that what you bloody fellows have been carrying around these past weeks is indeed a blue star sapphire weighing over 500 carats."

"The Bureau and I," says Weber, "are still of the opinion that the cartel never intended to have Mendoza send the stone as he did. Then when they learned how the gem was being transported, they panicked by insisting that the package be retrieved. It was why Roger was contacted in Acapulco and why Winter tried in Golfito."

"What will now happen with Roger?" asks Allen.

"He will have to stand charges for aiding and abetting. I'll recommend leniency, but it will ultimately depend on a judge's decision. In the meantime he is to remain in your custody," he says looking at Allen. "On your safe return to Puerto Vallarta, arrangements will be made to have you brought to Houston for arraignment," he continues now focusing his attention to Roger. "Understood?"

"Yes, I do. Thank you," answers Roger.

"What is the status of the boat's sale?" asks Allen.

"I represent the prospective owner," says Matt. "I have a letter from the bank authorizing that the boat be delivered tomorrow to the boat yard located next to the yacht club for haul out and survey. Does 09:00 fit your schedule, Captain Daniels?"

"Perfectly," answers Allen.

"Upon delivery and acceptance by the boat yard, you and your crew are free to head for home. Patrick will assume responsibility for documentation and transfer of ownership."

"My office can help with airline reservations and accommodations in Panama City if needed," says Patrick.

"What does the new owner intend to do with her?" asks Allen.

"He sees her doing charter work on Lake Gatun."

"We'll have her there at 09:00."

"Oh, one last thing," says Weber. "I do have one final piece of information that I feel will be of interest to the four of you. Gaston de la Hoya was not entirely truthful in what he told you about his identify. He was a double agent. When his position within Guatemala was compromised, he elected to try to escape to Mexico where he had many friends. Unfortunately, his planning was flawed to the degree that when he and his daughter and son-in-law encountered tropical storm Blanco they were blown out to sea and away from his intended landfall in Mexico."

"That is when we found them?" I ask.

"Yes. Had you fellows not come along, they could still be bobbing around miles from anywhere. Anyhow, when the bureau notified the state department, a rescue at sea was authorized because of the sensitive nature of what de la Hoya was working on."

"Why did he take his life?" Allen asks.

"Not certain why. His daughter thinks that the shame of his having been caught may have been the cause. At this point only he knows".

"And the envelope," I ask.

"It contained the location of highly sensitive information, now in the hands of the state department."

"And baby Allen?' ask Paco.

"Safe, together with his mother and father. All three have been given political asylum and will apply for citizenship as soon as possible."

"All I can say is that you blokes certainly have had one hell of a wild time. Allen, are all of your deliveries this full of adventure?' asks Patrick.

"No, thank goodness. And special thanks to agent Weber for keeping us safe."

"With that I'll say my good byes and be on my way. It has been a pleasure working with each of you," concludes agent Weber with handshakes for each of us. Matt and Patrick leave soon thereafter indicating that they will be at the boat yard in the morning.

Famished, we eat with very little conversation. I find myself relieved that the long delivery and package drama are drawing to a conclusion.

22:30 Finished with dinner, we retrieve the dinghy and take the choppy ride out to Athena. She waits silently for us as we make a 360-degree security turn before going aboard. Unwilling to leave the dinghy in the water over night, we bring it aboard.

Without hesitation we say our goodnights and retire to our cabins. Exhausted, I fall into bed. I'm too tired to think about tomorrow and what probably will be the final day onboard.

CHAPTER TWENTY NINE

Homeward Bound

$\mathbf{D}$ay 32. Friday

The day begins bleakly with dark clouds that race across the sky driven by winds of ten to twelve knots from the southeast. Quite a contrast to the sun washed skies of Panama City/ Balboa of the past few days. The temperatures are the same I presume, warm and sticky.

Showered and dressed, I pack my duffel bag before going above.

Now with full daylight I am able to see just how large this body of water is where we are anchored. I learn from our chart that this is the world's second largest duty-free port. As the Atlantic entrance to the Panama Canal it is literary 'the crossroads of world commerce.'

08:45 We release Athena from her mooring for the short trip to the boat yard. Two boat handlers meet us at the visitor's dock where they tie us down.

The boat yard is massive, spread out over several acres. I count three railways each capable of hauling boats up to one hundred feet in length and easily thirty feet wide. In addition, there are three Travel Lifts for smaller boats at other haul out locations. Numerous metal buildings are grouped together housing engine repair, metal fabrication, and welding and electrical facilities.

Matt and Patrick are not long in joining us. After a few documents that require Allen's signature are completed, Matt tells us that we are free to leave. Patrick offers us a ride to Panama City where we can book reservations home from his office.

"Give us a few minutes to get our gear," asks Allen.

I take the now familiar route through the cockpit, exiting down four steps before turning left to enter Paco's and my common bathroom and then into my cabin. All I need to do now is gather the last of my odds and ends.

The realization of having spent the last four weeks here surprises me. It seems like yesterday that I had brought these very items aboard. I have felt very comfortable here, somewhat removed from the rest of the crew in my own little world. The rhythmic vibration of the port engine drive shaft, the whine of the 5kw generator, the sometimes odiferous smell from the nearby head, the low overhead and narrow bunk are all very familiar.

Without further reflection, I stow away the last of the items and make my way above with a final look the main salon, galley and finally the cockpit area. It truly is like leaving an old friend. Silently I wish her well.

I swing the duffel bag over the side to an awaiting deckhand before lowering myself onto the dock where Paco and Roger are waiting. I take out the camera for one last picture of Allen, Paco, Roger and myself taken by Matt. Patrick has brought his car to the head of the ramp leading up from the dock. We load our gear into the back end of the Land Rover.

"Please say hello to Helen, Meredith and Sara from me," I say to Matt with a strong handshake. "Come visit us in Maine."

"We shall for sure," he says on closing my door before Patrick engages the clutch and we peel out of the boat yard. Not surprising I realize the Rover is right hand drive.

The ride back to Panama City is a thrill. Patrick drives with one hand on the wheel while the other is in constant jester as he describes our surroundings traveling at twenty miles over the speed limit. Sitting in the back seat wedged in between Paco and Roger I have a clear view of the road ahead that at times I wish I didn't.

The two-lane road can best be described as secondary. It winds and twists as it rises and falls with the terrain leading up to the peak or spine of the peninsula. To some extent it follows the railroad bed of the Panama Canal Railroad that in turn follows the shoreline of Gatun Lake where there are many open vistas overlooking the lakes wide expanse. At other times we are deep in the jungle with limited visibility except for an occasional village or open space.

Continuing to climb we find ourselves in the clouds as we pass over the mountain peaks before starting down towards Balboa. Before long we break out into the bright sunshine of what seems like another world. Again we join up and run parallel with the railroad. We pass well-groomed grounds with the Canal Zones signature white stucco and red tile roof buildings. We come close to Miraflores locks where I can clearly see the control tower and viewing stands seen yesterday. At one point we cross over the intersection of the Pan American Highway leading to the Bridge of the Americas.

Patrick's office is located in a modest building located not far from the Balboa Yacht Club. He introduces us to his secretary Lois who proves to be efficient and well organized. He excuses himself to enter his office.

"Does it make sense for me to return to Puerto Vallarta when it may prove less expensive to fly directly home?" I ask.

"Let's check it out," she responds.

"Meanwhile, there are soft drinks and coffee in the conference room. I'll let you know when I have anything." In other words, get lost so I can do my job.

The conference room consists of an oval table with eight semi-comfortable chairs, a sideboard cabinet with coffee and soft drinks. We make ourselves comfortable. I find a recent issue of Newsweek, the first news I've seen in weeks.

"Bob, American has a flight to Miami this afternoon. Unfortunately I cannot get you up to Maine until tomorrow. You'll have to spend tonight in Miami. Is this OK?"

"Sure, that's fine," I respond.

"There are numerous flights to Puerto Vallarta. I'd suggest the three o'clock with one stop. That way you can all go to the airport together," Lois tells the other three.

We all agree. She leaves in order to make the final arrangements.

Allen calls me aside to settle our account. I am paid in U.S. dollars.

"Thanks for all of your help and support," he says with a firm handshake.

I assure him that it was my pleasure and that I look forward to our next time.

We depart shortly after noon for the airport with a brief stop for lunch. Panama's Tocumen International Airport, on the eastern out skirts of the city, is a forty-five minute drive via the southern corridor toll road. Patrick drops me off first where I say my good byes with bear hugs and handshakes to my companions. I again thank Patrick for my copy of 'The Path.'

"You're welcome my friend, come see us again soon," he says before putting the Rover in gear and roaring away.

A skycap helps me with the duffel bag to the ticket counter where I find my ticket waiting. "Please proceed directly to the gate Mr. Devine, we are about to start boarding," informs the agent.

My seat assignment forward of the wing affords me an excellent view of the Canal, the port of Colon and the Caribbean Sea as we climb to altitude. I try, to no avail, to find the boat yard below where just a few short hours ago I had left Athena.

Two hours later, after a snack with a beer followed by a nap, we are on final approach into Miami International Airport. South Miami Beach with its colorfully painted art noveau hotels and white sandy beach on Biscayne Bay slides under us just minutes before the wheels touch down.

"Mr. Devine, I'm sorry but there is nothing available to Boston or Portland this evening. This is the start of the Fourth of July weekend and we are booked," says the reservation agent at Delta. I thank her as I had the other three airline representatives that I had pleaded with earlier. I conclude that I am out of options and resign myself to a one-night stay. It is now a matter of finding a hotel room.

In baggage claim, standing before a large display listing numerous hotels in the area, one in particular catches my eye, The Pelican Hotel on Ocean Avenue in South Beach. Without hesitating I push the corresponding button on the display and raise the telephone receiver. After several rings, a pleasant voice answers, "Pelican Hotel, may I help you?"

"Is there any possibility you have a room available for one night for a party of one?" I ask.

"I have a small room at the back of the hotel on the ground floor with a double bed, shower and telephone for one hundred dollars. Would this be of interest to you?"

I reply in the affirmative, provide a credit card guarantee and indicate I'll be there within the hour. I negotiate a price with a taxi driver outside baggage claim and settle into the back seat. A check of my watch shows it is six PM.

Within thirty-five minutes I am at the hotel entrance in the heart of what I have heard described as an adult Disneyland. Ocean Street is awash with cars and pedestrians and sidewalk cafes each vying for the same space on this narrow strip of real estate.

"Down this hallway, last door on the right," the front desk clerk and telephone voice instructs me upon handing me the key. The room turns out to be not bad. It is clean and neat. It has two windows with metal security bars on the outside, both looking onto a side street. The bed is soft and the water is hot. "What more can I ask for," I say as I stretch out on the bed for a five minute power nap.

The five-minute turns into a thirty-minute siesta. I wake to find it nearly dark outside as my watch now shows it is eight o'clock.

"Hi honey, how are you?" I ask Pat using the room phone. She is surprised and happy that I will be home tomorrow. We chat for a few minutes before saying good night.

Refreshed, I decide to go out for a late meal.

The young lady at the front desk recommends the food at The Cleve-lander Hotel located a short walk to my left up Ocean Avenue. "It's a funky place to see and be seen," she says with a wink.

I step out of the lobby and into a sea of humanity that I navigate as best I can in the given direction. I find that by staying on the outside edge of the sidewalk, I am swept along with the masses. Car traffic is virtually at a standstill, managing at times to move a car length at best, whereas foot traffic moves steadily along.

The Clevelander is an art deco hotel much like the Pelican. Built in the twenties for the growing tourist trade of south Florida, many of them had by the sixties and seventies fallen into disrepair, abandoned and some torn down. Now however there is a wide spread effort to restore and rebuild the grand old dames. South Beach, as this stretch of real estate is most often referred to, is enjoying an unprecedented comeback. Tonight is no exception. Fueled by the long holiday weekend, the night is filled with the likes of the jet setters of Europe, the celebrities of the enter-tainment world and the regular folks like me. It is a hot spot, a fun-filled sun worshipper dream come true during the day and an Epicurean's and entertainment delight at night.

"Hi, my name is Cindy. Can I bring you a drink?" my voluptuous bar maid asks.

"A Budweiser," I answer, finding it difficult not to stare at her near nudity.

"I'll be right back," she says with a flirtatious smile.

The mob that has collected here is enormous. It is a young crowd, mostly in their twenties and thirties. The music is thunderous, emanating from a five-piece band located at the far end of the outdoor court. I am about as far away from them as possible, yet the din is extreme. But no one seems to pay them any mind. Most of the patrons I conclude are here to get drunk and make out.

"Five dollars, please," states the scantily clad nymph.

I pay up, take two or three long pulls from the long neck bottle and settle in to, as my hotel gal suggested, "see and be seen."

"May we join you?"

"Please," I respond.

"My name is Dorothy," says one. "I'm Dolores," says the second as they swing their hindquarters onto two of the three empty barstools at my table.

"I'm Bob," I respond at their sudden intrusion.

Both are in their middle to late twenties, one moderately overweight and neither particularly attractive.

"Thanks for the seats," offers Dorothy settling in. I detect a slight accent.

My near naked waitress takes their drink orders, two rum and cokes.

They both light long slim cigarettes, exhaling in a cloud of smoke above their heads. Oblivious to my presence, they engage in conversation in a tongue that I recognize as Portuguese having at one time visited Brazil.

With little interest in their conversation, I busy myself with the art of "people watching" of which there is a lot of that to do.

"I brought another Bud for you. It's on me," says Cindy as she places napkins on the table to deliver drinks.

"Thank you," I respond providing a generous tip.

"You must come here often to get such good attention," says Dorothy.

"No, first time," I answer.

The wave of humanity ebbs and flows past my observation post. Although not at the epicenter of festivities I do have a good vantage point from which to watch. Unexpectedly, from within a group of well-dressed women, I see someone. It is someone that I know I know. Our eyes meet and in an instant I realize it is Maria from Mexico. I slide off my stool to weave and dodge my way through the mob towards her.

"Bob, what are you doing here?" she asks as I approach.

"Waiting for an airplane home," I reply.

"What a pleasant surprise," she says before we embrace with a kiss on the cheek and a long hug.

"I never thought I would see you again," I say. "You look wonderful."

"Thank you. May I introduce you to some of my friends?"

Her five companions are similar in age, each well dressed, extremely polite and with the appearance of being well educated. I shake each of their hands as I try to remember names.

"Come join us in the back," Maria offers. "There is a table set up for us."

I follow as she makes her way through the crowd, around a swimming pool that I wasn't aware of existed, past the bandstand and to a dining area under cover of a red and white striped awning. A black rod iron fence provides seclusion for the patrons inside. A security guard stands vigilant at the only opening.

Maria drops back to join me by taking my hand; the same warm, soft hand I held at Puerto Madera. Her big brown eyes flash as she smiles to reveal the same perfect teeth. "I'm glad you're here," she says with a squeeze of my hand.

The gate attendant immediately steps aside allowing the seven of us to enter. Led by Maria, I follow her to the back area where a long rectangular table is set for as many as twenty people. The table is festooned with flowers, balloons, crepe paper streamers and confetti. There are a number of women milling about, many now coming over to say hello and offer their congratulations to Maria. She in turn introduces each to me.

"Make yourself comfortable. I have a few things to attend to," says Maria as she turns to leave.

"May I get you something to drink?" asks a waiter.

"A beer, please."

"A Budweiser?"

"Yes, thank you."

Left somewhat alone, I have a brief opportunity to try to determine what this occasion is all about. What I do know is that it is a party celebration and there is a good chance it has something to do with Maria. It is clear that everyone here knows one another and they know why they are here. It is also clear that I am the only male in the group.

"Hello, my name is Lupita. I understand you are a good friend of Maria's?" asks a pleasant faced woman with a wide smile and sparkling brown eyes.

"A friend, yes. I haven't known her for very long. My name is Bob," I answer as we shake hands.

"It is a pleasure to meet you. How do you know Maria?"

I explain our chance meeting in Mexico and how, just moments ago, we have met once again. "It is uncanny that twice we seem to have been in the same place at the same time," I conclude.

"I see," she responds.

Seizing the opportunity, I say, "May I ask, what is the nature of this celebration?"

"Maria is being married Sunday. This is her bachelorette party," answers Lopita with a puzzled look. "Didn't she tell you?"

"No. We haven't had much of a chance to talk."

"Does this surprise you?"

"No, well yes I guess it does. In Mexico she led me to believe she would probably never marry. She indicated she had no beaus and was too busy to consider having another person in her life."

"Frankly, her decision has many of us worried. It has come about all too quickly."

"Your drink, sir" offers the waiter.

"Thank you," I reply but before I can offer a tip, he turns and departs. Seeing That Maria is returning, Lupita excuses herself to drift back into the crowd.

"I see you've met Lupita. Nice gal would you say?"

"Yes, we had a good chat, namely about you."

"I bet it had lots to do with my sudden decision to get married, right?"

"Yes."

"And how I had no intentions of ever getting married?"

"Yes."

"And you said the right man would come along."

"Yes."

"Well, shortly after returning to Miami from that trip, I met a man who has kindled deep emotions and feelings never before felt by me."

"In other words, you are in love."

"It was if we knew one another for years and that we were meant for each other. Don't ask me to explain, Lord knows I've tried to explain to my Uncle and my friends."

"You don't have to explain to me," I say. "By the look in your eyes, I can tell you are in love. Congratulations."

"Will you come to my wedding? Please."

"I wish I could, but I need to return home where I have an anxious wife and many projects waiting."

"Of course, I understand."

"But please, tell me about your man," I say.

Day 33. Saturday

07:00 "Welcome aboard," says the pleasant flight attendant upon my entering the main cabin of Continental flight # 31. "You are seated on the right side of the aircraft in row twelve, seat A."

Once strapped and settled in, I look forward to an uneventful ride to Newark with a connection on to Portland. I close my eyes to rest and relax. I am somewhat hung-over from the events of the past several hours and wish not to be disturbed. Fortunately the middle seat beside me remains unoccupied. I hear the main cabin door close, followed soon after by the gentle push from the tractor on the nose wheel moving us away from the gate.

"Sir, can I interest you in breakfast?" asks the flight attendant with a gentle tug on my arm.

"Yes, please," I respond realizing that we are airborne and at level flight. I must have crashed once seated. I don't recall taxiing out or takeoff.

Breakfast consists of dry cereal, banana, and a small container of orange juice with coffee. I enjoy and consume it with vigor, in spite of all I had to eat and drink last evening.

Finished, I recline my seat and allow myself to drift wistfully back through the evenings activities. I recall that Maria insisted on my staying where I enjoyed myself as the only male. I cannot recall the number of times I danced or the number of beers I drank. I do remember the food and service was excellent. I can remember offering a toast of best wishes to the bride to be followed by a long embrace.

Sometime, well after midnight, the party broke up. After which we walked back to the Pelican where we exchanged our best wishes and said our final good byes.

Returning to my room I was startled by how noisy it was due to the number of partying pedestrians outside my windows. It was useless to try to rest, particularly after a heavy object smashed into the rod iron bars of one window. At five AM I showered, dressed and drug my duffel bag to the front desk to check out and to call a taxi. My arrival at the Fort Lauderdale Airport was none too soon to catch this flight.

The smaller, two engine turbo-prop climbs out of Newark Airport and starts a gentle right hand turn to take us directly over lower Manhattan. The view from my mid-cabin right side seat is unprecedented. The entire ride to Maine proves to be a breathtaking experience under a cloudless sky of bright sunlight.

Outside of baggage claim I look for our familiar white Jeep Cherokee. Before long it comes into sight with Pat alone at the wheel. She stops at curbside where I throw my gear into the back. She greets me with a big hug and a long kiss. She looks good, rested and relaxed.

The drive north on US 295 of 75 minutes is spent mostly in catching up with each other's activities. "I'm glad to have you home," Pat says upon entering our driveway. "A month is far too long to be without you. Please don't ask to do that again."

And with that, my big adventure is over, at least for now.